Maratek's Journeys – more than 12 000 miles...

On the way to the army:
Wyszogród – Płock – St. Petersburg

On the way to the war:
St. Petersburg – Irkutsk – Moukden – Harbin – Moukden

On the way home from the war:
Harbin – Irkutsk – Tomsk – Wyszogród – Szczerców – Łódź

On the way to Siberia:
Warszawa – Transit prison – Labor camp

Escape from Siberia:
Barabinsk – Chelyabinsk – Irkutsk – Warszawa

Searching for a wife:
Wyszogród – Szczerców – Nowy Dwór

SCALES

Statute Miles, 660 = 1 Inch.

0 100 200 300 400 500 600 700 800

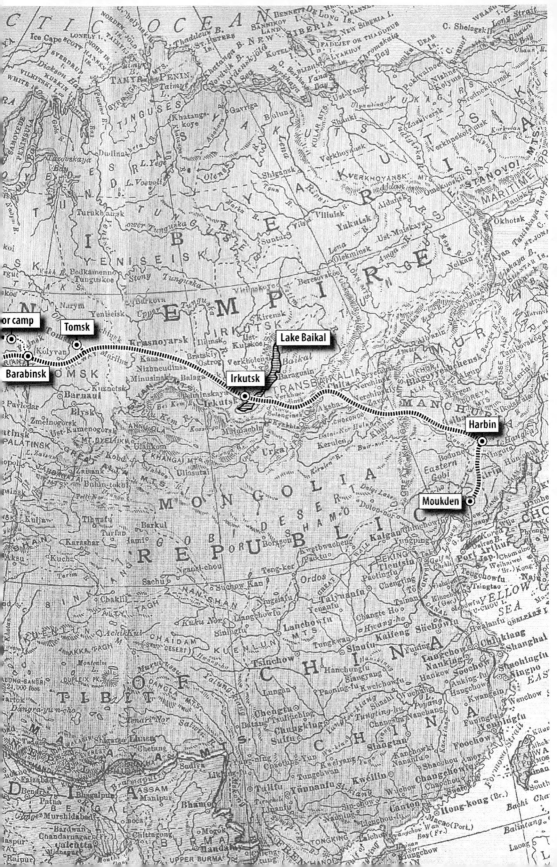

BRYNA KRANZLER
THE ACCIDENTAL ANARCHIST

FROM THE DIARIES OF JACOB MARATECK
TRANSLATED BY SHIMON AND ANITA MARATECK WINCELBERG

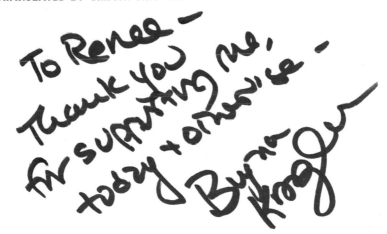

To Renee —
Thank you
for supporting me,
today + otherwise —
Bryna Kranzler

CROSSWALK PRESS
PO Box 928723
SAN DIEGO, CA 92192-8723

Wielmożny Jakob

Merstek ich bzya zy bin

opnisiad

12

23562
76497
34797
65476
23456

23456

23456
76543
84321
45678

No 142
95
23560

CROSSWALK PRESS
PO Box 928723
San Diego, CA 92192-8723
www.theaccidentalanarchist.com

BRYNA KRANZLER
© 2010 Bryna Kranzler

KRANZLER, BRYNA.
THE ACCIDENTAL ANARCHIST: FROM THE DIARIES OF JACOB MARATECK / Bryna Kranzler ;
translated by Shimon and Anita Maratek Wincelberg.
   p. cm.
   ISBN 978-0-9845563-0-4
1. Marateck, Jacob, 1883-1950. 2. Jews —Soviet Union —Social conditions. 3. Russo-Japanese
War, 1904-1905 —Personal narratives, Jewish. 4. Jewish soldiers —Soviet Union —Biography.
5. Poland – History—1864-1918 —Personal narratives. 6. Russia —History —Nicholas II,
1894-1917 —Personal narratives. I. Wincelberg, Shimon. II. Wincelberg, Anita. III. Title.
DS135.R95 .K73 2010
947.08/092/4—dc22   2010905536

Kranzler, Bryna
The Accidental Anarchist: From the Diaries of Jacob Marateck

Portions of this book appeared in a slightly different form in:
The Samurai of Vishigrod: The Notebooks of Jacob Marateck, Retold by Shimon and Anita
Wincelberg, © 1976, 1st ed., Published by the Jewish Publication Society of America,
Philadelphia, PA; Also in: Commentary, Hadassah Magazine, The Jerusalem Post, Jewish
Frontier, Jewish Heritage, Jewish Horizon, The Jewish Observer, Moment, and National Jewish
Monthly
"Down and Out in Chelyabinsk," by Shimon Wincelberg, appeared in: Judaism, A Quarterly
Journal of Jewish Life and Thought, September 22, 1995.

Printed in the United States of America

Cover design & layout by: Anton Khodakovsky
Edited by: Cerian Griffiths
Logo design by: Mike Kranzler
Author photo by: Joanne Janc

DEDICATION

THIS BOOK IS DEDICATED TO MY MOTHER, ANITA MARATECK WINCELBERG, who never gave up her father's dream of seeing his story told. By sharing her personal memories of him, as well as his diaries, she has given his voice an ever-lasting resonance while making sure that his unique sense of humor was never lost.

It is also in loving memory of my late father, Shimon Wincelberg, who spent many years working on his father-in-law's diaries, and published the first portion of them, but sadly was unable to see the project through to completion.

Above all, this book is my gift to Jacob Marateck, the grandfather I never met, and an individual I wish I had known. His story is proof that it is not the circumstances of our lives that determine who we are, but rather the way we choose to interpret them that defines our personalities and, to some extent, our destinies.

For Jay, who made it possible for me to write this book

*And for Mike and Jesse, who amaze and inspire me daily.
I hope you will cherish your legacy and, some day, share
it with future generations*

ACKNOWLEDGEMENTS

had been looking forward to writing the Acknowledgements to this book, not only because it would give me the opportunity to thank a number of people who were instrumental in helping me complete it, but more importantly because it would mean that I had finally finished a process that began 105 years and 3 generations ago.

But now that I have the opportunity to do so, I find that it's more difficult than I had expected. No matter how effusive I am with my thanks, or how many people I acknowledge, my words will be inadequate to express my heartfelt appreciation for their contributions, and I will, inevitably leave someone out. The following, then, is my humble attempt to recognize certain people who helped me in ways beyond what they may realize, and to broadly thank other friends who read advance copies of the book and made helpful suggestions.

For their friendship, encouragement, literary and spiritual support, my sincerest thanks go to my friends and colleagues: Arlene Pollard and Don Lipkis, Barbara Field, Cissy Wolfe, Hallema Sharif, Josh Hugo, Patrick McMahon and Zoe Ghahremani.

My brother, Rabbi Yakov (named for Jacob Marateck) Wincelberg, corrected and expanded upon matters of Jewish Law that are found in the text and footnotes, and also told me about some Marateck relatives of whose existence I had been unaware. And my son, Mike, revealed previously unrecognized talents when he did more than listen to me describe plot problems but offered creative solutions. He also continues to assist with enumerable, ongoing tasks, from editing marketing copy, designing promotional materials, serving as my Social Media Marketing Ambassador, and providing technical guidance for website problems. At least equally valuable is his continued enthusiasm for the book. Finally, I also want to highlight the special contribution made by Anton Khodakovsky, the very talented designer of this book whose cover art captures the time, place, and surprising tone of the contents.

Working on The Accidental Anarchist has given me the opportunity to learn about my grandfather in a way that might not have been possible had he lived. In the process, I also learned about myself, and developed an even greater appreciation for the value of friendship.

TABLE OF CONTENTS

1

IN THE BEGINNING

have no excuse, save for the ignorance of youth and a desire for grand adventure, which may have been one and the same thing. Consequently, the seemingly minor decision I made to end my education before the age of thirteen led me down a path from which each future choice was misdirected by the previous foolish one.

Not that I didn't have a loving family to guide me, particularly my older brother, Mordechai, who had seen me risk my life repeatedly but was unable to convince me to make at least one sensible decision. There was simply too much fun to be had.

The result was that, in a little over ten years, I went from being a *yeshiva*[1] student, a baker's assistant, and labor organizer, to a corporal in the Russian army during the war in Manchuria (in which the men under my command wanted to kill me, simply for being a Jew, as much as the enemy did, simply for being in the way), to a revolutionary. For my efforts, I earned my first two death sentences, which was a little more excitement than I needed.

This limited my curiosity as to whether my end would come from freezing or starvation, from Japanese artillery or Chinese bandits, and whether it would be today or tomorrow. From my experiences with the comically inept Russian army (at least, it would have been comical had our lives not

---

1 Hebrew: Jewish educational institution at elementary or high school level, or beyond

been at stake), I learned that, no matter how terrible it was for anyone to be in the midst of a war, it was a hundred times worse being on the losing side.

Still, I was slow to put into practice the lessons from my youth and, following the war, became a revolutionary who wanted to overthrow the Czar. This got me involved in amateur spy missions that would have gotten a Hollywood screenwriter fired, but got me sentenced to death for the third time.

As a result, I travelled the width of Russia, from Petersburg[2] to Siberia, where my adventures were to have come to an end. But even if my record wasn't clean, my conscience was; everything I did was done with the most honorable intentions.

And ultimately provided enough excitement to last a lifetime.

I grew up at a time when most of Russian-occupied Poland was living in poverty. Hence, it was not unusual for a child to leave home at the age of twelve to get a job to support the family. The only alternative was studying in a *yeshiva*.

Spending one's days indoors, rocking over a book of the *Talmud*[3] and arguing about the minutiae of Jewish law was never a profitable occupation, but it was the only "trade" in the Jewish community that really mattered. It also wasn't entirely impractical. There were rich Jews who wanted their sons to study with learned men, and were willing to pay good salaries to have one as a private tutor. Sometimes, one even heard that the tutor had gotten to marry a rich man's daughter.

When it was my turn, I looked at the professions being learned by my friends. None exactly made my mouth water. And since I wasn't a fan of hard work, I decided to follow in my brother, Chayim's, footsteps. He hadn't been interested in learning a trade, either, but became possessed by the crazy idea that he would become a great scholar. Since our parents could not support him, he went off to another village where the boys survived on the generosity of the equally poor householders who had been shamed

2   As St. Petersburg was known at the time

3   Hebrew: Commentary of the great rabbis from centuries past; focuses on Jewish laws, customs, etc.

into providing meals for the boys. Under those circumstances, as you can imagine, some hosts 'forgot' their obligations.

I, too, wanted to become a scholar, but unlike Chayim, I was unable to adjust to eating only every other day; starving I could do from the comfort of home.

Which was why I ran away from the *yeshiva* after barely a week. Unfortunately, I had neglected to tell anyone about my plan to return home, which resulted in no small amount of confusion.

Shortly after I was discovered 'missing' from the *yeshiva*, a boy about my age was found to have drowned. Using good Polish logic, the authorities put the missing boy together with the dead boy, and wiped their hands of both cases with remarkable efficiency. Consequently, my parents were notified of my death, and they sat *shiva*[4] for me for the first, but not the last, time.

One would think that, after my return from the dead, my parents would have been overjoyed to have me home. But it wasn't long before they reminded me that, having closed the book on the life of the mind, I needed to find a job.

But the limited exposure I'd had to the outside world when I ventured beyond my small, provincial town of Vishogrod[5] made me realize that there was a bigger world out there just waiting to be discovered.

Even at thirteen, the great world drew me like a magnet with its promise of new experiences. I wanted to go far away, perhaps as far as Warsaw,[6] which I pictured as a vast, modern metropolis, glittering with golden opportunities. Conveniently, Warsaw was where my older brother, Mordechai, worked as a baker. When I told him that I was sick to death of Vishogrod, he said he could get me a job as a baker's assistant. Coming from a state of perpetual hunger, the prospect of spending my days in a large, modern bakery, with its delectable smells and the unceasing availability of something to eat, gripped my imagination and wouldn't let go.

In principle, my father had nothing against Warsaw, but he held to the belief that a boy's only assurance of seizing his golden opportunity in life lay in having a skilled craft. So he arranged for me to work in a series of

4   Hebrew: Seven-day mourning period for the dead

5   Spelled, in Polish: Wyszogrod

6   Spelled, in Polish, Warszawa

apprenticeships with various tradesmen in town. Why 'a series' of apprenticeships? Because I proved incompetent at even the simplest task. As a result, most jobs didn't last a week; some didn't last the day. At least one boss predicted that, before long, I would end up in front a firing squad, about which he wasn't too far wrong.

Soon I found myself in Warsaw, working twenty to 22-hour days (and before *yom tov*,[7] a full 24), something that Mordechai had neglected to mention in his infrequent letters. The only salvation was *Shabbos*;[8] without that one day of rest, none of us could have survived.

Having made such a fuss about needing to get out of Vishogrod, I could hardly turn around and go home. Nor did I have enough money to return, even if I wanted to. So, for the next seven or eight years, I worked as a baker's assistant, and in a variety of other mindless jobs, not one of which had a future.

But what would have been the point of thinking about the future when, at the age of 21, I would be conscripted into the Czar's army. In the meantime, work was simply a way to stay alive, and sometimes barely that. My sympathies, as I rolled from one deadening job to another, were with the exploited souls who were enslaved by their employers – not that the bosses had it much better.

Meanwhile, my young blood craved adventure. Aside from the revolution, which I personally felt in no position to start, I could try to improve the lot of the people around me. At the time there was no such thing as a "union." Each worker was on his own. And merely talking about organizing workers was an engraved invitation to scrutiny by the secret police.

But by the time I was seventeen or eighteen, I was fed up with being powerless. So one day I went to the boss and told him that his three best clerks and I were quitting. The boss was furious. He accused me of being a Bolshevik, a hooligan, a nihilist, and a spoiled young man who'd never be satisfied with anything short of total chaos, anarchy, and the destruction of the social order.

I got angry, too, but instead of quitting, I called a strike, and demanded – and this was unheard of in Warsaw – a reduction of our working hours from

7 Hebrew: Refers to any Jewish holiday
8 Yiddish: The Sabbath

twenty to twelve hours a day. I was in a position to do this because I didn't have to worry about losing my job as I was approaching the age of mandatory army service. Which, after working 120-hour weeks and more, didn't sound like such a bad alternative.

Our little strike spread throughout Warsaw as workers and apprentices began walking out and demanding a 72-hour week. Under the guidance of an experienced *Bundist*[9] who showed me the ropes, I managed to "unionize" over 3000 workers in less than a month. The police harassed me at every turn, arresting me several times, and beating me up once or twice. Although they had me on their list as some sort of political troublemaker, they never figured out exactly what I was up to.

After such a fine start, the strike went off like a ship without a rudder. No one had any idea of tactics or negotiating positions. While I had a knack for agitating, making speeches and signing up members, I had none at all for strategy or administration. We also didn't bother our heads with theories and ideology. We simply wanted to support the cause of oppressed workers.

As a result, the strike dragged on until, gradually, each boss came to some sort of quiet arrangement with his workers. It was like a husband and wife deciding it was better to live together in hatred than to have their self-respect and lie in the street. So one morning I awoke to find myself a strike leader without a strike to lead.

But even though we hadn't achieved our goal of a shorter work week, at least we had shaken Warsaw to its very foundation, and given thousands of workers a sense of revolutionary consciousness.

And it gave an ignorant boy who, once upon a time, had set out for Warsaw to conquer the world, a taste of what he could do.

9   Yiddish: Member of Jewish Socialist Labor Party

2

HOW TO BECOME THE CZAR'S SON-IN-LAW

As summer dwindled to an end, a familiar pall of fear began to descend upon our village. Soon it would be the fifteenth of September, a date that struck terror even in the breasts of mothers who were still suckling their sons. For on that day, all young men of military age became subject to immediate conscription into the Russian army.

Do I need to paint a picture of what it meant in 1902, particularly for an Orthodox Jew, to be pitchforked into the Czar's army? Our parents' terror was due only in part to the knowledge that we would be exposed to the traditional dangers and discomforts of military service, but also that we would be subjected to the mercies and whims of superiors who would as soon torment a Jew as scratch themselves. (Such inconveniences were not exactly unknown, even in Vishigrod, among one's own, good Polish neighbors.)

But what Jewish parents dreaded most was the prospect, amply shown to be true, of returning soldiers who, within less than four years, would come home coarsened, brutalized, Russianized and with scarcely a spark of human (that is, Jewish) feeling left in them. Thus, every home rang with heated family conferences, all dedicated to the search for some means by which an innocent child could be preserved from the fatal clutches of *Vanya's*[10] army.

10 A nickname for 'Ivan' used as a general term referring to all Russians

For the rich, there was no problem: they bought their way out. For the poor, however, there was only one avenue of escape: self-mutilation. And since there were any number of equally frightful possibilities to choose from, long evenings of consultation took place.

My Aunt Tzivia strongly recommended a man who would draw out all my teeth. Feibush, the bath attendant, held that the surest remedy would be for me to blind myself in my right eye, without which one cannot aim a rifle. And my Uncle Yonah, never at a loss, knew a man skilled in the art of severing a tendon at the knee. Had I accepted even half the suggestions offered to me, I should not only have escaped military service, but would have ended up a cripple such as the world had never seen. None of these schemes, I am glad to say, found favor with my parents.

Although no one had bothered to ask me, I hadn't the slightest intention of maiming myself. In fact, the prospect of becoming the Czar's *eydem oyf kest*[11] for three years and eight months did not strike me as the world coming to an end. I hadn't spent but a short time back in Vishogrod before I became eager for more thrills. I longed only to be sent to the front lines and earn my share of adventures and medals before it was all over and I was obliged to return to Vishogrod and put the humdrum remainder of my life into some matchmaker's hands.

When we prepared to leave our home town – I, full of idiot enthusiasm, and my friend since boyhood, Chaim Glasnik, with a prophetically long face – his mother seized my arm in two trembling hands and pleaded with me to stay close to her son so that we might protect each other. She swore that, if anything happened to him, she would not survive him by even one minute. By the time she was done, my eyes were drowning in tears, while Glasnik merely stood to one side squirming, pretending that she was someone else's mother.

Too tearful to speak, I simply nodded my agreement. When I felt comfortable exercising my voice again, Glasnik and I pledged to each other that, should either one of us not return from the war, we would take each other's parents into our own home and "honor and support them all the days of their lives." So inspired were we by our generosity that we went

11 Yiddish: Supported or 'kept' son-in-law

8

further, adding that, if either of us returned to find ourselves orphaned, "My father will be your father, and my home will be your home, for all the days of your life."

On the appointed day, in such a downpour as might have swamped Noah's Ark, I was accompanied to the meeting place not only by my near and distant relatives, but also acquaintances who seemed to have come solely for the purpose of adding their tears to the puddles made by the rain. As I said my goodbyes, I stood tall and upright, trying to look older than my face, which only sparingly released those quills of manhood. But anyone would have looked taller than Glasnik whose head seemed poised in advance of his body, never quite certain where it wanted to be.

In that gloomy spirit, we climbed into one of the open wagons with the other 21 year old boys from our district who hadn't found a way to avoid serving in the Czar's army. My soldier's baggage consisted primarily of a canvas-covered box that my mother had filled with bread, herring, chicken fat, and sausages. (Those who did not intend to touch Vanya's unclean food until they have absolutely no choice had to stock up on such things).

As our wagon prepared to depart, my father, alone, expressed his sorrow by remaining mostly silent. But it was only his three parting words that continued to ring in my ears long after the cart had taken me away. All he said was, "Be a Jew."

3

A SMALL CHEER FOR CORRUPTION

With a good deal of comradely passing of vodka between Jew and gentile, we jolted toward Plock, the capital of the gubernya.[12] From Plock, we departed from by barge, which rocked along the Vistula River under a weeping sky. I could still faintly glimpse the nebulous hills of my birthplace and, with the sudden sharp realization that soldiers don't always return alive, I wondered if I should ever see it again.

Crowded below deck on account of the rain, we conscripts stood in steamy, suffocating closeness: Jew and Pole, Balt, Ukrainian, and transplanted German – and although the recent Syedlitzer[13] pogrom was still green in our memories, we managed, somehow, not to be at each others' throats. This may have been because of our common fate. Or because few young people had remained untouched by the prevailing revolutionary spirit with its rosy premonitions of universal brotherhood.

Some time around noon, determined not by the absent sun but by the hunger pangs in our bellies, the barge stopped and we were marched, in a straggling column of twos, toward a passenger train. We were loaded into

---

12 Russian: Province

13 Spelled, in Poland: Siedlce. *NOTE*: The Siedlce pogrom actually took place in 1906, not prior to Marateck's conscription in 1902. It is likely that, since he didn't write down many of his stories until years after the events described, Siedlce had been the pogrom foremost in his memory, and he had simply confused the dates.

boxcars that had signs advising that occupancy was limited to eight horses or 40 men, but with a little effort were able to hold many times that number. Although it was unheated, we could, at least, sit down.

While waiting for the train to depart, we shared another bottle of vodka providentially carried by one of the Polish boys. A *Vanya* non-commissioned officer with a stripe on his collar came pushing in with a stack of papers and started calling out names. Having, to his visible astonishment, found us all accounted for, he launched into a pompous sermon on how we should conduct ourselves as good, pious subjects of the Czar, meaning we were to jump to obey all of *his* orders. In the meantime, we would shortly be issued our subsistence pay.

Before Glasnik could wonder aloud if this was the right train and not some cattle express bound for Manchuria, another *Vanya* walked into our car bearing a sack of coins. I knew that the Czar didn't pay princely wages, but even I was unprepared to be handed seven groschen for a day's subsistence, which was not quite enough to buy a pound of bread. Among those who raged against this Russian stinginess were some of the gentile Polish boys who had been raised to believe that Poland was their country, and not a Russian colony.

There was a roar of protest, which the second *Vanya* tried to appease by pointing out that at each stop we would also get free hot water. The two non-coms seemed on the verge of being overwhelmed by a spontaneous uprising.

For my part, I wanted nothing to delay my getting to Petersburg, and tried to calm down the Poles by pointing out that it was undoubtedly not the non-coms who were robbing us, but the greater thieves at the top who took the money allotted for soldiers' food, and put it in their own pockets.

I never would have dreamed I'd said anything out of line, but the two non-coms I had saved from a taste of hearty Polish violence, asked me gratefully for my name and let me know they'd have their eye on me now as a revolutionary agitator. Following which, they began to bless us all impartially with good Russian benedictions, ending with the assurance that there was an excellent chance the lot of us would end up sampling the inside of a prison fortress for attempted mutiny.

By this time, being a soldier of the Czar had lost much of its charm. I resolved for the balance of my enlistment to keep my nose out of all brawls, mutinies, riots and revolutions or, in fact, any incidents other than those involving what I grandly thought of as "the honor of the Jewish people."

After a couple of hours, the train finally left Poland and, in the gloom of a sunless afternoon, began its grudging progress through a desolate landscape of meager fields, occasionally populated by skinny Russian horses and skeletal cows hunting for blades of grass. The Russians may have been a great military power, but they had a lot to learn about farming.

Night fell, and the train sped on without stopping for the promised hot water, while the lot of us scratched our unwashed bodies and groped peevishly for comfortable positions in which to sleep. Finally, due to the suffocating air and the foul smell of our bodies and feet, most of us fell into a state that was not so much sleep as loss of consciousness.

It seemed that I had barely closed an eye when the train screamed and shuddered to a halt. It was shortly after midnight. Military voices roared at us to get off with all of our belongings. We tumbled out, still half-asleep, and were driven like cattle through narrow, dirty streets until we reached a row of barracks where we were permitted to let our gear slide off our backs.

In the mess hall, long tables had been hammered together out of splintery boards. Atop them sat tin bowls filled with lukewarm, dirty water. Floating desperately on top of this brew were a few scraps of roasted pigskin that had probably been too tough to make into boots.

We were each given wooden spoons. And while the others fell upon this soup as though it were fresh-baked bread, none of the Jews in our group tasted a drop. We tore into the provisions from home. Not that we wouldn't, eventually, have to eat the same unclean food as everyone else, but in this way we put off that moment for a little longer.

At two o'clock in the morning, we were herded back to the station. Along the way, our comrades discussed their first military supper. One said it was perhaps a little too salty, another complained there wasn't enough fat in it. A third guessed that the cook had washed his dirty clothes in the water, and a fourth agreed that the soup did have a slight taste of army soap. And all of them roundly cursed *Vanya* for his stinginess with food.

We returned to the box cars, traveling under those inhuman conditions for two days until, at four o'clock one morning, we reached Petersburg. My older brother, Mordechai, who had attained a position of some influence, had planned to meet me at the station. But to my great disappointment he was not there. (It turned out that he had already been to the station several times. In fact, that very morning the stationmaster, with that wonderful Russian efficiency even the Communists could never change, told him that our train was not due until the following day.)

No one at the station was prepared for our arrival with even a caldron of tea. The first snows of September had just fallen. We trudged through this with our belongings along endless Petersburg streets for what seemed like a good five hours. Finally, panting, staggering with exhaustion, and drenched with sweat, we reached the Novocherkassky Barracks.

Our feet were swollen, and a man would have needed an ice pick before he could blow his nose. On top of which, we were hungry as wolves, and our revolutionary spirits were at a pitch not to be reached again until 1904.

I must admit that, on this occasion, *Vanya* treated us all – Jew and gentile, alike – with perfect equality: none of us got a thing. One of our guards explained that they could not give us food because our names were not yet on the roster. They did, however, give us free hot water and I, for one, was relieved to hear nothing more mentioned about our "mutiny" on the train.

By ten o'clock the next morning, we were at the induction center, mother-naked (which raised some comments on the sacred art of circumcision), for a medical examination by several army doctors who fell all over themselves to pronounce us fit. I suspected that, by this time, they had probably seen such an epidemic of remarkably similar injuries that they assumed the boys from the occupied portions of the Russian empire were unusually clumsy or particularly unlucky, and considered their afflictions an acceptable norm.

Later, we were measured like yard goods, next to be assigned to platoons according to our talents. Toward this end, we were asked our civilian occupations. I already knew from some of the veterans back home that getting into a good platoon made all the difference in the world. A 'good' platoon meant sitting in an office and being part of *natchalstva*, officialdom. A bad one was bitter as death. As my brother's letter had advised (no doubt afraid that, in my youthful stupidity, I would give my profession as "labor organizer" or "terrorist"), I called myself a tailor (which was Glasnik's occupation), even though I had never threaded a needle in my life. But, possibly because of the incident on the train, I was put into the 15th Company, which had the reputation of being the "Convicts' Company." From the first morning on, I understood why.

In other companies, the men were treated in a fairly civilized way. They were awakened at six o'clock in the morning, cleaned their floors, and polished their boots and brass buttons until seven, when they were taken out into the waist-high snow and made to run for an hour.

With the 15th they were less gentle. We were roused at four o'clock in the morning, driven out into the snow at five o'clock and kept running until eight o'clock, by which time the others were already sitting comfortably at breakfast, which consisted of tea with sugar and chunks of shriveled bread.

Since I was healthy enough not to be among those who collapsed during our morning run, I still had not fully realized what I was in for during the next three years and eight months. But I soon received Czar Nicolai's proper *sholom aleichem*,[14] and that sobered me a little.

What happened was this: having not tasted hot food for three days because our names were still not on the roster, I awoke early one morning with a powerful thirst, and took my own little teakettle over to the cookhouse. The mess attendant explained he was not allowed to give out any hot water until the bugle had sounded. I slipped him a cigarette, got my hot water and ran happily back to my cot to drink my tea.

I was about to pour the first cup when a Ukrainian non-com with a face like a sheep and a nose like a bulldog, the kind of treasure whom, in Russian-Yiddish, we called a *katzap*,[15] entered the barracks. Reading from the ominous roster in his hand, he asked for, "Marateck, Yakub."[16]

---

14 A Yiddish greeting. Here the term is used sarcastically

15 Russian-Yiddish: Nationalistic term for a Russian person; someone who is wholly Russian, not a hybrid with another nationality

16 Russian: Jacob

When I answered, he took one shocked look at my cheerfully steaming kettle and promptly gave me a Russian *misheberach*,[17] that is, a blow across the face that sent me sprawling.

Blood-spattered and stunned, I had barely managed to get back on my feet when he screamed, "*Zhydovska morda*! Jewface, pick up your hand and salute!" (Except *morda*, more precisely, refers to the snout of an animal).

Until he said that, I had been willing to overlook his bad manners. But I grew to manhood in a section of Warsaw where a man does not lightly let someone spit into his kasha. So without thinking, I snatched up the full kettle and walloped him once across the head. While I was at it, I also allowed my fist to find a resting place on his broad nose. In the commotion that followed, with plenty of warm encouragement for both sides, he ended up on the bottom and I on top while the blood from our mouths and noses mingled fraternally on the floor.

At the hospital, my injuries turned out to be hardly worth mentioning: a tooth knocked out by the first blow, and a finger cut to the bone by the sharp edge of my own smashed kettle. But the staff insisted on putting me to bed so that my opponent who, among other things, had lost part of his nose, should not suffer by comparison.

It was here that Mordechai found me at two o'clock the next morning. He'd brought his own little welcoming delegation of Jewish soldiers from our home town. But when he found out I had committed violence against a Russian of superior rank, Mordechai, in his loving anxiety over my ignorance and dimming prospects for survival, started to shout that unless I learned to control my "Polack temper," I would spend my army years going from one prison to another until I forgot what a Jew was.

I listened to him with respect. He was, after all, something of a big shot in *Vanya's* army. Only later did I find out what made him so important. As Quartermaster, he was in charge of the warehouse from which the men obtained their uniforms. The way the *natchalniks*[18] in the Quartermaster worked their racket was as follows: each soldier was entitled to a new uniform once in three years. The old one was supposed to be ripped apart and used for rags to wash the floors. But many of the old uniforms were still in

---

17 Hebrew: A prayer said for someone who was ill. Here the term is used sarcastically

18 Russian: Authority, or Official

good enough condition to wear so that, if cleaned up, and with in a new lining sewn in, they could be sold again, or even issued in place of new ones. There were large sums of money to be made out of these "resurrections," and everyone from the colonel on down had a lick of this juicy bone.

Mordechai was the only Jew in that entire operation and I suspected that they kept him only because they needed at least one honest man in the management of the warehouse. So, my brother went about burdened with money he couldn't send home without confessing to our father how he had come by it. He knew that, for all his grinding poverty, our father would not have tolerated such a source of income and Mordechai would have been forced to ask for a transfer.

But having been away from our father's influence a little longer than I, he explained that whether money was tainted or not depended largely on what you did with it. And since Mordechai lacked any inclination for gambling, drinking, or whoring, all he could think of doing with his cursed wealth was lend it to those of his officers who never could manage on what they had, or buy vodka for his Russian comrades and superiors who would lap it up, cross themselves, and wish him eternal life.

It mattered little to him that few of the officers ever repaid his favors or loans. As a practical man, he reasoned, what Jew in *Vanya's* army could ever know when a little influence in the right place might not, one day, mean the difference between life and death? Thus, almost despite himself, my brother became a man of some influence.

One of Mordechai's best "customers," but someone who at least acknowledged some vague obligation to pay him back, was his own captain. A relative of Czar Nicolai Alexandrovich, himself, Captain Mikhailoff was a wealthy man. Yet he knew nothing about holding on to his money, and freely admitted that his army pay, alone, couldn't have kept him in cigarettes. Like most Russian officers, he was a passionate card player, and whenever his luck turned sour, he would tiptoe into Mordechai's quarters in the dark of night, like a drunkard fearful of waking his wife. He always unerringly found his way to my brother's bed, and Mordechai, still half-asleep, would automatically slip him a hundred or two. (We have a saying, "Lend money and you buy yourself an enemy." This, as it turned out, did not apply to Mikhailoff. He proved to be a good soul with a merciful heart, which naturally led to slanderous rumors about his having had a Jewish mother.)

The question in my present circumstances was whether Mordechai possessed sufficient influence to keep me out of jail.

In *Vanya's* army it was virtually unheard of for a blood-raw recruit, a "Polack Jew," at that, to raise a hand in anger against a non-com, regardless of provocation. It was sadly agreed that my sentence upon conviction could well come to twenty years. What's more, there was the reputation of the other Jewish soldiers to consider.

Although Mordechai was still in the midst of scolding me, some of his friends reminded him that I had, after all, defended the honor of the Jewish people. Had he forgotten how many Jewish recruits the sheep-faced Ukrainian had beaten and tormented in the past? One man now also recalled having heard him boast that, in a certain pogrom, he personally had killed two Jews.

At this, my blood was boiling again. I bravely announced that, if I'd known this, I wouldn't have stopped until I had dispatched him to the Other World, prison or no prison. This instantly rekindled Mordechai's anger, but he raged at me like a loving father and I didn't take it too much to heart.

One of his friends now said to him, "All right, big shot. Let's see what connections you have at headquarters to keep this from going any further."

My brother mumbled and grumbled that his supposed influence was severely limited and that he didn't even know to whom to go. His captain? He couldn't be sure. The very idea of a Jew committing violence against a Russian of superior rank had too much of a "man bites dog" novelty about it to be hushed up. Further, knowing the Russian officer class a good bit better than I, Mordechai had genuine doubts about whether his considerable investments in good will over the past two years would actually prove negotiable.

But Mordechai came through for me. Captain Mikhailoff appeared genuinely glad to have an opportunity to repay his many favors. Mikhailoff assured Mordechai that I had nothing to worry about, nor would I need to incur the expense of a lawyer, for he, himself, would defend me.

I had no way of knowing whether he actually understood the nature of the crime with which I had been charged, or what kind of legal training qualified him to defend a soldier in a court-martial. It did me no good to suggest to Mordechai that, since it was my life, or at least my future for the next twenty or 30 years that would be determined by this military court, perhaps I would be better off with a professional lawyer. But as my brother pointed out, who was I to say "No" to a blood relative of the Czar?

The day of the trial arrived and I still had not so much as set eyes upon my 'defense attorney.' The Devil-only-knows how he intended to present my side of the case. In between biting his lips and shouting at me not to be such a worrier, Mordechai conceded that there were some grounds for uneasiness only when the trial had actually begun, and there was still no sign of Mikhailoff.

Meanwhile, my accuser entered the courtroom as though he, personally, were about to sit in judgment of me. I noted that the repairs on his nose and face had been carried out so artistically that, although he still bore a brotherly resemblance to a sheep, he looked notably less ugly than before.

The prosecutor painted our little brawl as an outrage committed by me, alone, an act of unprovoked savagery and insubordination that, unless punished so severely as to set an example for future generations, surely would lead to a speedy and total breakdown of all military discipline and inevitably to the dreaded revolution – a word that, in those days, tended to be followed directly by a death sentence.

I saw immediately that the judge was not in my corner. Any minute now I would be called upon to speak in my own defense. And what could I talk about? "Jewish honor?" I could already see myself blindfolded and tied to a stake.

Especially since my aristocratic defender, who had finally strolled in and taken his seat, one hand vainly attempting to comfort a throbbing brow, listened to the prosecutor like a man who couldn't wait to put this tedious performance behind him and get back to bed.

The aggrieved sergeant, bearing his scars as officiously as battle wounds, took the stand first. He delivered a good, strong recitation on how I had attacked him, totally without provocation, in what he could only assume to be a Polack Jew's typical frenzy of rebellion against good, Russian discipline. With each minute he spoke, I could almost see the judge adding another soldier to the firing squad.

At this point, Mikhailoff, who until now had maintained a morose, hungover, rather self-pitying silence, rose to my defense. Once he had found his feet, he straightened his body with remarkable steadiness. To my horror, though, he did not seem quite certain who in the room was the defendant. Nor, once he found me in response to Mordechai's frantic chin-wagging, did he pay the slightest attention to any of the charges against me. Instead, he launched into an impassioned attack on those non-coms who, by their unrestrained brutality and total disrespect for the proud traditions of the Imperial Army, had already turned Heaven-only-knows how many innocent and patriotic recruits into embittered revolutionaries against his relative, the holy Czar.

It sounded like a speech he had long been eager to get off his chest, and I suspect he would have made the identical one had I been on trial for blasphemy or wetting my bed. Although my defender was plainly the sort of man who had more growing under his nose than inside his head, I saw the judge repeatedly nod in respectful agreement. However, that still did not dispose of the crime for which I stood trial.

Only when the captain had, at last, finished delivering his heartfelt harangue and seemed ready to sit down did he briefly take note of "the so-called defendant." True, he conceded, perhaps a more experienced soldier might have tried to moderate his righteous anger. But as what I had done was so patently an attempt to defend the honor and security of the Czar, Captain Mikhailoff simply failed to comprehend why it was me and not the other man who was on trial. Much as I wanted to agree with my defender, even I had to admit that his argument lacked logic, not to mention common sense.

But to my astonishment, the judge showed himself to be totally persuaded by this line of reasoning. While I was let off with the most gentle of reprimands, Pyotr, my opponent, who hadn't been accused of anything, suddenly found himself reduced in rank. But that was not the last to be heard of him.

How much this verdict cost my brother, he never let on. For all I knew, my advocate may have defended me in all sincerity. But the outcome certainly made me a good deal more tolerant toward the all-pervasive atmosphere of corruption in the Russian army. Without this constant lubrication of the wheels, the most appalling injustices would have passed unnoticed, and men in positions of power might never have felt the slightest inducement to lift a finger for another soul.

4

THE FALL OF 'HAMAN'

After some months of basic training in the so-called "Convicts' Company," which Mordechai felt I was in danger of enjoying more than was appropriate for a boy of my refined background, I was unexpectedly transferred to the regimental tailor shop. Here out of eight men, two (including Glasnik) were actually tailors and therefore obliged to cover for the rest of us. However, no one complained because it was apparent that each of us must have had some pull with the natchalstva. Mordechai hoped that having me assigned to this platoon of 118 men, 42 of whom were Jews, would keep me out of further brawls and courts martial. (The biggest joke of all, as I read years later, was that at this very time the proportion of Jews in the Russian army and navy was almost forty percent greater than its proportion of the population. The reason for this I'll leave to greater philosophers to figure out.)

To my brother's dismay, within less than a month I began to crave some outlet for my youthful energies and thirst for new experiences. Against Mordechai's vehement advice, I applied successfully for a transfer to the 14th Company, which was under the command of my defender, Captain Mikhailoff. It was, after all, peacetime and while life in the infantry might have been a little more strenuous than smoking my pipe in the tailor shop, being among real soldiers was as exciting for me as going to summer camp would be to an American child.

Our noble Mikhailoff was a man who not only enjoyed life, but also did not begrudge others. He believed, for example, that in peacetime there was little sense in tormenting your men with a lot of useless exercises. So, while some companies were sent on field maneuvers, forced marches and other entertainments of that sort, our excellent captain took us to a shady spot in the woods where we were permitted to amuse ourselves with such leisure activities as trick riding and marksmanship. While we were well aware of our good fortune in having such a humane and easy-going company commander, we continued to talk among ourselves of the necessity of overthrowing our abominable Czar, Nicolai Alexandrovich, and abolishing such instruments of tyranny as the army.

In anticipation of the revolution, and thanks to Mikhailoff's generosity with ammunition, we soon became so handy with our rifles and horses that we routinely won a good many of those regimental competitions on whose outcomes our officers loved to place wagers. In fact, we did Captain Mikhailoff so proud that he was presently relieved of his command, promoted to colonel, and placed in charge of an important customs post on the Manchurian border where, it was understood, a man would have to be made of stone not to pile up money like manure.

Very well. We'd had a sensible and humane officer and instead of simply thanking our good fortune, we'd gone right on plotting the overthrow of his wretched relative. Now fate rewarded us for our zeal in wanting to liberate one hundred and thirty million of our countrymen with a new commanding officer.

On a cold Wednesday morning, we were promptly called into formation where we were allowed to shiver at attention for some time. Presently, our new boss introduced himself as Captain Fedorenko. He was unnaturally tall, and had shoulders like a barn door. Upon them rested a small Slavic head with a broad nose and little pig eyes. In fact, all the parts of his body seemed not to be quite in proportion so that when he walked, he looked not so much like a man as how you might picture the original *golem*.[19] Before the day was out, his nickname among the Jewish

19 In Jewish Folklore, the golem was created from mud, and became animated when the name of God, written out, was placed in its mouth

soldiers was 'Haman'[20] because one of his first official acts was to deny some thirty five of us permission to attend the reading of the Scroll of Esther[21] on the morning of Purim.[22]

Before he even knew our faces, he let us know he was well aware that the 14th Company, under its previous commander, had become disgracefully lax, undisciplined and unsoldierly – a virtual vacation resort. Well, he was here to put an end to all that. Those of us who had forgotten we were soldiers whose bodies and souls belong to the Czar, would very quickly find ourselves "vacationing" in Siberia where we might get the chance to do some real soldiering against a race of yellow vermin laboring under the illusion that Asia belonged to *them*. In particular, he advised the Jews in his company to cease conducting themselves as though they were still in some synagogue of theirs. This final observation did not go down well with the boys in my platoon.

Not only did Haman put us through the kind of training schedule ordinarily imposed only on the Convicts' Company, but he also let it be known that he was not afraid of us, singly or all together. In fact, he boasted that he had been transferred back here from Siberia, where he'd been perfectly happy, only because he had killed two men who'd made some threatening remarks to him. He sincerely hoped we didn't think he would hesitate for one moment to do the same thing, again, if he had to. The worst that could happen to him would be merely a transfer back to his beloved Siberia. As a result, it was we soldiers who felt obliged to eat and sleep with our rifles close at hand in case Haman thought he heard any one of us use his name in an unflattering context.

To the great misfortune of my poor friend, Vassily Divanovsky, whom I had met when we were both raw recruits on the train to Petersburg, Haman had taken a singular dislike to him. Vassily – Vasya to his friends – couldn't understand why Haman, who had already driven several of his men to suicide, should want to persecute him. "After all," he told me, "I am

20 Chief Minister of King Ahasuerus of Persia (aka Xerxes, 486-465 B.C.E.) who wanted to exterminate all the Jews in the kingdom, using a lottery to choose the date on which to do so.

21 This Biblical text retells the story of Purim, and Esther and her cousin, Mordechai's, roles in preventing the destruction of the Jewish people

22 'Purim' comes from the Hebrew word for 'lottery.' The holiday celebrates the Jews' reprieve from Haman's plan to determine the date for annihilating the Jewish people by drawing lots

an educated man, a graduate engineer, with a good knowledge of military fortifications. The Czar needs people like me. What's more, I don't drink, I don't get into fights, and I intend to obey every lawful command. So why should even the worst of officers have a quarrel with me?" (In justice to Haman, it must be said that, while he treated all his men with the same whole-hearted barbarity, he always seemed to have a little bit extra left for those Jewish conscripts who lacked the money, influence, or common sense to get themselves out from under his iron thumb.)

Nothing could persuade Vasya to use his family's connection to get himself transferred. He had, he told me, a domineering father who had tried to pressure him into an 'advantageous' marriage. To assert his independence, Vasya volunteered for military service.

But within weeks under Haman's tyranny, Vasya's features turned as gray as dust, and his skin barely clung to his bones. His hands shook uncontrollably, and his eyes bore the look of a man who would welcome death, the sooner the better.

Part of this may have been Vasya's own fault. What terrible thing had he done? One day, in response to some trifling injustice, he had politely pointed out to the tyrant that, according to Army regulations, volunteers were exempt from the more menial tasks such as kitchen and latrine duty.

Haman received this information in a state of marvelous astonishment. Then he screamed, "*Volunteer*? I'll show you, Jew, for what you volunteered!"

To begin with, Haman put Vasya into a solitary cell where, for 24 starved and sleepless hours, Vasya shivered like a skeleton. From there he was sent straight to the parade ground where the company was put through a long day of what Haman called "maneuvers," none of which would have the slightest usefulness in combat. He soon drove Vasya to the kind of despair that could lead even the healthiest of men either to take his own life or undergo a momentary loss of self-control that would get him shot for "mutiny."

Meanwhile, I had turned to my brother, Mordechai, who exercised his connections to get me transferred back to the 15th Company (that was previously known as the 'Convicts' Company,' but which now had a decent *polkovnik*[23] in the excellent Colonel Lakheff, and a large proportion of Jewish soldiers).

Early one evening, while some of us sat in a shady grove idly pitching pebbles into a tranquil pond, Vasya suddenly materialized before us, pale as fog. He drew me to one side and wept bitterly over his folly in having volunteered. If he could not get an immediate transfer out of the 14th, he would do something desperate.

I took the problem directly to Mordechai. But before proceeding on his advice, I thought it only right to tell Vasya what I had in mind to do. And to caution him that it was not without risk. That if I failed or, worse, Haman got wind of it, Vasya would suffer the consequences.

He said only, "Yakov, if you can get me out of the 14th, I will owe you nothing less than my life." And he vowed he would not forget my "heroism" till he went to his grave.

Unfortunately, our Colonel Lakheff, who was related by marriage to the Czar, was about to take a month's vacation in the Crimea. And since Vasya did not seem likely to survive another month of Haman's benevolence, I had no choice but to seek him out that very night.

A trek through mountainous snow banks and stinging frost brought me to Lakheff's mansion on Nevsky Prospekt. When I got there, I was dismayed to find the front yard packed with fine coaches, whose horses and drivers huddled and dozed under thick blankets of wool and snow.

I saw that I was intruding on some festive occasion. It seemed unlikely that, even if I managed to gain admission and found my colonel sober enough to hear me out, I would be able to draw his attention to the ill fortune of one young volunteer.

But having come this far, I also recalled that our good colonel, having married somewhat above his station, was in endless need of additional income so as not to disgrace his highborn wife. And that, in his elaborate network of graft, he *needed* people like my brother, both to protect his interests and, in case of a scandal, to absorb the full load of blame.

My arrival coincided with the exit of two portly civilians with cheeks like polished red apples, eyes dancing with satisfaction, and dabs of grease still clinging to uppermost of their several chins. As the doorkeeper scur-

23 Russian: Colonel

ried to awaken their driver, I slipped into the mansion, not at all confident I would emerge as lighthearted as the departing guests.

As it happened, one of the colonel's footmen was an old comrade from my days in the Convicts' Company whom, I assumed, owed his position more to his criminal expertise than his social polish. Ilya sympathized with my problem, but that night his master was entertaining guests of such fearful importance that it could cost Ilya his job if he permitted someone of my rank to barge in. Especially on a matter as frivolous as saving a friend's life. I suggested that he drop Mordechai's name, and he promised to see what he could do. Then, like Joseph, who waited two years for the Pharaoh's butler to remember him, I prepared to wait for my audience with the colonel.

I gazed into the ballroom that scintillated with electric lights. On a bandstand in the far corner, four men scratched out waltzes or minuets or whatever type of music it was that set couples to rotating like puppets. And then my heart suddenly froze. One of the dancers forcefully navigating a large, stone-faced battleship of a woman was Haman, himself. This meant either he was the colonel's good friend or, worse yet, they were partners in some handsome piece of graft.

I was ready to retreat when Ilya nudged me. To my astonishment, Colonel Lakheff came out almost at once. Apparently, Mordechai's name had done its job. The colonel, encased in a dress uniform that was crusted with medals, was almost too drunk to stand up but he recognized me readily and motioned me into his study. He slumped into a chair and said, "Now, what is so important that it can't wait till morning?"

To strike a more positive note, I said, "Your Excellency, do you remember how, last year, you saved my life?" This won me nothing more than a blank look.

"I was then in the 14th Company which, particularly for a Jewish soldier, was not a healthy place to be, then or now. And you, as a kindness to my brother, Mordechai, got me transferred into the 15th."

"Yes, yes, and what do you want now?" the colonel said with just a touch of impatience.

"Another transfer out of the 14th."

His fish-eyes bulged. "Again?"

"Not for me. For a good friend, a graduate engineer whom the company commander has threatened to destroy."

"Why?"

I hesitated. What reason would it be safe to give? "My friend made the mistake of calling the captain's attention to certain Army regulations."

"What's wrong with that?"

To this I had no ready answer. And I could see that the colonel was quickly losing interest.

"Write a letter to my adjutant. I'll take care of it next month when I come back."

"In a month, my friend will be dead."

Fortunately, Colonel Lakheff was too drunk to notice the insolence of my tone. He suddenly turned to me and said, "Wait here."

I had neglected to consider the loyalty among officers. Now the colonel would bring in captain Fedorenko so that I could repeat my accusation in front of him. Once again, I wanted to flee, but I didn't want to appear the coward. So rather dwell on the range of punishments that Haman would have in store for me, I tried to focus on the décor of the colonel's study. It was hard to overlook one very large painting, in particular, on which, amidst exploding shells and decorative splashes of blood, horsemen in plumed hats and spotless uniforms charged with drawn sabers into the mouths of massed cannons whose gunners, with admirable forbearance, fired carefully over their heads. If our officers thought that image truly resembled an actual battlefield, no wonder they couldn't wait to go to war.

When the door burst open, I spun around. Behind Colonel Lakheff were a number of other field-grade officers, including an unfamiliar general and two high-ranking ancient specimens with whom I did not usually slurp out of the same trough. All looked at me as though I had been caught selling the High Command's secret plans for the defense of Moscow.

I sat on my bed of nails while a battery of piercing eyes demanded to know for what world-shattering purpose I had interrupted them at their frolics. Suddenly, I stopped worrying about my doomed comrade: now I was worried about myself.

The colonel broke the silence. "Gentlemen, we are all familiar with the conditions in the infamous 14th Company."

"Getting no worse than they deserve," muttered the general.

"Quite so. But there have been times when the company was under strength, and regular conscripts were assigned to it, some of them valuable men, such as this soldier here."

The general finally disfavored me with a direct glance. "He wants a transfer? Let him apply through regular channels." Having said this and been roundly seconded, he and his aides seemed ready to return to the dance floor.

Unasked, I finally made myself heard. "No, sir. I got my transfer, thank Heaven, some time ago. I now ask the same for a friend, an engineer, expert in the design of fortifications." I saw no profit in mentioning that Vasya had also committed the indiscretion of being a Jew. "His company commander has vowed publicly that my friend will not live out this month." That seemed rather feeble, even to me. But, to my surprise, the other officers began now, with some circumspection, to admit that they had heard similar tales. I could see the general was not pleased to hear such matters aired in front of a common soldier. But in the end, impatient to be done with it, he instructed his adjutant to cancel Captain Fedorenko's promotion and arrange for Vasya's transfer by noon tomorrow. He punctuated his ruling with a terrible look in my direction that dared me to object that that was not soon enough.

As a consequence of my tampering with the time-honored way in which things were done, Haman was duly removed from command of the 14th. I suspected he had a fairly good idea who had been responsible for blocking his promotion. And neither I nor my friend doubted his ability to settle scores.

By this time, Vasya was no longer quite such an innocent and didn't leave his survival to fate. He promptly cabled an influential relative named Brodsky, the sugar magnate and philanthropist. And shortly Vasya found himself snatched out of his sleep and hauled off to the hospital where a civilian specialist, likewise uprooted from his bed, determined that my comrade had an "inflammation of the heart," and should never have been accepted as a volunteer in the first place.

While Vasya waited nervously for his discharge papers to be processed, his father, although still displeased by his son's show of independence, relented enough to send him the money for train fare home.

Unfortunately, Vasya's months in the Convicts' Company had turned him into a somewhat reckless gambler. And on the very night before he was to leave for home, his luck ran stubbornly against him. Although he waged a tenacious battle until dawn, he ended up with his pockets cleaned out to the last kopek.

Given his history with his father and his own idiot stubbornness, Vasya was naturally too proud to cable him for additional money, even to save his own life. This left him with a choice between remaining in the army, nakedly exposed to Haman's whims, or borrowing the immense sum of 50 rubles for train fare.

As it happened, I had a little money saved up. And as our unit had already been placed on alert for shipment to Manchuria, I lent Vasya the money and told him he could pay me back when and if I returned. Or, if I were killed, he should send the money to my parents. He swore, again, that he owed me his life and that if I ever needed anything ...

Once Haman no longer had Vassily Divanovsky on whom to exact his sadistic intentions, he turned his attention to me and asked if I'd like to be sent to the front lines in Manchuria. Since it was obvious that he was not making this offer out of kindness, I gracefully declined, and told him that, all things considered, I would prefer to go with my own regiment. At which he smiled and allowed that he'd long had his eye on me; oh, yes, he knew I was behind his cancelled promotion as well as other misfortunes that had befallen him since assuming command of the 14th. And if I thought that being out from under his direct authority afforded me any kind of protection, I should be aware that the clerks who handled the paperwork that kept our army operating so inefficiently would fall over themselves to fulfill his demands in order to ensure that they didn't become of the next objects of his attention.

Fortunately, before Haman could sign my transfer order, one of my Ukrainian comrades made an unnecessary remark about Jews lacking the proper warlike spirit, and by the time they pried us apart, he was bleeding admirably from the head, and I had deep and painful teeth marks in my right hand, which I couldn't take to the hospital because they would have wanted to know how I had acquired them.

As a result, the day before I was due to board the train to the front, my hand was swollen like a sausage. I could barely pick up a rifle, let alone fire it. With uncharacteristic concern for a soldier's welfare, the general in charge of medical services decreed that I should remain in Petersburg, so that when the hand had to be amputated, it could be done under the best conditions.

In a few weeks time, thanks to the fact that I'd been afraid to go to the hospital for treatment, my hand recovered. And Haman, for the moment, had other things than me to worry about.

5

MINISTRY OF MISINFORMATION

We had long been hearing talk about the inevitable war with Japan, and our company's five-man revolutionary committee, of which I was a member, was well aware that if the revolution were put off much longer, we might soon all find ourselves fighting for the Czar's honor in a far-distant Chinese province called Manchuria, where we had as little business being as the Japanese had being in Korea.

But the despised Japanese attacked, and crippled our navy at Port Arthur.[24] Our Little Father,[25] whom, I suspected, had been praying devoutly for the enemy to do him just such a favor, quickly declared war, confident that the resulting upsurge of patriotic fervor would take people's minds off such nonsense as revolution.

In the days that followed, we learned about the enemy we were about to fight. We were shown pictures that emphasized his smallness, and his brutish, simian features. It was surprising to realize that such a scarcely human creature actually had hands like us, capable of firing a modern rifle, and not mere paws for swinging from trees.

24 The Japanese attacked the Russian Pacific fleet in Port Arthur, Manchuria (which was of strategic importance to both Japan and Russia), on February 8-9, 1904. It was the first battle of the Russo-Japanese War, which Russia formerly declared on February 10, 1904.

25 Respectful way of referring to the Czar

The job of driving these overbearing little creatures back into the sea was not sufficient reason for a great power like Russia to exert her full might. As a result, all the regiments being shipped to Manchuria were under-strength, half-trained, and not even fully equipped.

Meanwhile, our newspapers and officers regaled us with such golden good news about how easily we would win the war that all of Petersburg became infected with war fever. Any thought of revolution went out the window.

So on a frosty summer morning, we lined up for the train to Manchuria. Our lieutenant, a moody graybeard in his sixties, told us that we were lucky. How were we lucky? We would get to ride to the battlefield in comfort while the enemy, primitive little beasts that they were, would have to walk. He made The Battlefield sound like a scheduled stop on the Trans-Siberian Railway.

My nearsighted friend, Glasnik, suggested that I let the lieutenant know that we, too, would be happy to walk, and with a little luck the war would be over by the time we got there. But I was a one-striper, a corporal, so I kept my mouth shut.

The train had 96 cars, each packed to at least three times its capacity. This way the railroad was able, on one track, to deliver its quota of thirty thousand replacements a month. I tried not to think about the men we were replacing.We sat in our compartments, barely able to stir an elbow, everyone hoarding his own fears and memories. For the moment, Russians, Ukrainians, Poles, and Jews sat packed together in a pleasant atmosphere of revolutionary harmony. Until somebody wondered aloud how many of us would return alive.

Days passed in such comfort. The half-blind windows of our car offered us only the brutal monotony of barren hills, rotting fields, and mute, hollow-eyed villagers. We were all stiff and irritable from the lack of space, and no one talked revolution any longer because by now we hated the stink of one another.

Soon, however, we came to appreciate our crowded compartments. The train had to cross Lake Baikal on rails laid over the ice, which at times suddenly cracked open into yawning rifts and crevices. To keep the cars from being too heavy, the officers were taken across by horse-drawn sledges. The rest of us walked forty miles across the windswept ice, our rifles, with their eternally fixed bayonets, resting on one shoulder, with only brief pauses for hot soup from our mobile kitchens. By morning, a number of men had disappeared, either deserted or drowned, and many more suffered from frostbite.

Then back into the unheated boxcars for another week of crowding and starvation, another week of wallowing not only in our own filth, but in that of the boxcar's previous, four-legged passengers.

One morning, we awakened to a strange landscape in which the roofs of the houses curved upward like boats, and the trees put me in mind of things that might grow on the moon. This was Asia. The people here had darker skins and narrow, villainous, Oriental eyes. Most of the men believed them to be 'Japs,' having little notion that we were almost as far from Japan as we were from Moscow.

We were headed straight for the battlefield, somewhere between Mukden and Port Arthur, where heavy fighting was taking place. We were said to have lost over sixty thousand men in one battle alone.

Officers came through the cars now to deliver inspirational talks. About how our Little Father, the Czar, was counting on every one of us. But mainly about the enemy's cruelty to Russian prisoners. This was to inflame our thirst for blood. In actuality, it had the opposite effect. Most of us were left subdued and depressed. Who wanted to get involved with such uncivilized savages? We all knew what we were in for, but there was no way back except in some condition we'd rather not think about.

The next day, our train lumbered to a halt near a village used as a transfer point for the wounded. I heard no sound of guns yet, but our commandant said we were very close to the battlefield.

Our hearts beat more quickly as we were marched through the village. Its principal building served as a field dressing station, and the streets were full of haggard men in Red Cross armbands wearing smeared butchers' aprons. The huts, wherever you looked, were filled with men groaning, gasping, or horribly still. Some of them also lay on the ground outside, listlessly waiting to die.

I asked why the wounded weren't taken to hospitals. Answer: because there were none, at least in this sector. Our high command had expected to engage the enemy much farther to the east, near the Yalu River. The

Japanese, however, had treacherously refused to cooperate. There was a hospital train on the way, but it had been due several days ago and seemed to have disappeared.

Spending a couple of idle and oppressive days among the piteous cries and foul smell of the injured and dying left most of us praying for a quick death, rather than the slow one of a serious wound.

Then it turned out that our commandant had read his map incorrectly and stopped the train in the wrong place. A dried-up, snowy-haired little man, General Zasulich consulted, by the flicker of a trembling candle, a large, tattered old map from which he seemed to extract as much enlightenment as a chicken studying the commentaries of Rashi.[26]

The fighting was said to be at least another half-day's journey away. They packed us back into the train, and all ninety-six cars continued on their blind search for the war. But we still didn't reach our destination. This time it was because the Japanese had blown up a bridge about ten minutes before we got there. We were saved only because God is good and our train, as usual, was late.

The adjutant cabled a message to Harbin for engineers and materials to repair the bridge. He was told that we were needed urgently at the front, and he should find boats and ferry us across, then force-march us the rest of the way, some hundreds of miles, with no mention of food.

Fortunately, none of the boats we were able to commandeer was big enough to carry our field pieces, ammunition, or horses, and our commandant, bless him, refused to send us into combat empty-handed.

We soldiers were quite content to remain where we were, and wouldn't have cared if they never fixed the tracks. Except that another troop train now arrived, and suddenly there were thousands of us stranded with barely enough food for a day or two.

Being on a single-track line with no nearby spurs for detours, we couldn't even send the second train back to get us food. Meanwhile, more trains would be arriving daily, all filled with hungry men.

We were given ammunition for our rifles and told to live off the land. While the Russian soldier, with his peasant background, was a natural-born forager, nothing edible had been growing in this rocky, frozen soil for

26 Commentator on the Torah (Hebrew Bible), who lived from 1040-1105

the last hundred miles. In fact, the only cultivated fields we'd seen all day were of poppies, grown for the Chinese opium trade.

Some men formed hunting parties. They were warned not to go too far afield. The area was notorious for bands of "Chunchus" ("Red Beards"), Chinese brigands who were so powerful, and so well organized, that they didn't hesitate to attack and rob even armed Russian patrols.

A day or two later there was more bad news. Thirty miles behind us, the Japanese had blown up the train carrying food. None of *us* had known it was coming, but *they* did.

Meanwhile, an engineer had arrived and told the adjutant that the bridge couldn't be repaired. A bypass would have to be built on pontoons, farther downstream. Although no building materials had arrived yet and the tracks behind us now were torn up as well, we were assured that the job would be done in two weeks. A silent cheer rose from the company when we heard the news. Not a man believed that we would be out of there in less than two or three months. By now, even the most patriotic Russian blockhead knew that in *Vanya's* army nothing ever went in a straight line.

6

THE LOST AND FOUND BATTLEFIELD

When you consider that we had come from the opposite corner of the world for no reason other than to liberate the Chinese empire from Japanese domination, it was strange that even the Manchurian coolies our army employed as laborers along the Trans Siberian Railway appeared, with some mad sense of Asiatic solidarity, to be spying for the Japanese against us, their liberators. This bizarre loyalty explained how the enemy knew about our imminent arrival before we did. To no one's regret, the blown-up bridge postponed our arrival at the battlefield by nearly a month, giving many of us four weeks longer to live.

Unfortunately, in time, our engineers managed to put up some sort of temporary bridge, which it was best not to examine too closely, and our train resumed its breathless progress toward the theater of war. This time, we traveled with leaden hearts, knowing we were in for a fight to the death against an enemy who had no appreciation for Europe's civilized traditions of warfare.

Meanwhile, we heard from soldiers guarding the railroad station at Mukden that our losses on retreating – or to be accurate, escaping – from Port Arthur had run into the tens of thousands. Thus, our train was needed to evacuate an endless stream of torn and broken men for whom no hospital beds were available locally, while its current, human freight was needed to fill the gaping holes in what was left of our front lines. So we were ordered out of the damp and airless train cars and were obliged to continue on foot. We were headed for the battlefield, and this time, nothing but a miracle could delay us.

From what I saw as we reached Manchuria, the best proof of how little the Russians actually expected a Japanese attack was how totally and nakedly unprepared our army and navy were, both for the fighting and its natural consequences. (To be fair, I am not certain that, even if our generals had been diligently planning this war, day and night, for the past ten years, they would have done much better.).

To begin with, we had learned nothing about modern advances in infantry tactics, while the despised Japanese, in their shameless eagerness to be westernized, were up on all the latest tricks. Our leaders were also smugly ignorant about the Japanese mentality, their fanaticism, their patriotic fervor, their incredible endurance, their horribly unpredictable methods of attack, and willingness to squander 100,000 lives for the capture of Port Arthur.

Meanwhile, the doctrines of infantry combat had been totally overturned several decades earlier by the American invention, or perfection, of the machine gun. Not that our Maxim wasn't at least as good as the Hotchkiss used by the Japanese. The difference was *they* knew how to employ it with some tactical effectiveness, while to us it was just another burden some poor donkey or foot soldier had to haul over the frozen ground.

Our repeating rifle was actually superior to those with which the Japanese were armed. Unfortunately, the invention of smokeless powder, about which no one had bothered to inform our officers, had increased the range, accuracy, and penetrating power of rifle bullets. This allowed the Japanese foot soldiers to be armed with lighter rifles while carrying twice as many bullets.

Unlike the Japanese, we had almost no mountain artillery, nothing but heavy stuff, useless for mobile warfare. It soon was obvious that most of our officers still visualized ground combat in terms of the last war they had fought – against the Turks thirty years earlier.

Add to these lapses the fact that the Russian infantryman, for all his stubbornness and bravery, was obviously not insane enough to try to outdo his Asiatic enemy. Especially in our regiment where the majority of soldiers were not Russians at all, but Poles, Jews, Ukrainians, Balts, and even Germans, all of whom felt toward the Czar about as much warmth as a chicken has for a fox. Throughout the army, the only force able to stir the average czarist soldier out of his brutish apathy, aside from self-preservation, was talk of revolution.

On our first night's excursion in search of the battlefield, there was a lot of grumbling about the cold, the lack of food, and, more perfunctorily, about the 'Japs,' a term that, for us, also included Siberians, Manchurians, Koreans, and Chinese. Despite all the "inspirational" talks about Japanese atrocities we'd been given en route, we didn't really hate them. The Japanese we merely feared, although not as much as we feared the villainous incompetence of our own junior officers.

Even I, a squad leader, found it difficult to work up much enmity. I knew that for each official enemy in Japanese uniform, I had a far more dedicated enemy at my side or behind my back. Prominent among these was Pyotr, the Ukrainian sergeant to whom I'd had such a murderous introduction almost as soon as I arrived in Petersburg. Having been demoted as a result of the trial, he was now under my command, and Glasnik frequently warned me that "the sheep-faced *katzap*" remained determined to settle old scores. And since I now outranked him, he was merely biding his time until the chaos of battle would make it quite impossible to determine precisely whose bullet had killed whom.

Meanwhile, I was quite content for our blundering general not to find the battlefield.

Tired, footsore and having gone without hot food for some twenty hours, some of my men were audibly grumbling. I advised them to shut up and count their blessings: if our commander knew his business, we would have been in battle already and possibly dead.

We plodded on past devastated villages and frozen, long-unburied corpses until, at sunrise, our general, perplexed, halted the column and politely asked some blank-faced Manchurian peasants if they could tell him where to find the battlefield. They glanced, open-mouthed, at his map and professed not to know what he was talking about. Meanwhile, the treacherous Japanese remained the Devil-only-knows where. By noon, we were totally exhausted, but also relieved to know that we had been granted another day of life.

Out of the icy morning fog that smothered the ground, we saw a convoy grinding toward us. Each wagon was piled high with dead or wounded soldiers, some of the latter still capable of moans and shrieks that scarcely seemed human. This, it turned out, was the unit at whose flank we were to have fought this morning.

None of us said a word, but it was easy to guess what each man was thinking. Those were men, full of life like us, and look at what had happened to them in only a few short days, perhaps only hours. Following the convoy was a file of stretcher-bearers carrying those wounded men whom they still had some wild hope of saving. Some of the stretcher-bearers seemed to make a professional assessment of us, as though estimating how heavy we would be to carry after the next encounter. I could hear a few of the men wishing they were already wounded and on their way back; at least they would escape something worse.

It was not until I recognized one of the walking wounded that it suddenly hit me: this was my younger brother's company! With a beating heart, I fell in beside one soldier and asked about Avrohom.

He made a negative gesture and averted his eyes.

I clawed at the front of his coat. "What happened to my brother?"

He shrugged.

"Is he dead?"

"I don't know."

"*Tell* me."

"Half the company is missing."

"Captured?"

"I don't *know*!"

In the end, all I could get out of him was that he had not actually *seen* Avrohom's body, but my brother's platoon was the first to be thrown into the attack, and hardly a man among them had survived. I held out little hope for my younger brother, who had never shown any interest in physical exertion, and I suspected hadn't taken well to soldiering.

I dropped to the ground, choked with tears, and bitterly regretted having enjoyed our reprieve. If only our imbecile of a general had found the battlefield in time, my brother's platoon might not have been wiped out. I darkly consoled myself with the thought that it mattered little which one of us was the first to die when it was plain that, eventually, we all would end up buried forever in this strange soil.

Some of my squad tried to console me. But I was most conscious of the one man who stood aloof and grinning.

We were suddenly halted and ordered to start digging trenches. I noticed that our officers had us deployed on the back slope of a hill in such a way that, while we wouldn't see the approaching enemy, we would, at least, be able to run away more easily. It was nice to see how much faith they had in the Russian infantry's ability to stand fast under frontal attack.

The trenches were to be about twenty feet apart and four-and-a-half-feet deep. The digging went easily because the ground was soft and muddy. But, for the same reason, the sides of the trenches kept caving in.

Before sunset, we were summoned together at the foot of the hill, where our commanding general delivered a talk. He was unquestionably a talented orator, at least as measured by his effect on the Russian and Ukrainian boys. He recounted the greatness of Holy Mother Russia, of how we had never lost a war, and of how devoted our Little Father, the Czar, was to the welfare of his people, regardless of their nationality or religion. Therefore, each man, whatever his origins, should consider it an honor to give his life for the Czar. After the war, things would be different: peasants would receive more land, workers would get higher wages, and even the Jews would have the right to own land wherever they wished to live.

Glasnik was the first to grasp that there was a small catch to these wonderful promises: to see them carried out, one merely had to get killed, first.

Our general had reassurances for skeptics like Glasnik. Our enemy, he said, was more monkey than man, so puny and primitive and so laughably unaccustomed to modern warfare or true Russian patriotic fervor that all we needed to do was scarcely more than throw our caps into the air to send him into headlong flight. I thought of the men who had passed us earlier today and wondered why they hadn't thought of that.

With evening, it grew piercingly cold. We lined up at our soup wagons. The food did little more than warm our stomachs for a moment. The real hardship was that we couldn't smoke because our lit matches might reveal our location to the enemy. I suspected, however, that the Japanese knew exactly where we were, probably better than we did.

Presently, we were issued bales of straw to spread on the muddy floor of the trench where we lay down to sleep.

By morning, all of us were furiously hungry, but nowhere was there so much as a glimpse of food. What I did see were hundreds of soldiers, roaming around in defiance of orders, collecting clean snow to boil for tea and to wash themselves. I ordered my men not to leave the trench, and to take just enough water from their canteens to rinse their mouths and eyes. So we waited and yawned and scratched ourselves, and cursed the bitter cold that knifed right through to our bones. By now the frost was so sharp that spittle turned to ice even before it dribbled down your chin.

After lying all night on the damp, muddy straw, my uniform and even my underwear were frozen stiff, as though they'd been heavily starched. I jumped around and thrashed my arms to work up some body heat. If the Japanese had attacked at that moment, I'm quite sure I would not have been able to hook a finger around the trigger. I could only hope that they were as uncomfortable as we were.

Toward noon, as an emaciated ray of sun broke through the grey, we heard shouts of joy. The soup wagons had arrived. Wild with eagerness, the men started to dance around in total abandonment. But, just as we lined up for the soup, without a thought for cover or concealment, our uncivilized enemy decided to open up with his heaviest artillery. In spite of General Zasulich's aristocratic contempt for geography and terrain maps, the accommodating Japanese, whether out of Oriental courtesy or simple impatience, had come looking for us.

Before we knew it, we were in the midst of a formidably accurate barrage. I saw horses, wagons, and men flung through the air like toys. All around me, soldiers, torn by shrapnel, were screaming. We rushed back to our trenches, full of hatred for the Japanese. But they were too far away for us to reach with our rifles.

We were, however, consoled by the promise of an opportunity to make a bayonet charge on the enemy's trenches, as soon as we knew where his main strength was concentrated. Meanwhile, far behind us, dispatch riders were hurrying in all directions to call for reinforcements, and our adjutant was telegraphing frantically for counter-battery fire. (This skirmish, I learned later, was known as the Battle of Liao-Yang,[27] and it involved more men than any battle fought in modern times, including Waterloo. And yet, no one in America seemed to have heard of it, which, for the sake of Russian honor, may be just as well.)

Our artillery finally came to life, dropping its first rounds on *our own* forward positions. This was done, I was told, to help them find their range. The shelling continued sporadically until nightfall while we cowered, starved and useless, in our trenches. After dark, we received a small ration of hardtack[28] that would barely sustain us for the night. With our stomachs feeling dry and shriveled, we huddled together and tried to sleep. Each squad had been issued a large straw torch and a bottle of kerosene. If attacked, we were to light the torch so the unit behind us would know to counterattack. That wouldn't help us any, but at least there was the plan.

But the Japanese, as usual, didn't wait for a formal invitation. At two o'clock in the morning on September 2, 1904, while I dreamed about sitting with a girlfriend in an ice cream parlor in Warsaw, someone shook me and yelled, "Brother, get up!" I jumped to my feet and immediately had to duck again. Machine guns were raking our position, and bursts of shrapnel squealed over our heads. Our batteries replied stingily and without much visible effect.

As the shelling grew steadily more intense and more accurate, I feared we wouldn't survive the night. I'd never had any romantic notions of combat being anything other than terrible, but I had not expected it to be this frightening.

I prayed for daylight, although that offered no guarantee that the shelling would stop. Suddenly my lieutenant screamed, "Lord, have mercy!" and fell on top of me. Covered with his blood, and unable to support his weight, I grew dizzy and, within a moment, found myself lying pinned to the bottom of the trench.

---

27 The Battle of Liaoyang, one of the major battles of the war, took place from August 24-September 4, 1904

28 A simple biscuit or cracker used during wars, extended seagoing voyages (where they are known as "sea biscuits,") or wherever perishable foods would not endure

Glasnik pulled me free and kept shouting in my ear, "Marateck, are you wounded?" I stood up and checked where my uniform was bloody, but it was all the lieutenant's blood.

The wounded man whimpered, "Mother! Mother!" None of us knew how to tie a bandage that would stop his bleeding. I tried to give him some water, but his mouth was tightly clenched from the pain. I knew if we didn't get him to an aid-station at once, he'd die from loss of blood.

Above us, the bombardment was thicker than before. But four of us decided to risk it. Crawling on our bellies, we dragged our lieutenant toward the rear. After slithering like this for about an hour, we dropped into an empty trench to catch our breath. The sweat had congealed on our bodies, and we started to shiver from cold. I struck a match to see how the lieutenant was doing. He was without a head, and probably had been for some time. Two of the soldiers began to cry.

Returning with some stretcher-bearers to pick up wounded men, we saw that many no longer needed assistance. Too weak to keep warm by moving around, they had frozen to death.

Later, during a letup in the shelling, one of our regimental staff officers came by on horseback and told us that we had won a great victory. Despite heavy losses, we had held our position. I was too tired to point out to him that the hill belonged to China, not to us, and that the Japanese infantry had not as yet made an actual effort to take it. Further down the line, a cheer went up as the next platoon was informed of its "victory." I sat on the damp straw and prayed to be spared any more such military triumphs.

In mid-afternoon, there was a fresh artillery duel, but the enemy had shifted its interest to another sector, and we were able to sleep. Toward evening, I crept out of the trench to see whether there was any soup left. With a shock, I discovered that all the nearby trenches were empty. Our battalion, it seemed, had been ordered to retreat while we slept, no doubt by the very same officers who had confirmed our "victory," and no one had bothered to wake us. The wind and sleet had covered all tracks, and it was impossible to tell in which direction they had gone. As it was getting dark, we knew that if we went looking for them we could easily stumble into enemy hands.

There we were, alone on a huge sloping field, surrounded by the twisted bodies of men and horses, piles of empty ammunition boxes, boots, shovels, mess tins, broken carts, fur hats, blankets, and scraps of clothing. To my great disappointment, I saw that Pyotr, my devoted enemy, hadn't fled and was, in fact, full of vigor. But he had the excellent idea of searching the dead for any hardtack, sugar, or tobacco they might have on them. Soon the rest of us were doing it. We found very little, until we searched the pack of an officer, which yielded a small bottle of vodka. It was quickly shared, no more than a lick for each man, but it left us somewhat more cheerful.

A machine gun suddenly opened up on us and we raced back to our trench, surprising a number of large rats that had been gnawing on a body we had been too tired to bury. One of our men got a bullet through his thigh, but he was so numb with cold he didn't even feel it.

Night fell, and we were not sure of what to do. Stay there, or try to find our battalion? It was a serious question, not only because we might, at any time, be overrun by the Japanese, but also because if we rejoined our unit after we had been officially listed as dead or missing, we would automatically be declared deserters. Which could mean the firing squad.

We decided to stay put, at least for the night. But it wasn't safe to sleep. I don't know which we dreaded more, the Japanese or the rats. To keep warm, we huddled together, helping one another stay awake. Sometime during the night, however, sleep won out.

By morning, snow had covered us with such a thick blanket that we might have been in a feather bed at the Hotel Bristol in Petersburg. My first thought was that I had died and been buried; it was a miracle that we hadn't frozen to death. The only reason I knew I was alive was because I was hungry. And because I heard my comrades' snoring.

It took all my strength to dig myself out. By now the snow had nearly filled the trenches. Above me, there was no sky, and almost no air. Around me, I saw not another living soul. Where had they all gone?

It was impossible to breathe without inhaling snow. The wind was like a dagger in my lungs.

I took a little of the crisp, dry snow and washed my eyes. My watch had stopped, and I didn't know if it was morning or afternoon. Somewhere in the distance, cannons were booming. Apparently not even the Japanese were interested in our little group.

I envied my comrades who were still sleeping, and thought about burying myself once again in the snow. But with bloodstained clothes frozen to my body, I couldn't loosen anything without tearing off patches of skin.

Fed up with being alone in my misery, I tried to awaken Glasnik. But even after I had removed his heavy covering of snow, he continued to snore. Finally, I had to pull his hair to get his attention.

It took him some time to recall where he was. Then he helped me dig out the others. The boy who had taken a bullet in his thigh absolutely refused to budge. I pressed my ear against his heart; it was silent as a stone. We managed to awaken only three more soldiers. As far as I could tell, the others had died during the night.

One of the live ones was Pyotr. He had a slightly insane glimmer in his eyes, the kind of a look you might see on a man who is ready to kill himself ... or you. Meanwhile, the storm piled snow into our trench as fast as we could shovel it out. We finally decided to abandon the dead (they were as well protected as if we had buried them properly), and try to find the rest of our battalion.

I saw some faint indications of where the road our battalion must have taken had once been, but by now the snow was hip-deep and we couldn't make much progress. If we didn't move quickly enough, the snow would bury us, and our bodies would not be found until the Chinese farmers returned for the spring planting. We decided to return to our trench to share the night with our comrades, but we could no longer find it.

Glasnik suddenly refused to go on. He took out his *tefillin*,[29] bared his left arm, which instantly turned as blue as skimmed milk, bound the leather straps around his arm and skull, and prayed by heart, saying the *shema*[30] with all the fervor of someone bidding farewell to life. I watched him enviously. My own *tefillin* were in my pack, but my fingers were too frozen to unbuckle it.

Pyotr, who in Petersburg had, more than once, been known to tear the *tefillin* from the head of a Jewish recruit, stared at Glasnik like a cat ready to pounce. I braced myself for the showdown. Better to die this way than

29 Hebrew: Phylacteries. They consist of leather straps and two square leather boxes, and contain four sections of the Torah written on parchment

30 Hebrew: Short for Shema Yisroel, a central Jewish prayer: "Hear O Israel, the Lord is our God; the Lord is One"

get a bullet in the back. But instead, Pyotr crossed himself. Was he trying to provoke me? But as Glasnik removed the *tefillin* and touched them to his lips, Pyotr suddenly lunged and seized them. Before I could intervene, he dropped to his knees, kissed the *tefillin*, and begged them to spare his life.

While I stood open-mouthed, he handed them back to Glasnik and insisted that, before he died, we must forgive him for the sins he had committed against Jews. I got fed up with his whimpering and threatened him. If I heard any more talk of dying, I said, I'd shoot him down like a dog. We had to think about surviving. Pyotr gave me a strange, frightened look, but calmed down.

We kept moving along what appeared to be the road, but the snow was falling so heavily that we could barely see one another. I ordered each man to hold onto his neighbor's belt. Partly walking, partly crawling, we dragged ourselves through the waist-high snow. Surely, somewhere in this vast, empty country there must be some remnant of a Russian army.

Pyotr suddenly called my attention to a group of dark figures on the horizon just ahead of us. They were impossible to identify, but they didn't move like Russian soldiers. We loaded our rifles and waited, but the dark figures seemed content to let us to make the first move. Half-blinded by the white steam pouring out of our mouths, we aimed our rifles, and I gave the order to fire. Our rifles exploded in a deafening volley. The recoil made my shoulder feel like a block of ice struck by a hammer. I motioned to the men to take cover, but there was no return fire. Nothing but a couple of high-pitched howls. Now we could see that the dark figures were wolves, feasting on our dead, and no doubt waiting to make a feast of us, as well.

It tore at my heart to think that, somewhere in this glacial wilderness, my brother's body might be lying exposed to the hot, sharp jaws of such creatures. I was so incensed by the wolves' disrespect for our fallen comrades that I began to fire. Whether or not my comrades understood my thinking, they began to fire, too, until we had killed most of the wolves.

Suddenly, I wondered why I had ever have thought of wanting to die. I needed to hold on to hope that I would still find Avrohom alive. Who was to say that he wasn't, at the same time, praying for his own death out of grief over my probable demise? Then the two of us would be complicit in unnecessarily causing great pain to our parents. That gave me strength to urge myself and the men forward.

Afraid to abandon ourselves to the deadly seduction of sleep, we plodded through a wilderness of hills and valleys choked with snow. The following day, we were briefly encouraged to find other lost soldiers, numb, half-dead, emaciated, and with blackened faces, who attached themselves to our little column. Not one of them said a word.

Toward nightfall, we gained the top of a hill and saw beneath us masses of Russian soldiers lying sprawled on the ground. It was a bivouac area where other refugees from the battle had assembled, waiting for someone to feed them, help them to write a few words to their families and, only if absolutely necessary, re-form them into battle-worthy units.

Drawing closer, I was startled to hear someone call my name. It was Berezin, a friend from my original platoon. We embraced each other, and I asked about our Jewish friends.

The news was mixed. Korotkin and Smelnikoff had been killed or captured in the last battle. Our strong man, Grabasz, was unharmed, but my friend Rosenberg, while in the hospital, had fallen into the hands of a "tailor" who had shortened one of his legs. And Krug had gotten a bullet through his eye and, by now, was probably dead.

I begged Berezin for some bread, which I shared with Glasnik and Pyotr, who suddenly burst into the most bloodcurdling oaths that he would be a friend of the Jews for the rest of his days. I was baffled by his passionate conversion. Glasnik's *tefillin* and my piece of bread hardly seemed enough to induce such a miraculous transformation.

But late that night, as we sat huddled around a small fire, Pyotr, who had managed to wheedle a drink or two, came lurching over to us insisting that he owed us his life. In what way did he owe us his life? Because in the brutish, *Vanya* view of the universe, it was a miracle that Glasnik and I hadn't murdered him or left him to die during our long trek back from our positions, though we had had countless opportunities to do so. And, in his superstitious mind, it was equally obvious that only the magical powers of Glasnik's *tefillin* had somehow kept us from fulfilling our bloody intentions.

As proof that he no longer harbored any ill feeling toward us, he demanded to be allowed to kiss Glasnik's *tefillin* once again. I braced myself for an eruption of drunken rage. Just as it looked as though blood were about to flow, Glasnik put a finger to his lips and, round-eyed with solemnity, explained that the *tefillin* were sleeping now.

Pyotr seemed to consider this and then nodded, sat down by the fire, and was soon snoring. Glasnik and I, strolling out of range, agreed it would be unwise ever to turn our backs on this man. His oaths might have sprung from a heart bursting with sincerity, but how far could one trust a man who remained convinced that only "magic" had kept us from doing to him what he would cheerfully have done to us?

7

THE PHANTOM SYNAGOGUE

With our new regiment, we were loaded onto trains, overcrowded as before. After the Devil-only-knows how many days of such tourism, we awoke early one morning to find our train pounding into a city we were told was Harbin. A maimed soldier had once told me that Harbin, a Chinese city, had a sizable Russian colony, largely owing to the capital and enterprise of Siberian Jews[31]. And while he had not seen it with his own eyes, he also thought there might be some kind of synagogue, established by either Russian or Cathayan[32] Jews.

I was relieved to hear this because I had, for some time, been anxiously counting the days and, according to my calculations, *Yom Kippur*[33] began that very evening. Harbin was the only place in all of China where I might yet have a chance to spend *Yom Kippur* in the midst of a congregation.

It was not altogether a matter of piety, on my part. After hearing some of the returning wounded tell of what went on at the front, I was not very optimistic about surviving the year to come. This made me doubly determined

---

31 Convicts and Jews made up much of the early population of Siberia, however there was strict regulation of Jews' movement and actions. Later, when the Pale of Settlement in far western Russia became overcrowded, Siberia became the only other location in which Jewish settlement was permitted.

32 Cathay is another name for China

33 Hebrew: The Day of Atonement

to be in a place of holiness tonight where I might plead, for my parents' sake if not my own, to be inscribed and sealed in the Book of Life. Perhaps I also had a more selfish reason: if Avrohom was still alive, no power on earth would prevent him from attending, either.

No one knew whether our regiment would remain there for any length of time, or would be sent directly into another battle. Our lines were crumbling in the face of the Japanese advance and anything was possible. But I had made up my mind: if there was a synagogue in Harbin, nothing, not even the prospect of standing trial for desertion, would stop me from finding it tonight.

At the depot, I picked up the hopeful rumor that we were to spend the next few days at an encampment near the city. "Near" turned out to be a march of several hours through a swampy, roadless, and thickly wooded wilderness through which there was no assurance I'd be able to find my way back.

As evening approached, I was left with a heavy heart. Our camp was in such a state of disorder that none of the officers knew about food or tents for the newly arrived regiment. It was obviously futile, amidst all this chaos, to ask for permission to return to Harbin. Especially for an errand as frivolous as asking the faraway God of the Jews to forgive our sins.

Some of the Jewish soldiers in our regiment had already begun talking about organizing services right in the camp. However, they were strangely convinced that *Yom Kippur* did not begin until the following evening, and I could not persuade them otherwise.

Yet, even those few who agreed with me that *Yom Kippur* began that very evening, felt it was hopeless to try and walk all the way back to Harbin that night. First of all, no one knew the way. Second, although none of us knew how many kilometers or how many hours we had walked, no one felt we could possibly arrive in time for *Kol Nidre*.[34]

Plus, the area we would have had to cover on foot was reported to be swarming with Chinese bandits who had already killed, robbed and mutilated a number of our stragglers.

I tried to convince the others that the rumor about bandits was spread by our own officers to keep us from wandering off. In the end, I persuaded

34 Aramaic: Prayer said on the eve of Yom Kipper before beginning the service

only Glasnik to accompany me by painting the prospect of being invited to a fat, traditional Jewish meal after the fast, and perhaps even spending that very night in a warm, clean feather bed. But I had no doubt that it was out of friendship, not holiness, that Glasnik agreed to go with me.

We carefully loaded our revolvers and filled our pockets with bullets. I gave someone my watch with instructions to send it to my parents in case I was killed en route.

It took no effort to evade the few tired sentries guarding the camp, and as darkness fell, we were well on our way, blundering through a misty landscape strewn with unseen rocks, knee-deep patches of mud, and unexpected rivulets that left our boots filled with water.

I felt reasonably confident that I knew the way into town. But with no visible moon or stars, and no landmarks to guide us, we walked and walked and Harbin seemed as far away as ever.

Presently, we came upon a narrow road. I was certain that if we stayed on it, sooner or later we were bound to come to a village in which we could ask directions.

The path meandered through a dense and dripping forest. Any tree might be sheltering a bandit waiting for foolish travelers such as we. Although we tried to walk without making noise, our frequent stumbling made this impossible.

After another hour of walking without making visible progress, Glasnik said that the way he felt, anyone who would stab or shoot him would be doing him a favor. I helped restore his energy by pointing out that, from what I'd heard, when Chinese bandits caught a Russian soldier they didn't kill him all at once. They had a method called "death of a thousand cuts" by which they whittled away at the prisoner piecemeal until, after several days, he was fortunate enough to expire.

By then, it was dark; it would be long past *Kol Nidre* time, but if we were headed in the right direction, there was still a chance we might find a Jewish home where we could get a warm bed tonight, and a festive meal tomorrow night.

We had left camp at half past six, and it must have already been close to midnight. The forest seemed endless, and I felt tempted to lay down under a tree and go to sleep. But we had to be closer to Harbin than we were to camp, so we continued in the pitch darkness.

Almost immediately, Glasnik walked straight into a swamp. Trying to help him out, I promptly sank in up to my hips. And then, as if to tantalize us in the midst of our struggles, the lights of a city appeared to be glowing just beyond the forest.

Caked with mud and soaking wet, we stumbled into the silent city. By the light of a dim street lamp, Glasnik and I regarded each other's inhuman appearance, and decided to look for a pump where we could wash our hands and faces. After blundering through half a dozen streets or alleys, we spied a light burning in a little hut, and decided to knock on the shutters.

A Chinese man opened the door and gaped. Behind him, a squirming mass of seven or eight children started to cry at the sight of us. The man whispered something to his wife, who shot out the back door, screaming.

We tried with gestures to explain that we only wanted some water to wash off the mud. Other Chinese now came running out of nearby shacks. I realized, indignantly, that far from being terrified, they were laughing at us.

I waved a ruble at them, and within moments, two pails brimming with water appeared. A Chinese man who seemed to know about a dozen words of Russian offered, for another ruble, to act as our guide. He looked at least a hundred years old. But the way I was feeling at that moment, money was no object if he could lead us to the synagogue, which we tried to represent, with the aid of Hasidic[35] gestures and contortions, as a place of prayer.

His face lit up with sudden understanding, and he motioned for us to follow him. After some twenty minutes of walking, we came upon an old frame building. Candles were burning inside. With great skepticism, Glasnik asked me, "You know how to pray in Chinese?" I, too, was somewhat unconvinced. Meanwhile, our guide had gone into a corner to argue, negotiate, or plot with the caretaker he had aroused. It was ominously clear to me that they were discussing us. And I couldn't say I much liked the way they looked in our direction.

---

35 Hebrew: Pertaining to a Hasid, a member of a strict sect of Orthodox Jews

I interrupted our guide in the middle of his earnest conversation and asked him whether there was some kind of inn or hotel anywhere in the vicinity.

Our interpreter suddenly seemed to have forgotten even his modest repertoire of Russian words. He smiled and nodded reassuringly while echoing my question in his own singsong. His repetitions were so musical that Glasnik wondered if he were the cantor of the synagogue.

We continued wandering through lanes ankle-deep in mud, looking for the Russian quarter. Before long, Glasnik began to complain to me as passionately as the children of Israel had once protested against Moses for having taken them away from Pharaoh's fleshpots, and made them blunder through the endless desert. The difference was Moses, at least, could talk to God whereas I couldn't even talk to a Chinaman.

Passing a drab wooden building without windows, we suddenly heard ghostly, disembodied voices that sounded like reverberations from the bottom of a well. We drew closer to the entrance, which consisted of a large, flapping rag, and our noses were assailed by a strange odor. I told Glasnik this must be a Chinese restaurant. Glasnik sniffed once again and refused to believe that the odors could have anything to do with food for human beings.

I shared his distaste, but I reasoned that even a primitive restaurant might offer accommodations for the night. Just as poverty could break iron, so, I supposed, that exhaustion could tolerate the smell of Chinese food. We entered cautiously, our hands on our revolvers.

Inside, rows of Chinamen were sitting on the bare floor with their feet folded beneath them. A man I assumed to be the owner came out and began to talk at us, presumably asking what we wanted to eat. I tried to explain that we were looking only for a place to sleep, but Glasnik interrupted, indicating with gestures that we wanted food, lots of it.

The owner smiled, nodded, and went into what, from the stench, had to be the kitchen. Glasnik pointed out that I had no proof that *Yom Kippur* began that night,[36] and was it not a *mitzvah*[37] to eat well before the fast?

36   Jewish holidays begin on the eve before the holy day
37   Hebrew: A good deed

"I've heard about these Chinamen," I told him. "He'll bring you a roasted cat, or a boiled dog, or a pickled snake." Glasnik turned green, but bravely insisted that the food could not possibly taste as bad as it smelled.

A waiter finally came out of the kitchen, and set two steaming bowls in front of us. Glasnik sniffed at his portion and seemed ready to gag. He said, "I want to see you eat first."

I shook my head. Glasnik dug his chopsticks into the bowl and tried to pick up a mouthful. It fell back. The Chinese men started to laugh. Glasnik promptly put down his chopsticks and commenced eating with his hands. The other customers now roared with laughter.

Suddenly, Glasnik gagged, and spit out his mouthful, accidentally splashing one of the nearby customers. I saw now that all of them had been waiting for an opportunity to start a fight. They crowded us into a corner. As I reached for my revolver, the owner of the restaurant forced himself between us and seemed to warn the others we were armed.

I suggested to Glasnik that we leave. My typically meek friend said not until he had beaten up the Chinaman who had started the fight. But I had seen the flash of knives in the dimly lit room, and managed to convince him that some of those people were probably bandits, and we'd be lucky to get out of there alive. We edged back towards the door like cowboys, holding our revolvers pointed at the crowd.

Outside, in the smudged gray dawn, I saw some Russian-looking men at the end of the street, and ran toward them. They took one look at us and turned to run away. We had to chase them for several blocks before I could corner them and ask if they knew of a synagogue in town.

One of the men replied in Yiddish that he didn't know about a synagogue, but a Jewish-owned restaurant was not far away; we could inquire there.

Glasnik and I brightened at the thought of a hot Jewish meal after the fast or before if, as he insisted, I was wrong about the date. We raced in the direction the man had indicated.

Before we found a restaurant, we came upon a building that was unmistakably a synagogue. We were just in time to see the cantor mount the pulpit and hoarsely announce that he had caught cold, and therefore his prayers would not be up to their usual standard. When he started to sing, I suspected that he would not have done much better without a cold. Still, he was the *shaliach tzibur,* the "intermediary of the community," and if the words that came groaning out of his mouth satisfied the Almighty, who was I to complain?

Starved, exhausted, and muddy as we were, we had achieved our goal. It made all of the hardships of the night before worthwhile. Heaven surely would take note of the trouble to which we had gone. That was when I felt Glasnik nudging me, guiding my eye.

I looked around and saw no sign of Avrohom. But there were at least one hundred soldiers from our regiment. Instead of setting out blindly the night before, they had arrived just ahead of us, clean, well-rested, with a good dinner under their belts, proper authorization, and even a guide to show them the way. Glasnik gave me a ferocious look.

I felt no envy at their neat, unruffled appearance, for when the moment came to cry out to the Almighty that I stood before Him, crushed and confounded, "having gone astray and led astray," no tears in all of Manchuria could have been more wholehearted than mine.

8

BANZAI!

By now it was deep winter, probably close to Chanukah.[38] After a mere three months in the bitter Manchurian wilderness, our regiment had lost more than three-quarters of its men. There was no longer a front line to speak of. It seemed as though the Japanese were every-where. Even our officers were eager to pull us back.

But that was not so simple. Though our company had tried not to end up as the Rear Guard, we now came under steady bombardment. Defensive actions had to be taken to protect the main body, or what was left of it. This time, enemy fire killed many officers. I suppose, having always been pampered, they found it difficult to cower and grovel in muddy holes and trenches like the rest of us.

Luckily for us, the enemy, acting out of some crazy Japanese notion of neatness, had paused to reorganize instead of staying on our backs and finishing us off.

Replacements belatedly started to arrive from Harbin. Among them was Vasiliev, our new company commander. He was a tall and handsome Mus-covite landowner, who appeared to take it as a personal affront that a good

38 Hebrew: Holiday commemorating the rededication of the Old Temple in Jerusalem following the Maccabean victory (165 B.C.E.). The eight-day holiday, which begins every year on the same date on the Jewish (lunar) calendar, falls on a different date on the secular calendar each year, either in late November, or December

percentage of the men in his company were Jewish. He was in no position to transfer us, but we soon found out he had other ways of reducing the burden we placed upon his tolerance.

One of our new commander's first official acts was to place me in charge of a post in a desolate stretch of forest where, several times in the past, the Japanese had crept up in the darkness, and killed and mutilated our sleepy, half-starved sentries. With me, he sent three other Jews and one new Russian boy, presumably to keep us from talking too freely.

I could see already what we had here, and I wasted no breath complaining. I did, however, ask him for a machine gun to help keep us from being overrun in a surprise attack.

He gave me a condescending look and said, "Just go and do what you're told."

"I need a machine gun. If you'll come with us, I can show you why."

"You think I've nothing better to do? I know you Jews. You'll fall asleep and we'll lose the gun."

I tried to control my voice. "Without the gun, you may lose five men."

"Four less of you to deal with after the war," he muttered, not quite under his breath.

This confirmed my suspicion that we didn't have a friend in this new *Vanya*, but what he said was nothing more than government policy at the time. For some reason, it didn't occur to this genius that if we were killed, the entire camp would be endangered.

After supper, we proceeded to our isolated post, holding on to each other's belts in the darkness. Our spirits were not exactly glowing. We knew that if we ran into trouble, we would be entirely on our own. But at least our shift was only for two hours.

We settled in with our meager five rifles poised on rotting sandbags. Seeing my look of disgust, Glasnik said, "Just wait until the next time the whole company comes under attack. One of us will see to it that our captain dies a hero's death."

I told him sharply in Yiddish to shut up; there was a *Vanya* among us. The new boy promptly answered in Yiddish, "I'm as much of a *Vanya* as you are."

I was doubtful. Many Russian peasants were fluent in Yiddish. I asked him to show me his *tzitzis*, the biblically commanded fringes that, during the war, were often worn even by non-observant Jews, if only to identify their bodies for a Jewish burial. He opened two buttons on his tunic, and we all relaxed.

The new boy told us he had known this officer for the last three months. He always sent his Jewish soldiers to the point of greatest danger, and with the same friendly explanation he had given me.

I looked at Glasnik. "Just wait," he said with a wink. It was probably idle talk, but I felt comforted. Although I didn't know if I could do it myself, I had no doubt that this type of officer deserved to be killed out of pure self-defense because he was clearly prepared, night after night, to give the Jews under his command the most dangerous assignments until he was rid of us all.

We watched, and listened, and waited. After three hours, no one had come to relieve us. Somehow, I was not surprised. But it was too dangerous to send one man back to seek our replacements, and more dangerous to leave only one man on guard. For all of us to go would have meant deserting our post, which might have been what our company commander was counting on. Finally, well past midnight, some shadows appeared. Upon being challenged, they gruffly gave us the password. Our replacements were Russian. They had a machine gun.

Too tired to go back to camp, we fell asleep in a nearby trench. A while later, we were awakened by sharp automatic fire. Our relief, it seemed, had all fallen asleep and one of them had been stabbed to death. But the attack consisted of only three Japanese, one of whom was killed by the machine gun; the second was wounded, and the third had surrendered. At daybreak, we marched back to camp with the two captives.

The wounded man gestured and pleaded pitiably. He seemed to be offering to tell us anything we wanted to know if only we would let him live. Someone went looking for an interpreter.

Meanwhile, our commander arrived on horseback, flashing his drawn saber and grinning like a sportsman at the two Japanese, who sank to the ground and started to plead. Vasiliev asked for volunteers to behead the captives. Most of the Jewish boys turned away in disgust. But the response was so enthusiastic from the other soldiers that the only solution would have been to draw lots. In the end, the commander decided he wanted to do the job, himself.

A stake was driven into the ground and the captives were tied to it in a manner that left their heads exposed. They were no longer pleading, but all my nerve endings could feel the hatred in their eyes.

Our commander drew back far enough to give his horse a running start. Now, with a shout of joy, he came galloping toward the stake. One slash, and both heads plopped to the ground. Some of the men started a make-believe football game with one of the heads, while the other was retrieved by a group doing a Cossack dance, while skillfully tossing the head from hand to hand.

I turned away, not wanting to watch any more. But I could tell that I had already become hardened because I felt no more than a mild twinge of disgust.

The next morning our retreat continued, although I was no longer sure we were heading in the right direction. Day and night, the sky was so thick with clouds of snow that we had neither sun nor stars to guide us. Nothing but our officers' doubtful ability to read their maps and compasses.

Though in retreat, we were still under orders to stop and fight, even counterattack, whenever conditions were favorable, to slow the enemy's advance toward Mukden. Even now our company commander acted as though we were heading into battle instead of running away from it. For days no one had mentioned killing him. We were far too tired, and he was far too alert.

Glasnik reported the latest rumor. Alexei Kuropatkin, our Minister of War, himself, was standing on one of the nearby hills to make a firsthand survey of the situation. It was said that he might take personal charge of coordinating our strategy. Strategy! I didn't know who was more foolish, our own proud General Zasulich, who was willing to suffer huge losses rather than retreat in time, or Kuropatkin with his policy: "No battle before we are in superior force." That would have suited me fine, except that the Japanese refused to cooperate, even though we outnumbered them four to one.

By the next day, the Japanese had finished regrouping and came after us in full force. Their artillery had found our range, which meant their forward observers must have been quite close, yet we never spotted them.

Since our group was closest to the enemy, we had to run the fastest. But I could see that our commander was looking for terrain on which he could halt us to stage a heroic Rear Guard action. Apparently, he feared he might never again get as good an opportunity to make a name for himself.

Even as darkness fell, the accurate shelling of the Japanese didn't let up. We kept running. Toward dawn, a messenger rode up with an order from headquarters: Stop and make a stand.

Our company commander was justly angry. Here the terrain was flat and almost indefensible. The ground was also icy and rocky – impossible conditions for digging trenches. We had passed up far better positions, to which it was now too late to return. But headquarters was adamant. The enemy was advancing too quickly. Time had to be gained to reinforce Mukden. We were ordered to build ramparts out of frozen corpses, the only material in abundant supply.

During the night, while small, Japanese units leapfrogged toward us in quick, terrifying spurts, the trench wall in front of me unexpectedly collapsed. It seemed that one of the frozen bodies was not yet dead, and had moved his legs.

Before we could think of repairing the breach, our commander ordered us to counterattack. If we had been fresh troops, properly equipped with normal artillery support, reserves, and enough ammunition, we might well have been able to give the enemy a bloody nose. But most of us were totally spent, and wanted no part of this mad scheme.

Seeing this, a sensible officer would have pulled in his horns. It was dead plain that we were in no condition to be inspired or threatened. But our commander was not one to take "No" for an answer. He worked himself into an almost insane fury, and began firing his revolver at those who made no move to get into position.

Several men were hit, and the rest jumped to obey. Glasnik whispered, "We should have shot him during the last bombardment."

I, just as angry, vowed, "He'll never see Russia again."

The Japanese were now firmly entrenched behind our own abandoned line of barbed wire. By the time we were set to counterattack, it was daybreak. When the sun came up, it would be directly in our eyes, casting a blinding spotlight on us. The whole enterprise was sheer lunacy, and I foolishly assumed that even our commander would have sense enough to call it off.

He wouldn't dream of it. What's more, he now ordered me to take five men with wire cutters and open a breach in the barbed wire.

I told him, "It's too light already. We'll never reach the barbed wire."

He reloaded his revolver, waved it in my face, and shouted, "Go on, Jew, before I make an example of you." It was either obey or get shot.

I looked at the other soldiers. Like sheep, they were ready to go, more afraid of his revolver than of the Japanese machine guns. I blindly picked five men, and led the way without even bothering to see if they were following me.

My prediction turned out to have been too pessimistic. By inching forward on my stomach, I reached the barbed wire, but I knew that the moment I rose up to cut it, I'd be an easy target. Still, now that I was here, what else should I do?

I looked back uncertainly at our lines. None of my five "volunteers" had bothered to keep up with me. I could see our commander surveying the enemy positions. If I took a shot at Vasiliev now, no one could say it was not an enemy bullet.

I crawled around until I could aim my rifle. I had him in my sights, but couldn't press the trigger. It wasn't my conscience that stopped me; my hand was either cramped or frozen stiff. As I rubbed my hand against my tunic to restore circulation, I heard the scream of the first shell. I lay pressed against the icy mud, but shortly I could tell by the location of the flashes that we were being pounded by our *own* artillery.

It was only after several minutes that our artillery seemed to realize that their range was too short, and stopped firing. I found out later that it was our commander, the man I had been about to kill, who managed to signal to them to cease firing.

There was no further talk of a counterattack, because with the first beams of sunlight, hordes of Japanese rose out of the earth and, like a tidal wave, came rolling steadily toward us. Accompanied by queer blasts on a bugle, a roar of voices rose in a single word: "Banzai!"

Our company disintegrated before my eyes. We turned and ran, stumbling heedlessly over the dead and wounded, alike. From time to time, we heard far behind us a hideous shriek, which I assumed to be one of our soldiers being sliced to death.

After a furious, pistol-waving attempt to rally us, our commander was now running as fast as any man in the company. I had trouble catching up with him until suddenly he staggered. A bullet had torn through his neck. He tried to keep going, which was a mistake, because he ran right into an explosion that tore off part of his leg.

I was closest to him, and instinctively picked him up and slung him over my back. At once, two men behind me shouted, "The dog! Let him rot!"

As I stumbled forward, trying not to fall, he gasped, "God bless the Jews! Dear God, let me live, so that I may earn their forgiveness."

He babbled on like this, while my comrades, Jew and gentile, muttered behind my back, "Throw him down, the filthy dog! Hasn't he killed enough of us?"

They were absolutely right. Yet somehow, having done this much, I couldn't just drop him. To a Jew, a *baal teshuvah*, a repentant one, is said to rank higher even than a man of lifelong piety. I didn't know how literally one should take this, or even whether this only applied to Jews, and I was nagged by the suspicion that my commander's repentance might not have been altogether sincere. But who was I to judge another human soul?

With each step, his weight seemed to double, like some demon out of an old wives' tale testing a weak man's resolve. Although it must have been agony for him to talk, he plainly felt his life depended on keeping me reassured of how much he now loved the Jews.

We stumbled past wounded men pleading with us either to take them along or to kill them. But none of us was able to think of anything beyond staying on his feet.

I suddenly felt a bullet barely miss my head. When I turned, I saw that the company commander was dead. I didn't want to see whose gun was smoking. I merely hoped that whoever did it, Russian or Jew, hadn't been trying to kill me, as well.

I let the commander's body slide to the ground. His warm, sticky blood had soaked through my tunic. I tried to wipe it off the back of my neck before it froze. For the rest of that day, I could not look anyone in the face. Not even Glasnik, whom I was sure was innocent. After all my loose talk about killing the commander, not to mention my own halfhearted attempt to do so, I felt like an accomplice to the murder.

9

THIS WAY TO THE FIRING SQUAD

ur retreat from Mukden had finally lost some of its nightmarish quality of headlong flight. Mainly because, after weeks on the run with virtually no food or sleep, we were worn down to the point where we'd not only ceased to resemble an army but barely invited comparison with human beings.

Meanwhile, Kuropatkin had now taken personal charge of stemming the tide of losses in the Harbin-Mukden sector. As was typical when a new man took over, Kuropatkin felt obliged to produce some immediate victories, regardless of the cost. In fact, his first order of the day was, "We will spare neither blood, nor treasure. All must be sacrificed for Emperor and Vaterland." But he took one look at the leftovers of our battalion and had us taken out of the line and quartered in an abandoned village.

That didn't mean we were free to recuperate. Although we moved about like shadows, there were still enough officers around to see that outward appearances were maintained. This included guard duty.

A call went out for all non-coms to report to the commandant. I pretended that I hadn't heard. For me, the final straw had been the week before when, under attack and almost out of ammunition, I'd been ordered to take a white flag and surrender the company to what turned out to be another Russian unit. But this recognition had not come until we had shelled each other enthusiastically for some hours and they, in their final blind charge, had been only inches from bayoneting me – white flag and all.

For my conduct in this lunatic affair, or maybe just to keep my mouth shut about it, the new commander personally assured me of a medal and a promotion. But I was finished with responsibility. Let them take my stripe. The pay, which we rarely received and had no place to spend, could never make up for all the terror, privation and exhaustion. I was ready to lie down and not get up for a month.

But before I had a chance to get myself demoted, one of the lieutenants tracked me down. I was told to take ten soldiers and mount guard. I told him I hadn't slept in a week, and to please let me rest for at least one night. He was not unsympathetic, but explained that there was a shortage of non-coms; I must do my duty and fill the gap.

It was a beautiful clear night with no more than a mild breeze. Having deployed my ten men and sternly warned them not to close an eye, I was tempted to sit down for a moment. But that was strictly forbidden. Besides, I knew I would not remember to get up again. Nevertheless, my lids kept drooping. To hold them open, I pinched myself, kicked one foot against the other, and generally struggled like a man about to drown.

Near midnight, a strange officer and two armed men shook me roughly, waking me. The officer demanded to know where my gun was. My heart stopped. I was without a rifle, and there was no sign of it anywhere. As we were miles from any Japanese, one of our own men must have stolen it. Fifteen minutes later, the new commander who, only two days earlier, had lauded my coolness under fire, told me what I didn't need to be told. The penalty for sleeping on guard duty was the same as that for losing one's rifle: death. About my only comfort was that they couldn't kill me twice.

The captain lectured me on what he thought of such undisciplined, ir-responsible soldiers as me. But he allowed that, from a Jew, what else could you expect? I noticed that I was not a 'Jew' two days ago when he promised to recommend me for a medal.

I was put into an improvised jail cell under heavy guard. The survivors of my company were furious. From behind bars, I could hear snatches of their reassuring arguments, not only about the injustice being done, but also their sporting curiosity about whether I'd be shot or get away with twenty-five years at hard labor.

Despite such stimulating thoughts, I slept like a corpse until noon the following day. It was only once I was somewhat rested that I began to realize the depth of the trouble I was in. Three days ago, I hadn't much cared if I lived or died, but having regained some of my strength, I also had gotten back my appetite to go on living. When they brought my ration of bread and water for lunch, I left it untouched. My heart was so bitter, I felt I would choke on a drop of water.

In the evening, Glasnik stopped at my window and consoled me with the news that I was the principal topic of conversation all over the camp. While most of the Russian boys were fairly nonchalant about my fate, the Jewish soldiers insisted, as a matter of principle, that I must not be executed. They'd circulated petitions asking men to sign a statement that they would refuse to shoot me. Those who wouldn't sign their names were warned that whoever took part in my firing squad would live to regret it – but not for very long. Since we Jews were somewhat in the minority, I was not only impressed with their boldness, but also concerned that some of them might yet end up joining me against the wall.

But strangely enough, the officers began to get a little nervous. Accustomed for years to shooting deserters and other delinquents without hearing a word of complaint, they realized that mine was not going to be a routine case.

Their uneasiness was not the result of my popularity, or fear of the Jewish soldiers. Their confidence in themselves as a class had been shaken by the recent succession of military disasters. They also couldn't help but be mindful of the current revolutionary ferment back home. (This had already led to hundreds of government-sanctioned pogroms, but at long last, it showed that Jews were capable of organized and effective self-defense.) The order was passed down that none of my guards were to be Jews.

There was one adjutant of whom, back in Petersburg, I had been clumsy enough to make an enemy while we were both somewhat drunk. (It was a little incident for which he couldn't have had me court-martialed, because that would have required him to explain what he was doing with another officer's wife.) Now it turned out that he had neither forgotten nor forgiven me for my unintentional rudeness. And with an efficiency that, if applied to his own duties, would quickly have made him a general, he rushed through the paperwork required to send me into the next world.

Glasnik, beside himself, raised his right hand and swore by Heaven and earth that if the adjutant signed the order for my execution, he, Glasnik, would personally kill him and then put a bullet through his own head. I begged him not to do anything that could not do me any good and might cause difficulties for other Jewish soldiers.

Meanwhile, five guards approached, leading a chained prisoner who was to share my hut. He was tall, taciturn, and eagle-nosed, but with some strange, livid marks on the tip of his nose.

"Where are you from, brother?" I asked him.

"Gruziya."

"And what is it they want from you?"

He spit and shrugged. "Let them shoot me. I've done what I had to do."

He was a mountain dweller, and his people were not noted for their patience. What was his crime? It seemed that one of his officers, when drunk, would amuse himself by stubbing out his lighted cigarette on this soldier's nose, the size of which appeared to offend him. One day, after the officer had repeated this game two or three times, my fellow prisoner lunged for the man's sword and lopped off his head.

I congratulated him on his quick reaction, but suspected that his chances of getting shot were even better than mine.

Like me, he had little appetite for his bread and water. But he slept soundly enough while I didn't manage to doze off until long past midnight.

When I awoke the next morning, I found him wrapped in a tallis,[39] saying his morning prayers. I jumped up, rinsed my hands, got my own tallis and tefillin, and tried to keep up with him. But his melodies and his pronunciation were so exotic that in the end I simply stood and listened to him until he was finished.

Now, for the first time, we shook hands. I addressed him in Yiddish. He looked at me blankly and replied in Hebrew. So we ended up speaking Russian to each other once more.

I spent the day "doctoring" him, that is, carefully enlarging the scorch marks on his nose until his whole face looked swollen and grotesque. That way, when he went to trial, perhaps the judge would recognize that, after such hideous abuse, even the mildest of men might reach for a sword. The

39 Yiddish: Prayer shawl

72

Georgian doubted it would do the slightest bit of good. But he saw I was dying of boredom and anxiety, and so he good-naturedly allowed me to distract myself by disfiguring him further.

Early the next morning, both of us were taken in chains to a nearby town where a military court was to sit in judgment of us. Both of us were given defense attorneys. My friend's lawyer seemed quite capable, and I was proud to see he made the most of his client's now really dreadful-looking nose.

About my own attorney, I was less enthusiastic. The one thing he wouldn't consider was letting me tell the truth – that a human being could go only so long without sleep. He probably knew his customers and what they would or wouldn't believe. He seemed to feel my only possible defense was to claim that, owing to food poisoning or drinking polluted water, I suffered from a strange sickness that, without warning, could cause me to lose consciousness.

I was desperate enough to try anything. But where on this green earth would I find a Russian army doctor who would favor me with such an improbable diagnosis?

My counsel agreed it wouldn't be easy. Especially since none of the doctors at this post were known to be Jews. But he was still making inquiries. So that was what my life depended on – a non-existent Jewish doctor.

After hearing my attorney's preposterous defense, the court surprised me. They agreed to postpone my case until I'd had a thorough medical examination. I felt more hopeful when I saw that the Georgian got off with only five years of hard labor. He was ecstatic, and threw me a kiss as they led him out.

I had one more night in my cell, guarded like the crown jewels. Tomorrow an army doctor would determine whether I really suffered from such a mysterious illness. Even my attorney admitted that if the doctor found me healthy, it was the firing squad.

Alone once more, I was seized by depression. I cursed my attorney for not having let me tell the truth. There were plenty of fresh troops to mount guard. Why pick on a man who'd barely slept a minute during the week-long retreat?

Late in the evening, a middle-aged lieutenant suddenly arrived to take me away. I was surprised to recognize him as a man for whom my brother Mordechai, back in Petersburg, had bought many a glass of vodka. Could he be here now to return the favor? If not, would it be tactful to remind him who I was? But his manner was so cold and forbidding that I kept silent.

He marched me with chained hands in the direction of the officers' quarters. Halfway there, he slowed his pace, moved up beside me and, without any change of expression, told me not to be frightened. "I'm only taking you to the doctor."

"At this time of night?"

"One of your doctors," he said in a whisper. "He's expecting you."

I didn't trust him. My attorney might dream of miracles, but Glasnik had checked that very afternoon and confirmed that there were no Jewish doctors at this post or anywhere nearby.

The lieutenant explained to me that this doctor was a converted Jew, which to him was plainly one and the same thing. I, on the other hand, knew that men who have turned themselves from bad Jews into bad Christians were apt to bend over backwards to show that they were untainted by old loyalties. But go explain that to a Russian officer. In any event, I had little choice in the matter.

Presently, I saw I was not being taken to the hospital but directly to the doctor's house, which I considered a mistake. It was late, and the doctor would either be angry at being disturbed, or the whole thing would look so conspiratorial that he'd feel himself compromised.

When we reached his house, there was some kind of party going on. Through the window, we could see our doctor with half a dozen fellow officers. They were eating, drinking and playing cards. It was quite obvious he was not expecting me.

I hid in the shadows while the officer rapped on the door. As I expected, the doctor was in a rage at having his party interrupted. His irritation was even greater when he found out it was not an emergency at the hospital, but merely a matter of life and death for a Jewish soldier. Still hidden, I prayed silently for the merits of my holy and beloved ancestors to intercede for me.

The convert finally deigned to let me into his house. He looked me up and down and pronounced, "There isn't a thing in the world wrong with this man." He was clearly ready to usher us right back out.

I stood my ground and replied, rather insolently, "Maybe there is, and maybe there isn't."

Now, a man with any spark of Jewish feeling would, at once, have responded to an observation like that. But the doctor only got more annoyed. "What are your medical qualifications?"

"Who knows how I feel better than I do?"

"And that gives you the right to come to me practically in the middle of the night?"

"I thought you understood," I said, more subdued. "I'm under a sentence of death."

"What's that to me?"

I turned helplessly to my escort. He shrugged. He'd done his part. Now he was ready to take me back.

But it seemed that the doctor knew, all along, why I was there. Perhaps he wanted to demonstrate that he was now a good Orthodox Russian, no longer a member of what our sages called rakhmonim bnei rakhmonim, "the merciful children of the merciful."

"Why did you fall asleep on guard?" he demanded.

I started to tell him how I hadn't slept for several nights, but I caught a warning look from my escorting officer. So I quickly launched into a recital of how I'd eaten some spoiled meat and drank polluted water, and while on guard duty that night had had convulsions and suddenly lost consciousness.

The doctor looked at me with what I couldn't help but regard as Jewish skepticism. "You look healthy enough to me now."

"Thank God, I'm feeling a little better," I hastened to assure him.

"Perhaps imprisonment agrees with you."

My hopes evaporated. He was playing with me. Of course. How could a creature like a convert leave himself open to the suspicion of helping a Jew? I bit my lip and stared at him with open contempt. Even though my life was at stake, I had no intention of lowering myself to beg such a swine as he for my life.

Folding his hands behind him, the doctor marched up and down in front of me like an actor on a stage, and studied me with an expression of great shrewdness. I could feel my life hanging on his mood, his whim, perhaps his own fears. After a long silence, he said, "Get back to your unit."

I didn't understand what this meant, but outside my lieutenant hugged me with relief. Then he took me back to my cell.

I was awakened at daybreak. Two men with bared swords were standing over me. My heart almost jolted to a stop, which would have spared the firing squad of wasting precious bullets. The guards told me to put on my boots; they'd come to escort me back to the tribunal.

I stood once more before my judges, and couldn't keep my eyes off the adjutant who had worked so diligently to have me shot. He smirked like a man who knew more than I did.

I had told my attorney what the convert-doctor said, and he repeated his defense argument about my strange illness, offering to support this with expert testimony.

The adjutant laughed in his face. I couldn't understand why, until I saw how well he had prepared himself. No less than four army doctors were ready to examine me. I looked frantically around for my convert. Sympathetic or not, at least he understood the situation. But now there was not a hair of him to be seen.

In less time than it took to undo a button, the four doctors pronounced me in perfect health. No need to even open my tunic. Bewildered, I began to wonder if I'd dreamt the events of the previous night.

But my attorney proved not to be a complete fool, after all. He ran quickly over to the clinic, burst in on my doctor, and dragged him away from a roomful of patients. When they returned, I was relieved to see that my convert outranked the other four doctors.

Fingers reeking of tobacco, he examined me right then and there, roughly separating my eyelids and shining a match in front of my eyes. I felt my lashes being singed. The Devil-only-knows what he expected to find. I heard the adjutant snicker.

The convert suddenly turned to his colleagues and shouted, "How can you say this man is well? Have you examined his brain?"

Flustered, the other doctors shook their heads. I could see they were skeptical but, thank Heaven, in *Vanya's* army, you didn't argue with a superior officer.

"You never noticed there is a spot on his brain?"

"And what is the significance of that?" demanded the presiding judge who outranked even my doctor friend.

"That spot is a symptom of a kind of sleeping sickness." He said it so convincingly that for a moment I wondered how long I had left to live. "A man with those symptoms may sink into a coma at any moment. He should never have been allowed to serve in the army. The only place for him is the hospital."

He told the other doctors to look into my eyes, and each of them dutifully lit a match, agreed with his diagnosis, and apologized to the court for having overlooked my brain. I was furnished hastily with a chair, and began to enjoy all this sudden solicitude.

Before returning to the clinic, my convert warned the court that such a spot on the brain, if not properly treated, could lead not only to sleeping sickness but also to insanity. With a disgusted look, the presiding officer ordered me taken straight to the hospital. I was not convinced that he believed a word of all this, but form had been satisfied, and if I could produce such an influential supporter, it was probably best not to shoot me.

I assumed that, now that the court-martial had found me not guilty, all of the hospital nonsense would be quietly forgotten and I'd go back to my unit. But my doctor seemed to have enjoyed his little joke too much to let it end there. Clearly, the Jewish spark in him was far from dead.

I was sent to a hospital in Mukden, where I met a number of my old comrades, some of them badly maimed, but all delighted to be out of the war. They told me how some units, owing to inadequate supplies or tactical blunders, were slaughtered even worse than our own. So a soldier who lost only an arm or a foot felt that the rest of his body was pure profit.

I was assigned a bed, examined by a brain specialist, and given food such as milk and white bread whose taste I had long forgotten. In fact, I was given everything but medicine.

After a while, it dawned on me that the doctors knew it was all a put-up job, but weren't sure who was behind it. So, to avoid trouble, they kept me among the critically ill and the dying, and I ended up eating not only my own food but theirs, as well.

Eight days of this golden life and I was abruptly pronounced cured and sent back to my company. I reported to my commander who had started all my troubles by putting me on guard duty. He wanted me to assure him that I was totally cured and in no danger of relapse.

I told him, "How can I be sure? All I know is the doctors in Mukden said that I was fit for duty, again."

My commander shook his head worriedly. Someone must have given him hell for entrusting the safety of the camp to a man with spots on the brain. "Well, just make sure you get enough sleep," he said. "And, for heaven's sake, don't fall out of bed."

10

THE SECOND ROAD TO THE LEFT

fter my discharge from the hospital, I found the remnants
of our tattered battalion overrun by hundreds of starved
and demoralized survivors from General Kuropatkin's latest
"counteroffensive."

Meanwhile, the units held in reserve for this particular counterattack
included survivors from the Third Company, First Novocherkassky Regiment, to which my brother, Avrohom, had belonged. I asked around, but no
one knew where to find the rest of them.

It had been a good many months since I had reconciled myself to the
likelihood that Avrohom was dead. Yet, discovering that some fraction of
his company had survived, I was suddenly flooded with fresh hope and determination to locate this remnant.

Meanwhile, my company, which was now down to maybe a fifth of its
original strength, had been waiting anxiously for the railroad to have pity
on us and bring fresh soldiers to replace the ones our generals had used
up.

And at last, we got our first carload of reservists. They turned out, for the
most part, to be elderly homebodies burdened with anxiety for their wives
and children, and they fit in with us veterans about as smoothly as a hunch-
back trying to make himself invisible against a wall. There were, however,
revolutionaries among them and they had interesting stories to tell about

new riots, massacres, strikes, and pogroms taking place back in the mother country. None of this added to my enthusiasm for my present job, which was to take the sad creatures they had sent us and drill them into ferocious soldiers ready to die rather than let General Oyama[40] march into Mukden.

I was, at this time, going through a period of depression, harrowed by dreams that were so real, I was certain they were trying to tell me something. But what? Having lost Avrohom, the one brother to whom I'd always felt closest, and without one letter from home in more than eight months, I'd begun to suspect, with certainty growing daily, that the outbreak of so many officially inspired pogroms following "Bloody Sunday"[41] in Petersburg must also have claimed the lives of my parents. After all, if they were still alive, would not at least one of them have written to me in all this time?

These gloomy thoughts led, in turn, to morbid fantasies in which I saw myself surviving the war as a helpless invalid and coming home to find not a single relative left to look after me. Would I, too, turn into one of those miserable, fiery-eyed, crippled beggars I remembered from my youth in Warsaw, men maimed in the Russo-Turkish War, who had been reduced to groveling in the streets like savage stray dogs?

In this bitter frame of mind, I forgot that no one else in my company had received mail during the last eight months, either. Which wasn't considered a problem since most Russian soldiers couldn't read.

Yet one morning, despite our army's slipshod ways with forwarding anything less exciting than ammunition, we found sacks of mail for our company. I called out the names on the letters, just like my father used to do in our hometown because our mailman also couldn't read. Before long, our happiness was tainted by other emotions. Almost eight out of ten recipients were no longer there to respond to their names, and no one knew the forwarding address to the Other World.

While some of the men kissed the letters they received or pressed them to their hearts, I called out names for another half an hour and not one of the letters was for me. My nightmarish fears began to choke me once again,

40 Aka Prince Oyama Iwao, Field Marshall and one of the founders of the Imperial Japanese Army

41 A demonstration by laborers on January 22, 1905 that was initially peaceful but turned violent when the unarmed workers were fired upon by troops, triggering the Revolution of 1905

and I found myself trembling, hardly able to read aloud. Among the last handful of letters, I twice shouted "Marateck" before realizing it was for me.

Once mail call was over, the men who couldn't read begged me to read their letters to them. But I had no head for anything other than the envelope addressed in my father's hand. I sat down and read:

> My dear son Jacob,
>
> This letter is written not with ink but with tears. So many months have gone by; this is already my twelfth letter and not a word from either you or Avrohom. Some people say that your entire regiment was wiped out, but we can only think about what has become of our two sons. Every minute to us is like a year. We spend whole days only awaiting the mailman. Your mother and your aunts run every day to pray upon the graves of their holy parents to intercede for you Up There. I try to console your mother that God will help and He will bring a good message. But deep in my heart I am afraid, because I know it cannot be that both of you have forgotten your parents. I no longer know what it is to sleep nights. I still say *tehillim*[42] for you daily, and so do the Rebbe and all his Hasidim, that you may be preserved from the great danger you are in. Dear son, if, Heaven forbid, anything has happened to either one of you, I beg you to write us the truth that we may know the worst. We greet you, your father and mother who hope to hear good news, Amen.
>
> *Shloime Zalman Marateck*

I sat down with paper and pencil and, without waiting for my tears to dry, at once replied that we both were, praised be His Name, in good health, only Avrohom was unable to enclose a greeting at the moment because he'd just gone to town to buy tobacco.

Having written this and handed it to the mail clerk, I was gripped by a ferocious determination to somehow turn my lie into truth. In what we all knew to have been little better than a complete rout, tens of thousands of missing Russian soldiers must surely be scattered all over Manchuria: in hospitals, villages, Japanese prison camps, or temporarily attached to other

42 Hebrew: Psalms from The Book of Psalms

units. If Avrohom were still alive somewhere, I was resolved to find him, even if, during my search for him, I was listed as a deserter.

Along with the mail, we'd received some three-month-old Petersburg newspapers, which were kind enough to inform us that our army was almost on the verge of expelling every last Japanese soldier from the Asiatic mainland. In fact, one got the impression that only the Czar's infinite kindness kept us from driving out all of the Chinese, as well.

The only uncensored news we had from home was a little magazine in Yiddish that printed a kind of comic strip about the activities of a scrawny little man called "Uncle Pinye" or "Pintshik" and his gigantic wife, "Raizel." It took no great cleverness to figure out that "Pintshik" was Japan (*der Yapantshik*) and "Meema Raizel" was *Matushka Rossiya* (Mother Russia). Under the guise of their little domestic tiffs, in which Raizel mercilessly bullied Pinye but her little husband always got the best of her, it was conveyed to us that not everyone back home was taken in by the bold-faced lies and boasts of the censored press.

I also found out from a wounded officer that, contrary to what we'd been told, Mukden had already fallen with losses (to us) of some 200,000 men. And that back home, there had been another unsuccessful attempt to assassinate the Czar.

I asked the officer what the chances were that the Czar would now agree to a negotiated peace. He was pessimistic. We had already lost the war, but the longer our Little Father kept us fighting, the longer he hoped to delay the all-but-inevitable revolution.

While we waited impatiently for the American president (Theodore Roosevelt) to help negotiate an end to this war,[43] and soldiers continued to be killed daily by Japanese snipers or Chinese bandits, we were still being exhorted to prepare ourselves, physically and spiritually, for the decisive Battle of Mukden. This, we were told, would determine the outcome of the war once and for all, and teach the upstart Japanese a lesson they would not forget for centuries to come. Which was that, as General Kuropatkin had lately inscribed on his banner, "The Lord Preserves His Own."

---

43 For his role in negotiating The Treaty of Portsmouth, which ended the Russo-Japanese War, President 'Teddy' Roosevelt was awarded the Nobel Peace Prize (1906)

To raise our morale, we were also informed in strict secrecy that, unbeknownst to our treacherous enemy, a vast Russian fleet under Admiral Makaroff had been sent all the way around Africa to come upon the Japanese from behind and blow them out of the water. (What actually happened, as I read many years later, was that in May of 1905, after months of hardship, incompetence and all sorts of bad luck, when the Russian fleet, actually under Admiral Rozhdestvensky, finally appeared in the Strait of Tsushima, the Japanese navy lost no time in sending it straight to the bottom of the sea.)

Meanwhile, I went on training our apathetic recruits, our pitiful replacements, how to make a bayonet charge against a trench defended by machine guns. And we all waited with great enthusiasm for the "Battle of Destiny."

There was another shipment of mail, although, once more, most of the 198 men to whom the letters were addressed would never answer to their names, again.

I had a fresh letter from my father. This time it was addressed to me, alone. My heart pounded as I tore it open. He wrote:

> This is the seventeenth letter to which you have not replied. Your mother is almost blinded with weeping. My dear child Jacob, I must also tell you that I have heard Avrohom is dead. However, the Gerer[44] Rebbe specifically assured me that you are alive and that you will, with the help of the Almighty, return to us.
>
> Today I got up from sitting *shiva* for your brother, may he dwell in a bright Eden. Your mother cries that her prayers were insufficient to save him, and that he has not come to a Jewish grave. I plead with her to regain her strength, so that she may live to see you and your other brothers come back to us in a good hour.

Choked with bitterness, I told Glasnik that Avrohom was dead. Therefore, I now intended to keep my end of the bargain, which was not to return without him.

---

44 Pertaining to the Hasidic dynasty originating in Góra Kalwaria, Poland; Ger comes from the Yiddish name for Góra Kalwaria

Glasnik, seeing that I was serious, argued angrily that the fact that my father had sat *shiva* was wholly insufficient proof that my brother was actually dead. Assuming Avrohom were married, would there not have to be two eyewitnesses to his death before his wife could be declared a widow and permitted to marry, again?

For once, I had no patience with this Babylonian[45] kind of logic. In fact, ready to do the job before Glasnik with his superior knowledge of *Talmudic* law (as he hadn't run away from *yeshiva* before the age of thirteen), could weaken my resolve, I fumbled for my revolver.

Glasnik looked at the weapon and shook his head. Did I really want to be buried here, in the alien soil of Cathay, where no one would ever find my grave? Was my determination so feeble that I was afraid I'd change my mind if I waited until we got to a town large enough to have a Jewish cemetery, where at least I'd be able to receive a proper Jewish burial? Glasnik promised that if I'd wait to kill myself like a proper, God-fearing Jew, he would personally dig my grave and say *kaddish*[46] for me. In fact, if the conditions were attractive enough, he might even keep me company and shoot himself, as well. (Perhaps I should explain that our frequent readiness to consider suicide was not a sign of madness or despair, but simply of weighing a reasonable alternative over something worse.)

It took me some moments to realize that he was joking. But suddenly, in dead earnestness, he said, "Brother, we belong to the nation of Israel, and we have survived far worse than this, and by the merits of our holy ancestors and the tears of our parents, you'll see, we will, with His help, return alive."

I looked at him and felt moved to tears. What a gift it was to have a true friend! He now tried to cheer me up by picturing our homecoming: Two young men, straight as arrows, whom the most beautiful girls in our district would consider it a privilege to look upon; the matchmakers would fall upon us like horseflies on a dung heap. But we would merely twirl our

45 When used generically, "the Talmud" refers to the Babylonian Talmud, which was compiled in Babylon in the 5ᵗʰ century. The study of Talmud, great rabbis' commentaries on the Torah, reflects a reverence for logic in which questions pertaining Jewish law are rigorously debated and analyzed from all angles with the goal of arriving at a final answer.

46 Hebrew: Prayer said by relatives of the deceased so that the deceased benefits from the merit earned by its recitation

mustaches, and if they asked how much of a dowry we demanded, we'd tell them not to come back and talk to us about anything less than a thousand rubles.

So, thanks to Glasnik's eloquence, I didn't shoot myself that day.

A few mornings later, in the midst of a blinding snowstorm, five horsemen approached our camp and begged for a bite to eat. The insignias on their uniforms identified them as being with Avrohom's unit. I asked if they knew a soldier named Marateck.

They said they'd never heard the name. I turned away, crushed. But one of the horsemen explained that they'd only been with the company for two days, and this gave me a moment of renewed hope ... until the second one said there were hardly any survivors from the original company. On the other hand, if I wanted to see for myself, they were stationed only about ten or twenty kilometers away.

I wanted to grab the horseman closest to me by the throat. Why hadn't he said that to begin with? Ten, twenty, 100 kilometers – nothing would stop me from finding out whether Avrohom was alive. I didn't let myself stop long enough to consider whether I might prefer to hold on to some shred of hope rather than discover a harsher truth.

Writing down whatever directions the horsemen could give me (which wasn't much since they were lost, themselves), I drew a rough map, which I tucked into my boot. They'd also given me the password, "Red Girl."

I ran to tell Glasnik I was going to find out, for certain, whether my brother was dead or alive. He argued with me that, despite all the rumors of peace negotiations, there were still believed to be Japanese snipers positioned on at least one of the hills I would have to pass. Even if I managed to get past them, a lone Russian rider was almost certain to be ambushed by some roving band of Chinese highwaymen. Furthermore, the snow outside the camp was almost belly-high to a horse, and even in what little shelter we had, the icy wind cut through you like a razor.

The conditions suited me just fine. In fact, I said, in such uncivilized weather, any sensible sniper or bandit would be huddling deep inside his cave, and I would have a much better chance of slipping past him.

The Russian soldier in charge of the horses was an old friend. When I told him of my plan, he advised me not to take a horse but a mule, which might go more slowly, but would have much better staying power under these terrible conditions.

My friends gave me some of their spare ammunition, and I left loaded down with 120 rounds, a rifle, a cavalry saber, and my revolver. Before leaving, I gave Glasnik my diary and begged him to send it to my parents as a remembrance if I didn't come back.

I climbed into the saddle, and the mule carried me into the night. By my watch, it was barely eight-thirty in evening. Ten or twenty kilometers, even under these conditions, should not take more than three hours. Whether or not I would try to return tonight depended on how much danger I encountered en route, but above all on the kind of news I got when I arrived.

Three hours later, I found myself in the midst of an endless forest but it had finally stopped snowing. Despite my fear of bandits, I struck a match to consult my map. If the map was even roughly accurate, I had covered less than half the distance. If I came out at the right spot when I emerged from the forest, I would still have to climb a considerable hill, and then cross a body of water, which may or may not be a river, and may or may not be frozen over.

The trees bent and groaned under the weight of the snow. Each one was a perfect hiding place for a Cathayan bandit, to whom the value of my weapons alone, not to mention the mule, would guarantee a life of luxury for at least half a year.

By the time I got through the forest and reached the edge of the water, it was long past one o'clock in the morning. In the moonlight, I saw the outlines of a ruined hut on the opposite shore. Its roofless walls might, unless inhabited by Heaven-only-knows who, give me and the mule a sheltered place to rest for a while.

As we headed for the cabin, the mule's clumsy hooves cracked the ice. Unable to halt in time, it stumbled headlong into the frozen water, spilling me into the water with it. Fortunately, the river or lake was only neck-deep. But as we emerged on the opposite shore, I was shivering like a leaf in a high wind, and the mule behaved as though it were having a fit.

The clothes began to stiffen on my body, and my head boiled with fever. I felt myself grow dizzy. For good measure, my vision also began to blur. As for my feet, they were as responsive as two blocks of granite. I said to myself, "Master of the Universe, have I come through all these hardships and dangers only to die here, where no Jew will ever find my body?"

When I finally reached the ruined hut, another blow fell. Beyond the hut were at least half a dozen possible paths. I consulted my frozen map. There was nothing on it to correspond to this tangle of roads. In the morning, even if I woke up with renewed strength, how would I know which path to choose?

A ravenous howl broke the silence behind me, and I suddenly realized I was surrounded by wolves. I quickly dragged the mule into the ruined hut and fell into a deep sleep.

In my dream, my grandfather, Reb Shmuel Schlossberg, of blessed memory, appeared to me, bearing in his hands a red clay vessel covered with white linen. Just as he had in my childhood, he seemed to have come in response to my moans of distress. He stroked my cheek, and had me drink from the clay vessel in his hands.

As I drank endlessly, feeling no need to pause for breath, he said, "If you take the second road to the left of the hill, you will find your brother." He even advised me where I would locate my mule, which I hadn't realized was missing.

I awoke, startled to find that it was night, although probably the following night. I must have been asleep for close to twenty hours. And the mule was gone. For some moments, I looked for my grandfather in order to continue our conversation.

Gradually, I realized it was a dream, and that I was now either awake or else had plunged into a new nightmare. I could not, for the life of me, recall where my grandfather told me to look for the mule. But never mind. Even if it meant continuing on foot, I was determined to follow his advice and take "the second road to the left of the hill," although I could not really picture what he meant.

When I came to the road I thought my grandfather had told me to take, I found my mule. The creature was calmly eating snow, as though to leave me in no doubt that my difficulties were none of his concern. I was filled with an unshakable conviction that if my grandfather knew exactly where I'd find my mule, why would he not also be right about my brother? I had always believed in dreams, and had no doubt that the dead knew things that were hidden from the living, though I wondered how my grandfather could possibly know my brother's address in deepest Manchuria.

I mounted my mule once again, and followed the path Reb Shmuel had instructed me to take. I tried to force myself to remain skeptical, as well as on my guard.

After several hours, I thought I saw a camp, and galloped downhill with a burst of impatience. I only noticed the sentry once his rifle was already tracking me. I managed to halt my mule, but the password had flown from my mind.

The sentry threatened to fire.

"Do I sound Japanese?" I asked.

He said he had his orders, and began to count to three.

At the last moment, I cried out, "Red Girl!"

The sentry reluctantly decided not to shoot me. I asked him about the Third Company, First Novocherkassky Regiment. He hesitated, because the Japanese were known to be using some Polish spies. He was convinced, no doubt correctly, that our own army didn't know of the existence of this camp. Which was why they received neither replacements, nor mail, let alone provisions, and had been forced to subsist entirely by foraging. In the end, he decided to trust me, and pointed to where I could find what was left of the Third Company.

In the dim moonlight, I recognized the cap worn by my brother's unit. But the faces were unfamiliar. It was clear that all my acquaintances were dead.

My heart beat unbearably as I ran from one group of figures to the next. Most were still awake, but none had ever heard of my brother.

I finally encountered a familiar face, a German boy named Friedrich Vogel, a notorious jokester who'd been part of the original company. He was carrying an empty pail, on his way to fetch water. When he saw me, he cried, "Marateck!" and dropped the pail.

I looked at him closely. He looked aged by a good twenty years. Only his squeaky voice was still the same.

Without any greeting, I demanded, "Is my brother still alive?"

"Who?"

"My brother!" I shouted at him. "Marateck!"

"Your brother," he said. "Ah, didn't you know?" He made a long face. "Someone else is walking in his boots."

"He's dead?" I cried. All the strength went out of me. So my grandfather's appearance in my dream was simply a cruel mockery. Then I remembered that he hadn't actually said I would find Avrohom alive.

The German stared at me with curiosity. Then he seized my arm and said, "Come. I'll take you to him."

"He's buried here?" Reluctantly, I let Vogel drag me a short distance. He stopped, and directed me to walk ahead of him. I took cautious steps, not at all sure I wanted to see what the German was avoiding.

As I peered around a corner, I was briefly blinded by the light of a glowing fire. The soldiers sitting around it were eating what looked like a freshly killed goat, its carcass lying on the ground beside them. A few smoked pipes and passed around a clear bottle of something that didn't seem to be water. One of the men resembled Avrohom, except aged, and not really healthy. But then, I hadn't looked at myself lately.

Could it—? How—? I turned toward the German. He smiled, pointed to his feet, and whispered, "Avrohom got new boots off a dead man. I walk in his old ones." I almost forgave the German for his German sense of humor. I urged him to keep quiet so I could surprise my brother.

For some time, I watched, and listened to them cozily chatting about girls, a subject about which they knew even less than I, and about the rumor that, to save Russian pride, America had finally helped both sides arrange an end to the war.

I stood in the darkness until I saw pain clouding Avrohom's face as he said, "Ah, if my brother, Yankel, were alive, what a celebration we'd have." Tears filled my eyes, and I suddenly felt choked and ashamed to be hiding from him.

I burst out of the darkness and cried, "Here I am!"

For a moment or two, he seemed to believe I was either some sort of a demon, or his friend's idea of a bad joke. His eyes had a haunted, feverish look. Half-smiling, half-crying, I quoted to him from the *Shabbos* morning

Psalms, *"Yipoil mitzidcho elef ... "* ("A thousand may fall at your side, and ten thousand at your right hand, yet it shall not come near you").

Still silent, he finally nodded, and shyly offered me the piece of meat he was holding in his hand. Only when I embraced him did he permit himself to relax and believe I was actually alive.

All the rest of that night, until daybreak, we sat and talked and laughed and ate and resolutely got drunk. By morning, Avrohom was able even to joke about the silly misunderstanding that had convinced him that I was dead. Now he only hoped our postal service had remained faithful to its traditions and lost the letter in which he had informed our parents that I'd been killed in action.

If, after having already sat *shiva* for him, our parents had also gone into mourning for me, they would, by now, be so experienced that they could go into business as professional mourners. And so drunk and hysterical were we at that moment that we thought even that was funny.

11
WALKING WOUNDED

When we were first sent us to Manchuria, we had understood it was purely to help settle a small quarrel between our Little Father, the Czar, and the insolent Emperor of a subhuman race known to us only as "the Chinamen." Later we learned that the people who shot at us were actually called Japanese, and did not live in China, but on a string of furtive islands somewhere in the Pacific Ocean. So much for geography. So much for history. Meanwhile, it was either still winter, or winter again.

While we huddled behind the slippery walls of our trenches, waiting to be told we could go home, our General Staff felt the sudden need for one decisive, last-minute victory, something to raise the spirits of our long-suffering negotiators at the peace talks.

In consequence, the next day we tramped uphill toward the broad, featureless plain on which our victory was to take place. Along the way, I overheard all sorts of subversive grumbling. Not only in Russian but, less cautiously, also in Polish, Yiddish and German, along with the kind of wild talk in which the living claimed to envy the dead. The dead, no doubt, would have gladly traded places.

Owing to a not-uncommon slip-up, some of the men in my squad had rifles but no bullets. Others, unarmed, had their pockets stuffed with ammunition but, for some reason, declined to share it. It didn't matter. Soon there would be no shortage of bodies from which to scavenge what we needed.

The battle began without waiting for us to settle in. Soon the bombardment became so savage, it seemed as though the only value of having infantry was to give each side a way of keeping score in numbers of men killed.

Amidst all the noise and smoke, it took me a while to realize that my rifle had stopped working. I still had my Browning revolver, one of the privileges of being a corporal. And in a pinch, there was always the bayonet, which, thank Heaven, I had never been forced to use. Glasnik offered to let me have his own rifle. Why? He had never taken aim at a living thing and saw no reason to start now. He had also grown tired of carrying and cleaning it. But if I accepted his rifle, how would he defend himself? I politely declined.

After four days and nights of steady bombardment, a frightening thing began to happen. Here and there, a soldier pushed beyond endurance by the unending shriek of incoming shells and the inhuman noises of the wounded, simply went mad and started knifing or shooting his closest comrades, mistaking them for "Japs."

Unfortunately, there was only one merciful way to cure such a delusion: kill the fellow as quickly as possible. Owing to everyone's stinginess with ammunition, this was usually done with a knife. And if you think it is easy to do away with a man who refuses to hold still, I would advise you not to try it.

One day, after shivering through seventeen straight hours of shelling, my ears still ringing with screams from a nearby trench that had taken a hit, I felt my own composure waver. As a precaution, I gave a handful of bullets to a few of my Jewish comrades and asked them to swear to me that, should I go crazy and need to be gotten rid of, they would use a gun instead of a knife.

Some of our boys who had remained in *yeshiva* longer than I had impressed upon me that, speaking in the abstract (since what I requested was forbidden by Jewish Law), death by knife with two smooth strokes – one severing the gullet, one the windpipe – was far more swift and painless than death from a bullet wound, which is why it was the *Talmud's* prescription for the humane slaughter of kosher animals.

I pointed out that, not being a kosher animal, I had the right to choose how I wanted to die.

During a lull in the shelling, a staff officer, whose warm quarters were in the rear, had made a quick motorized survey of the front lines, and spotted us sitting idly in our trenches; that is, we were eating, smoking, sleeping or scratching ourselves like normal human beings. Displeased to see the Czar's defenders drawing good pay for doing nothing, he ordered a frontal attack with fixed bayonets, "to stir things up a little," as he put it cheerfully. This was not an unusual example of our High Command's attachment to tactics probably last employed against Napoleon, using weapons from that same era.

I looked at Lieutenant Korolenko, who averted his face. He could not undo an order from a staff officer, but was honest enough to be embarrassed at having to issue the command. He also made it clear that he, at least, was not insane enough to lead such an attack. Then who would? I looked around. We had lost some good men only yesterday. That suddenly made me the next highest ranked.

I peered over the lip of our trench. Before me lay at least a hundred yards of churned-up open ground that was crisscrossed by a wilderness of barbed wire and Japanese machine-guns positioned to furnish interlocking fields of fire.

The best chance of surviving this crazy mission was by attacking in the dark. So at four o'clock the next morning, I blew my whistle. My men, sullenly cursing and rubbing the sleep out of their eyes, crawled out of the trenches in their usual, healthy competition to be the slowest. Meanwhile, we waited for the promised artillery to pulverize the Japanese defenses. Or at least force them to keep their heads down long enough for us to race across the field and impale our contemptible opponents as, we hoped, they groveled in their holes.

But our big guns prudently directed their firepower at the Japanese batteries that threatened only *their own* position. All this did was assure us that, if any of the Japanese machine-gunners had been napping, they were now fully alert.

Although it would be crazy to attempt an attack now, we had no choice but to continue creeping carefully through a jungle of iron barbs. We clawed our way into the dirt like moles, resigned to lay there until darkness fell again. Or until the war was over. But our enemy had no intention of letting us off so easily.

While we lay flat on our bellies, the Japanese suddenly trampled toward us with the all-too-familiar howl of "Banzai!" In sheer panic, we scrambled to our feet and tried to remember what we had learned in bayonet drill at the Novocherkassky Barracks back in Petersburg.

There was a moment or two of almost embarrassed hesitation, as if both sides were at a dance and had only a moment or two to choose a partner. Then we began to thrust and club and hack and stab at our enemy as frantically as soldiers have done for all the centuries before gunpowder allowed us to kill at a more civilized distance.

This highlighted a certain deficiency in the Russian soldier's training. The way we had been drilled in the use of the bayonet involved taking a step back, so that upon stepping forward it was possible to thrust the blade into the enemy's gut with greater force. On the drill-field, with straw dummies as targets, this worked very nicely. But while we tried to execute our elegant little two-step, tried to remember which foot came first, the enemy, unschooled in our European sense of fair play, lacked the decency to stand as still as scarecrows and let us run them through. Instead, under the barbaric Asiatic rules by which they had been trained, they felt perfectly at liberty to lunge at their opponents and impale them, or smash their skulls with a butt-stroke.

But if the average Russian soldier was hard to train, he was even harder to untrain. Thus, while a few independent souls quickly adapted to actual combat conditions, some of our ordinary peasant boys got so flustered in the fatal heat of combat that all they could think of was protecting their heads, which unfortunately left their bellies wide open.

Not that I was much better. I had only escaped having my own skull smashed in because my attacker's aim was blocked by the low-hanging branch of a tree. During that instant, I looked into the eyes of the squat, round-faced Japanese soldier who was momentarily off-balance. He was sweating, both with eagerness and deathly fear, and forgot to guard his belly against my bayonet. Had my rifle been in working order and my fingers not too mixed-up to work the bolt, I might have shot him. But having glimpsed, for the merest second, a terrified boy my own age inside that uniform, I, too, felt immobilized. That condition lasted just long enough for the chaos of battle to send us both spinning off in opposite directions.

Then, as abruptly as if the music had ended, the survivors on each side turned, and rushed back to the comfort of their trenches.

Not long after, we were ordered to withdraw to another defensive position. But the enemy was not finished with us. Within hours, we felt the Japanese hard at our back, and before long we were running for our lives. Whipped as we were, all we wanted was to reach the railroad that had brought us here, but our pursuers clung to us like the Egyptians following my ancestors out of Egypt.

During a brief pause in our flight, I looked around, and my heart lurched to a stop. Where was Glasnik? Had I not promised his mother that I would look out for him? For a moment I had the mad notion of turning back and searching for him. Or at least finding and burying his corpse. But the occasional muzzle-flash from behind jolted me back to reality.

Some time during the second week of our retreat, we stumbled upon a system of crumbling fortifications that had been abandoned by another Russian unit. They had left in such haste that many of the trenches still held unburied bodies that were slowly decaying in the cold sun. Happy to have found a ready-made defensive position, our colonel decided that this was where our Regiment would make one more stand for the tarnished self-respect of the Russian army.

Unfortunately, the trenches had been dug on flat ground. When the Japanese launched their attack, by tomorrow at the latest, they would be on hilly terrain from which they could look down our throats. What's more, the melting snow had filled the trenches with water deep enough to cover our boot-tops. The only creatures that thrived in this environment were the rats. Never before had I seen rats that could swim and even dive so expertly. This being Asia, who knew if they were rats and not some sort of Chinese four-legged fish? But the encroaching darkness left us no time to explore any alternative.

That night, not satisfied with keeping us pinned-down, hungry, soaked and shivering, some enterprising enemy soldiers had bellied up, like snakes, and placed bottles of vodka on little mounds of dirt almost within our reach. It was plain they understood *Vanya's* mentality a lot better than we understood theirs'.

I pleaded with my men not to fall for such a cheap trick. But it took a lot more than common sense, or my authority, to come between a Russian and his beloved beverage. Some of the men began, at once, to crawl out of their trenches, convinced they could snatch a bottle more quickly than a Japanese bullet could travel. They were mistaken. Which did not stop either the Japanese or our men from repeating the same game the following night, and the night after that, with the same depressing results.

Meanwhile, I squirmed in icy black water that had risen up to my groin. I drowsed, and awoke to visions of fat, black rodents with crocodile jaws. Some of my comrades were more resourceful than I. Lacking boxes, sand-bags or wooden logs to stand upon, not to mention hand pumps to drain the trenches, they kept dry by climbing on top of bodies that, under constant sniper fire, we had not had time to bury.

The following morning was deathly quiet. For some undoubtedly sinister reason, the Japanese had stopped shelling us. Could it be that the war had finally ended, but only the enemy knew it? It was more likely that they were only waiting for the inhumanly efficient Japanese government to send them more ammunition.

During the lull, we received orders to continue heading north. The men cheered. What else could that mean but that the war was truly over? Yet the Japanese, unpredictable as ever, kept right on our heels while their snipers picked off those who couldn't keep up.

The man next to me stumbled and fell with a sharp gasp of pain. He had a deep hole in his back, and purple blood squirted out of his mouth. I felt helpless; no one had ever taught me how to apply a tourniquet for a back wound. After a time, a sudden, ugly, wheezing gasp escaped from his mouth, and his arms went slack. I quickly relieved him of his rifle and his remaining bullets, and searched his pockets. He had been hoarding two cubes of sugar! I grabbed them, popped one into my mouth and immediately felt a surge of energy. I briefly debated whether to save the other sugar cube for later, but decided that I needed the energy now.

The second cube, however, was covered with blood. As hardened as I had become by the war, this blood came from a soldier I knew. Plus, Jewish law forbade consuming blood – animal or otherwise. I held the sugar cube between my fingers, turning it to examine it from all sides. Not even a small corner was unstained. But God is merciful, and His laws made it clear that it was permissible to violate almost any one of them to save a life. Was this not a matter of life and death – my own?

Saliva pooling in my mouth, I closed my eyes and tried to think of the taste of *faworki*[47], the sugary, fried pastries that bakeries in Warsaw prepared every spring, and lay the cube on my tongue. But as I had never had enough money to buy any of those treats, my imagination failed me. The taste in my mouth became bitter and metallic, and I spat it out cube. But a second sugar cube wouldn't save my life any more than a single one would.

Some hours later, the remnants of my platoon decided to rest for the night. It did no good to point out that the Japanese were only a rifle shot behind us. But since the men had made it plain that they no longer accepted my authority, I continued walking on my own.

It was at least another hour before I felt safe enough, for the first time in weeks, to abandon myself to a full night's sleep. While dreaming of such miracles as feather beds, my eyelids were ripped open by enormous flares bleaching the sky. In the distance, a couple of machine-guns spat at each other. Numb in every limb, I wondered stupidly whether it was safe to go back to sleep.

When the flares died down, I knew it was time to move on, no matter how sleepy I was. Near dawn, I spotted the fires of a large encampment. Theirs or ours? For some moments, I wasn't sure it mattered. If the Japanese took me prisoner, I assumed they would give me something to eat. That was more than I could count on from our own kitchens. On the other

47 Polish: Often known as "Angel Wings," these are ribbon-shaped pastries that are fried and then coated with confectioners sugar

hand, there were ugly rumors of Russian prisoners being used for bayonet practice.

As there were no visible sentries, I watched the fort from a distance for half the morning before I felt certain that the camp was Russian. How could I be sure? It was full of soldiers whom no one had told what to do as their officers had saddled up and ridden off.

I begged for some food and, after enduring a variety of insolent and foolish questions about what I was "doing" there, I was given some hardtack and hot water. It was my first hot meal in over two weeks.

In the evening I met a Polish clerk who had been in my battalion. My heart pounding, I asked if he had seen Glasnik.

He had not. On the other hand, he had also not seen his corpse. I tried to find some consolation in his words. Glasnik may have been only a mediocre soldier, but he had a talent for getting out of tight spots.

In the morning, I cadged another breakfast and continued heading north, part of an endless column of what had once been soldiers. Although the roadside was littered with gear our men had gotten tired of carrying, no one had the strength, or will, to stop and scavenge any longer.

To break the monotony, some of us paused long enough to turn and fire at the dim shadows behind us. Our pursuers signaled their annoyance at this by sending back a hundred bullets for every one of ours. One afternoon, I felt a violent blow against my neck. I was ready to hit back but the man beside me said, "Fool, your neck is bleeding. I think you were hit by a bullet."

He said this so casually, I assumed he was joking. Then I touched my neck; my hand came away wet. If my comrade had kept his mouth shut, I would have kept right on going, and maybe the wound would have closed up by itself. Instead, my eyes grew dim and my knees began to buckle. I tried to keep running, but the other fellow had ruined my concentration.

I awoke in a field hospital, heavily bandaged around the neck and shoulder. A nurse was stroking my forehead and trying to get me to drink some water. I wanted to thank her but my throat was on fire.

When I saw a doctor hurrying past. I stretched out my arm to stop him and asked, "Doctor, how am I?"

He said, "Don't you know?"

"What?"

"How you feel."

"I mean, how serious is it?"

"You were lucky," he admitted in what sounded like a critical tone. "The bullet came from a great distance; it didn't bite very hard. You were also lucky that it stayed in your neck and kept you from losing more blood."

The nurse held him back a moment longer. She showed him my bandage, which was soaked through. "He needs a clean bandage."

"From where? Take it off and wash it."

Vanya, as usual, had planned well. There were no more clean bandages left in all of China, so wounded men who came in after me were bandaged with whatever kind of soiled rag could be scrounged.

Unfortunately, my doctor was so proud of the job he had done that, long before I felt like giving up my comfortable bed, he pronounced me "cured" and sent me back to the field.

12

THE LONELIEST PLACE ON EARTH

Spoiled by days of lying in bed, I left the hospital and attached myself grudgingly to another column of stragglers. One of the officers who hadn't abandoned their units explained that we were not running away: we were "regrouping" to make a stand at Mukden. Assuming it had not already fallen. He readily agreed that, from a strategic point of view, it was not desirable to have the enemy both in front of and behind us.

The closer we got to the railroad in Mukden, the more bewildering the chaos became. At one point, I came upon sacks of mail lying piled behind a telegrapher's shed, all waiting to be returned as "undeliverable." Rummaging through them, I found a letter from my parents.

They wrote that my brother, Mordechai, not long after being reported dead, had come home. He had been discharged early on account of some undiagnosable illness. But once safely out of the hands of Army doctors, he recovered. Within days, he left for Warsaw. I gathered from their reticence about the reason for his departure that he had gone for some illegal or 'revolutionary' purpose. They also asked me if it was true that Glasnik was dead.

It had been three weeks since I'd last seen my friend. Yet each time I glimpsed a soldier with the hunched over, nearsighted posture of someone threading a needle, my heart skipped, and my imagination leapt to pin

Glasnik's features onto his body. While the Russians have a saying, "What lies under the earth is best forgotten," my memory of his mother's tears wouldn't allow me to forget.

I also worried about facing his father, a man of so little personal force I wondered how he ever managed to express the wish to have a child. How could I return in the full glory of all my limbs and organs to explain to this shadow of a man that one moment his son was at my side and the next moment he was gone? That I had "lost" my friend the way one might forget a newspaper on a train?

Yet my father said that Glasnik's father urged him to write to me because, with a stubbornness one would not have expected of him, Glasnik's father refused to believe that his son was dead. He wanted The Truth.

My father's controlled handwriting also pleaded with me to make inquiries about a number of other soldiers from Vishogrod and nearby villages who had been similarly reported dead or missing. Out of seven boys he named, I knew for certain that four were dead, and one was badly wounded. What would I say to their families? I suddenly dreaded the thought of going home.

Toward daybreak, after another night on our feet, we came to a stagnant body of water covered with a thick green scum that smelled worse than it looked. An order was passed down the line not to drink the water. By the time word reached our group, many men already were lying face down in the water, slurping like dogs. I tried, forcibly, to get them to stop drinking. One of the men threatened to kill me. Moments later, he doubled over in agony.

I, too, suffered terribly from thirst and for a moment, I almost decided that cramps would be the lesser torture. But then I saw corpses lying upstream. And the man who had just threatened me was wriggling like a half-crushed worm. He suddenly kicked, and then became still.

Later that day, I ran into Semyon, a Russian friend from my days in Petersburg, who had also lost his regiment but not his resourcefulness. As tens of thousands of famished and thirsty soldiers had already preceded us on this highway, he said, any Chinese farmer who might have had any food had long since been stripped of it. If we wanted to avoid starving, we needed to strike out cross-country.

We made sure that our revolvers were loaded, and slipped away from the column without anyone so much as turning his head.

Semyon had a fine sense of direction, and the hilly path on which he led us rose gently. Near the top, he claimed to hear the sound of mooing or bleating in the valley below us. "Milk!" he said. "Why should only officers drink milk?"

I heard nothing and saw no sign of any animal, but by this point, my thirst was unbearable, and that was reason enough for me to believe him.

We stumbled downhill toward a flowering meadow blanketed in ghostly shreds of fog. In the failing light, we spotted the burned and roofless huts of a Chinese farm. An ominous puff of smoke escaped from one of the ruined buildings. I hoped we had not stumbled into a nest of Chinese bandits, many of whom our boys had treated rather badly on the way to the front.

Darkness began to flood the sky, yet no matter how fast we walked, the meadow remained as far away as ever. Discouraged, I sat down to rest for a moment. By the time Semyon was able to rouse me, it was five o'clock in the morning. I shook off his hand and lost consciousness, again.

Later, I was awakened by a loud noise. "That is a goat or a cow crying to be milked," Semyon said. He licked his lips.

Ecstatic, and forgetting the risk of running into bandits, we ran toward the jumble of ruined clay huts. I stopped when I came face to face with a cow, its udders swollen with milk.

We searched around for a pail, any sort of container. This was no time to be particular. We were going to have milk, all we could drink!

Then I remembered the gasp of smoke from one of the huts. Even as I fumbled for my Browning, a ragged Chinese woman materialized between us carrying a small, crying child. In addition to wailing, she repeatedly bowed so deeply that I feared she would drop the child.

"She's afraid we'll steal her cow," Semyon said.

Addressing us in a bird-like chatter, she pulled us into a small, wrecked building, which gave off a ghastly sweet stench. Before us lay two bodies.

Judging by their age and her grief, I assumed they were her son and his wife. Both seemed freshly dead. Who was to say that the murderers were not still close by? It may only have been our arrival that kept them from killing the old woman and making off with the cow, too.

My friend gagged and ran outside to be sick. I followed, but kept my revolver in my hand. The woman tried to pull us into yet another small ruin, but the smell made it horribly obvious what we would find there.

Semyon said, "See if you can explain to her that all we want is some milk."

I was close to having lost my appetite, but for my friend's sake, I pointed to the cow. Even as the woman began to cry, again, I pumped my hands in what was meant to illustrate the way one milked a cow. It took a while before she fell silent and reacted to my pantomime. Then I tried to gesture to her that we needed a container.

She hesitated, then ran inside and brought out a small, muddy trough, the kind from which the poorer Polish farmers back home fed their pigs. She wiped it out with an equally muddy rag. Then, with trembling hands, she drew the first gush of milk.

Semyon and I fell to our knees. Bumping heads, we began to slurp up the milk. Thirsty and starved as I was, I could not help noticing that the milk had a peculiar taste. Yet neither one of us was able to stop drinking. We left just enough milk to cover the bottom of the trough, hoping not to find out exactly what had flavored it.

I tried to offer the old woman some money. Fearful that I meant to buy the cow, she slapped my hands away, then sank to the ground and kissed our boots. The infant, meanwhile, toddled over to the trough and sat on it to demonstrate the use to which it was normally put.

We waited until late afternoon to start up the next hill. That way, the sun's long shadow would blur our silhouettes to anyone who may have, for whatever reason, wanted to shoot at us.

Halfway up the summit, both of us began to get the very cramps we had escaped earlier by not drinking the polluted water. After all those months, we agreed, it must be that our insides were no longer able to digest milk.

Later, the cramps returned once more and nearly drove us mad. Semyon begged me to shoot him. But even had I wanted to, the pain in my gut would have made it impossible to aim straight.

Semyon cursed both me and the Czar with impartial ferocity. In between, he made the terrible sounds of a man dying. It tormented me not to know what to do for him. He was a fine young man from a noble family who could easily have become an officer. And in all the months of our acquaintance until this moment, I had never heard him say a bad word against either the Jews or the Czar.

In desperation, I rubbed some snow on his stomach. The cold seemed to ease his pain, and I continued rubbing his belly until he fell asleep. Only then did I feel darkness smother me like a cloak.

Curled up against my friend's body, I didn't awaken until the sun was high overhead. Semyon lay beside me in the same position I had left him last night. I tried to wake him. There was no response. In panic, I tugged at him so hard he rolled over, his eyes lifeless as marbles. At that moment, surrounded by blinding white silence, I felt like the last man on earth.

A savage burst of pain reminded me that my insides were still knotted with cramps. It was pure chance that he died and I, for some reason, was still alive. For now.

Searching Semyon's pockets, I removed his papers as well as the gold medallion from his neck. I also took his revolver and his bullets. Ignorant of Russian Orthodox ritual, I dug a hole for my comrade's body, and wished him a speedy transfer to whatever paradise he believed in. So that he would not journey alone, I also wished for him to have the Czar and his family for company.

Surrounding me in a limitless ocean of land were the four points of the compass, but nothing that would tell me which way was north. I was no longer sure whether, so close to the Arctic Circle, the sun set in the east or the west. Never had I seen a landscape so bitterly empty of human life, so naked of landmarks, so oppressed by a leaden sky in which neither sun nor stars could tell me if I was headed in the right direction.

For hours, I hauled my feet up and down those white, deserted hills. I knew China had a population in the hundreds of millions. Where had they all gone? And more urgently, where was my army?

On a path rutted by the wheels of heavy guns, I came upon a trickle of ragged Russian soldiers who were as lost as I. Some of them looked and sounded like rough characters. One of them kept insisting that he had heard there was a ten-day cease-fire, but was not sure when the ten days began. For all we knew, they may have just ended.

The sight of this disorderly crew made me wonder if I would not be better off on my own. But when the others groaned to their feet and, bunched together in a totally unmilitary cluster and started to walk, I found myself, out of sheer loneliness, drifting along with them

At nightfall, we were raked by a thunderstorm that wiped out all traces of the road. There was no shelter anywhere. Several of us took branches and braided them together into a kind of mattress that kept us from sleeping in the mud, although with little more comfort than a bed of nails. I found myself amidst a jumble of uniforms, some soldiers without boots, others without firearms, one armed with nothing but an axe, but all determined to fight to the last breath for a dry place to sleep.

I awoke in total darkness in a gutter carved by a small, icy river that rushed down from a nearby slope. It seemed that, during the night, a number of new men had joined us and I had been elbowed off the mattress. A savage argument was boiling up around me. Everyone was fighting to capture or retain a sliver of space on our common bed. Now there were close to thirty men struggling over a space that could barely hold ten.

I could see that, with this crowd, regardless who won, I wouldn't get much rest. Dark as it was, I decided to continue walking. My back was so stiff that I needed my rifle as a crutch to help me to my feet.

A sudden voice jerked me back. Someone with a Ukrainian accent had just called one of other men, "*Zhydovske morda,*" the same expression that had led to my first death sentence.

This time, however, I was happy to hear the slur; it meant I was no longer alone! There had to be at least one other Jew among this dark, scuffling mass of bodies. I felt instantly invigorated. I waited for my un-known ally to identify himself, preferably with his fists, to demonstrate that he had normal Jewish feelings.

But in all the shouting, I couldn't tell who he was or if he really exist-ed. I decided to pull rank and, with a parade-ground shout, demanded, "Who is the Jew that is causing all this trouble?"

Briefly distracted from their quarrel, the men gawked at one another. Accusations and denials flew through the air as they tried to help me unmask the villain. Seeing in me a kindred spirit, one of the ruffians gave me a hearty clap on the back.

I demanded silence, and then shouted, "Will the guilty Jew stand up and report to me at once!"

There was a stir among the bodies, some standing, some sitting in the mud, and all looking suspiciously at one another. I made a sharp sound of impatience, and a ghostly figure rose up before me.

"What did I do?" he complained with some vigor. The voice pierced me like a knife. Glasnik! He had not yet seen my face, and it took me several moments to calm myself.

I shouted, "Follow me at once," and headed down the dark, slippery road with Glasnik nervously dogging my footsteps while some of my comrades cheered me on.

When we were far enough from the others, I turned and said, "Nu, Glasnik, have you got anything to eat?"

13
THE GREAT CITY OF HARBIN

We all knew that the war was over ... as good as over ... the minute they signed the papers, somewhere in America, the only country in the world still on speaking terms with both sides. But it seemed that no one had told the enemy it was over.

Meanwhile, Glasnik and I joined the other half-starved stragglers marching toward Harbin. This time, our first stop was the telegraph office where we cabled our parents to kindly discontinue mourning for us.

Then Glasnik and I were shoved into a unit made up largely of milk-faced replacements that had just arrived from Europe and who, to their happy astonishment, were already being sent back. Giddy with relief, these young oafs thought the whole war thing was a big joke, and had only contempt for those of us who had been foolish enough to get involved in the actual fighting. This led to little flare-ups of brotherly bloodshed. But as long as it did not involve Jewish honor, I kept out of it.

One evening, strolling about the camp, I met Captain Lakheff – one of the few officers who, during our retreat, had shown as much concern for his leaderless troops as for his own skin. He shook my hand and apologized to me.

"For what?"

"Don't you remember my promise? I said I would recommend you for promotion to lieutenant."

"But I'm a Jew," I reminded him, lest he had mistaken me for one of his own.

"Other Jews have become officers. There was a great need for officers who would stay with their men, so the High Command lowered its stan—"

I interrupted him to ease his discomfort. "And what happened?"

"What happened, fool?" he said good naturedly. "The war ended too soon. A few more weeks of fighting, and you could have come home in an officer's uniform."

"A few more weeks of fighting, and I could have come home in a different condition, too."

"But there is one thing I can still do for you. When we get back to Petersburg, I will present you to my relative, the Czar, himself."

I didn't have the heart to tell him I could live very nicely without this great honor. But the colonel kept his word. And somewhere in a kitchen drawer of our apartment, amidst screwdrivers and tubes of glue and boxes of rusty nails, there may still be the medal I received on that occasion.

Over time, a few more of the "missing" began to reappear. Among them were officers whom we had believed were already back in Petersburg. But, poor fellows, despite their efforts to escape the indignity of our retreat, they had missed their train.

These generals and other high officials who had been preoccupied elsewhere during the fighting, now strutted about with bulging bellies and greasy cheeks, glittering in their parade-ground uniforms. They took every possible opportunity to make patriotic speeches, presumably to compensate for their absence during the fighting. Some were quite entertaining. Whatever military talents they might have possessed, I hadn't witnessed.

One general, who had been presumed dead (to the great joy of all who knew him), suddenly resurrected himself. He was the one who had vowed that, upon our return, we would find a Russia that had become liberal, democratic and every bit as modern as England or Germany. The Czar, himself, had promised there would be a true representative government in which even Jews would have a voice.

What all this meant was that our Little Father had been badly frightened by the previous year's ill-fated revolution, and wanted to make sure that, after all we had seen and endured, his returning soldiers still loved him as much as ever.

We broke ranks, and Glasnik called me aside. With an embarrassed look, he asked, "How much money do you have?"

"How much do you need?"

He dragged me behind some shrubbery. Then he climbed a tree to survey the area and make doubly sure that we could not be observed.

"Lunatic," I yelled. "What are you looking for?"

He climbed down and opened his tunic. Like many soldiers, he had sewn a secret pocket into his waistband. From this pocket, he took out more money than I had ever seen in one place, other than on the tables on which our officers played cards.

If I gaped stupidly, it was not because the amount was so large but because Glasnik was no more of a gambler than I was and, unlike most of us, was far too fastidious to rifle the pockets of corpses.

I finally dared to ask, "Where did you get this?"

It turned out that, the previous evening, he met an officer for whom, in Petersburg, he had once stayed up all night altering a uniform the man desperately needed for a reception at Court. At this event, the officer had met his future bride, and as part of her dowry, the bride's well-connected father had eased him into a position as regimental Quartermaster, the same role in which everyone but my honorable brother, Mordechai, had become rich. This officer, who had neglected, at the time, to pay Glasnik for his all-night work, suddenly remembered him for the small role he had played in making him a very rich man, and thrust a fistful of notes into his hands.

We sat down while Glasnik sorted and counted his shapeless lump of rubles. It added up to more money than his father had probably earned in his entire life. Only why was my friend making this sudden, somewhat dangerous display of his wealth?

"Because half of it is yours," he explained.

"How is it mine?"

"Don't you remember? Your promise? If I were killed and you lived, you would take my father into your house and honor him and support him all of the days of his life, exactly as you would your own flesh and blood. Just as I had vowed to do for your parents if things went the other way."

"So?"

"That makes us partners."

"Fine. But the war is over."

"You're still my partner."

"You're crazy."

Tears in his eyes, he shouted at me. "I never had a brother. You were more than a brother to me. I owe you my life a hundred times over. If you don't take half the money, I'll set fire to it this minute, I swear."

I did my friend the kindness of not forcing him to strike a match.

For two cultured young men bulging with money, there was only one thing to do in Harbin.

Although we had been severely warned not to set foot outside the barracks since our train might depart at any moment, Glasnik and I scraped off our beards, brushed our clothes and boots, and marched off to pay a visit to the world-famous (or so we had been told) Harbin Opera.

Out in the street, we followed a group of officers who looked as though they had already spent a good part of the evening consuming the city's more perishable pleasures, and now also seemed to be heading for the opera where they could catch a few hours of sleep before resuming their pursuits.

The Opera House was packed, mostly with officers and high Russian officials, all chattering loudly enough to cause you to wonder if they would condescend to stop when the music began.

Having shared a bottle of something the moment we left the barracks, Glasnik and I were intimidated neither by rank nor by the fact that each of our tickets cost almost a month's pay. We had not troubled beforehand to find out the exact nature of the entertainment in store for us. If it was good enough for the refined tastes of our nobility, who were we to ask questions?

The stage finally lit up and the performance began. We realized quickly that this was not what people in places like Petersburg or Warsaw would call "opera," where bloated singers waved their arms and gargled like a cantor at a rich girl's wedding. What the Chinese called opera was an endless succession of peculiar dances accompanied by high-pitched music that gave both of us immediate headaches.

I began to suspect that some of the singers and dancers were not women at all, but men who had painted female faces on top of their own, which was enough to spoil what little I might have enjoyed.

Since half the audience would probably rush for the exits after ten minutes of such entertainment, the performers took pity on the audience and gave us a demonstration of mock warfare, which was done with acrobatic skill and entertaining to watch. "If that is how they fight," Glasnik whispered to me, "no wonder the Chinese never win any wars."

To make our drowsing officers feel still more at home, the actors also tried to tell what they believed were Russian jokes, shrieking with helpful laughter each time they arrived at the punch line. While this encouraged some of the audience to join in the hilarity, it was obvious that neither the actors nor the spectators understood one word of what was being said.

I glanced at my watch and then at Glasnik. There was no telling how far into the night this would go on. We rose silently, and with a handsome apology for every polished boot stepped upon, we escaped into the open air.

It was far too early in the night to go back to the barracks. Since money was suddenly no object, we strolled up and down some of the busier streets of Harbin in innocent search of other diversion.

We followed some of the officials who had escaped from the entertainment to a place where one could get drunk at a reasonable cost, especially once the alcohol had sufficiently paralyzed one's sense of smell. The schnapps, in truth, tasted like a mixture of sulfur and rotten eggs, but had the power to make one drunk very quickly.

An elderly Chinese man accosted us on the street, and showed us some kind of magic lantern in which, for five kopeks, one could see things that were not usually seen in army camps. Truly, the variety of intimacies possible between a man and a woman seemed almost beyond imagining, especially in our depleted state, and I wondered whether I'd live long enough to ever taste the fruit from this Tree of Knowledge.

While we stood and gawked and came back for yet another fascinated look, a second promoter sidled up and, without the least embarrassment, let on that for only one ruble one could have the "full use" of a woman.

Glasnik and I looked at these Cathayans with their smooth faces and pigtails and skirts, but I was damned if I could tell which was a woman and which was a man.

The pimp continued to tug at my elbow and I couldn't decide. In fact, I found myself appealing to Heaven to restore my long-forgotten *yetzer hara*.[48] After all, here I was in the midst of a great and terrible war, even if it was 'officially' over, and who knew whether I would return alive? Let me, at least, have this one experience before I die. But I couldn't summon up the necessary lust.

Meanwhile, a group of Russian soldiers came out of the place, buttoning themselves and fairly bursting with satisfaction. Glasnik and I exchanged yet another uncertain look. It was a mistake for us to come here together because we were both a little embarrassed in front of each other. But in the end, with a bit of rough nudging from our gentile comrades, we went inside.

In a dim room without a floor or furniture, the first thing I saw was a creature wearing Chinese trousers and a short kaftan who gave me a broad wink. One of the Russian boys nudged me and said, "This one's yours." But I found that I was unable to make a move. Instead, I accepted another drink.

After a few more, I began to relax. Once my eyes became accustomed to the gloom, I realized there were some fine-looking women there. I kept refilling my glass, waiting for desire to sweep me off my feet. Meanwhile, my comrades continued disappearing into small adjoining cubicles shielded by ragged curtains that left very little to the imagination.

The Chinese person who had winked at me earlier now simply took my hand and drew me firmly into a windowless room. It was furnished only with a mattress made of bamboo sticks.

Waiting for me to make a move, she daubed her face and whitened it with powder, which I took was meant to make her more alluring. I stared at her more closely and, although I was almost totally anesthetized from

48 Hebrew: Inclination to sin

what I'd drunk, I realized that she smelled even worse than the schnapps, almost like a cellar full of onions that, over the winter, had begun disintegrating like corpses.

Now she crinkled her eyes and made inviting little gestures with her hands. I pantomimed with my hands and feet that I didn't feel quite ready yet and, in fact, hadn't actually made up my mind.

Her gestures grew more explicit, more coarse. The slender exotic flower was beginning to look to me more like a typical Petersburg whore, the kind known by the expression *oifes t'mayim* ("unclean fowl").

I continued sipping the vile stuff in my glass to endow myself either with lust or the courage to walk out. To gain time, I told her I still didn't believe she was a woman. She seemed to understand perfectly and, with a great show of girlish modesty, she tightened the greasy curtain, and then slowly removed her garment. What she put on display was a grimy, yellowish body that, without question, had all the necessary furnishings of a female. But despite, or because of, all I'd drunk, I was flooded with pure revulsion. I ripped aside the curtain and rushed out.

Glasnik joined me in the street. He could tell by my look that I had not been satisfied, either. But now the pimp and another gigantic Cathayan came running out after us, demanding payment for 'our' women.

This struck me as so unreasonable that when the big Cathayan suddenly flashed a knife in his hands, I drew my revolver and made an equally threatening move. At this, the men didn't merely return to their house of joy but took off down the street with piercing cries of indignation.

And so, still faced with the bleak prospect of dying without ever having known the full taste of a woman, Glasnik and I supported each other as we staggered back to our camp.

The next morning, I didn't feel virtuous so much as deathly ill. I bitterly reproached myself for having gone out with such frivolous and repugnant intentions. In fact, either the Chinese schnapps or my disgust at my weakness of character left me too sick to eat for several days, and too feeble to drill my platoon that, without any malice, I'm sure, would have been quite happy not to have me recover at all.

14

THE SIBERIAN 'QUEEN ESTHER'

n Harbin we were packed back into the boxcars that had delivered us to the great and terrible war. Although it was notably less crowded than it had been on the way to the battle, I found myself missing the airless shoving and endless bickering of my absent comrades. We sat on the train surrounded by thoughts of those souls who were not returning with us.

I don't know how many days later, our train stopped in Irkutsk for maintenance and restocking. There were rumored to be empty barracks in which we could bathe, do laundry, and even sleep lying down again, an invention I had never before fully appreciated. The danger, however, to being able to sleep in relative comfort was that images of the war, which we'd rather not have to look upon again, could return and smother us with their full power each time we lost consciousness.

Other than being the capital of Eastern Siberia, Irkutsk was known to be home to a great beauty, a wealthy young widow known as "Queen Esther." [49] She was legendary along the Trans-Siberian Railway, not only for her virtue but for hospitality of such royal lavishness that her guest book was said to hold the names of some 18,000 Jewish soldiers whom she had fed.

49 The heroine of the Purim story

This she did to honor the memory of her husband who had fallen early in the war while leading a squadron of cavalry against a fortified Japanese position (something that, in my private opinion, only a blockhead would have done). But by the time this unkind judgment had traipsed through my mind, I was not only in love with her but had made up my mind to reward her generosity by offering myself to her in marriage, sight unseen.

Naturally, my friends and I were determined to betake ourselves into the city and claim our share of the Queen's bounty – right after a good night's rest of twenty or thirty hours.

Unlike the Russian army, this jewel of a woman had anticipated our arrival. Like true royalty, she sent an ambassador to seek out the Jewish soldiers (meaning anyone willing to be so identified) and invite us to dine in her home the following night. The only flaw in this wonderful invitation was that tomorrow was not today, and to my hollow stomach, tomorrow evening was as far away as the moon, and we had a long, hungry night ahead of us with nothing much to do but sit around the barracks, clustered according to nationality, and play cards, pluck lice out of each other's hair, and talk about matters of common interest. The Poles dreamt wistfully of a day when their ravaged country would be free of Czarist domination, while the Russians reminisced with glum nostalgia about muddy villages and corrupt landowners, the joys of vodka and the price of pigs.

Meanwhile, we Jews diverted each other with tall stories of demons and *dybbuks*,[50] pious women and the occasional not-so-pious woman. Glasnik spoke of a holy man credited with being able to predict, and even alter, future events. He told the story of a poor widow who had come to the rabbi, desperate to marry off her daughter but unable to scrape together so much as two kopeks toward her child's dowry. Aside from which, the daughter was neither a beauty nor much of a housekeeper.

As Glasnik spoke, I felt my eyelids droop. I was not partial to stories about wonder-working rabbis; they made me nervous. Especially since I believed in them.

"The widow," Glasnik said, "poured out her heart to the holy man, and he told her to go home and be concerned no longer. Why? Because,

50 Yiddish: In Jewish folklore, a malicious spirit of a deceased person that attaches itself to a living one

within a week, a handsome young man would appear at her house and take her daughter just as she was, clumsy-handed and without a kopek to her name."

I sat up, outraged. No self-respecting rabbi, with or without miraculous powers, would make such an insane promise. Glasnik glared me into silence and continued.

"The daughter, naturally, laughed at the holy man's prediction. Especially when six days went by and no one had shown up who, in any way, matched his far-fetched description of the girl's intended.

"But late that evening in her little attic bedroom, she emptied out her chamber pot in the customary way, that is, by spilling it out the window. As luck would have it, a handsome young city official was passing by and got thoroughly drenched. He burst into the house, furious, and what do you think he did? He took the girl, just as she was, without a kopek, straight to jail."

Upon the arrival of morning, my friends and I learned that, while we had had the good breeding to wait until the time we were invited, some of our less scrupulous comrades had ventured out the previous night in search of the Queen's palace. After hours of blundering, they found the place at close to midnight and had the insolence to knock on her door.

Not only did this exemplary woman's servants not set the dogs on the men, but the staff bustled to relight lamps and stoves, and in short order set before the soldiers a late-night snack of the most exquisite leftovers. How was it possible not to fall in love with a woman like that?

We were strictly forbidden to leave the area, but since our officers were recuperating at a local hotel and no one seemed to be in charge, my friends and I contained our raging hunger only until mid-afternoon. Then, with rifles slung over our shoulders as though en route to a distant guard post, we strolled briskly into town.

Irkutsk, although in many ways a modern city, proved to be somewhat short of signposts and streetlights. Before long, we found ourselves so utterly lost in a spider web of alleys and lanes that Glasnik said we should have left a trail of breadcrumbs to help us find our way back. But, of course, if we had had breadcrumbs, we would have eaten them by now.

At last we spotted a policeman. Before he could open his mouth to ask what we were doing at large, I firmly demanded the address of the woman known as "Queen Esther." Like any good Russian civil servant, he pretended not to understand a word I said.

So with all possible tact, I shouted at him, "Get the dirt out of your ears! We are looking for the woman who is kind to soldiers."

At this, his face brightened in a repulsive leer, and he pointed to a dingy tavern whose upstairs rooms were clearly not designed to host prayer meetings.

At the end of my patience, I asked whether this pitiful town of his had a synagogue, and drew my bayonet. The policeman stopped trembling only when he saw me use it to draw a Star of David in the dirt. Suddenly, his faculties returned and, eager to be rid of such violent characters, guided us in the right direction.

What we found was, indeed, a synagogue, but most of the Jews gathered there for evening prayers were descendants of soldiers who had been forcibly resettled in Irkutsk. Exiled from Jewish learning and traditions for who-knows-how-many generations, their religious practices had decayed into such a sad patchwork of what they remembered (or misremembered) from their parents or grandparents that I could only marvel that they were Jews, at all.

At the synagogue, we were given proper directions, and at last found the Queen's mansion in the midst of a small private park whose trees and shrubs were aligned as neatly as troops on parade.

We were greeted at the front door by a tall, bearded, broad-shouldered Jew. Even in a butler's uniform, he looked more like a general than most of our generals. (It turned out that he had once been a high-ranking officer until ruined by a jealous rival.)

Following his instructions, we marched in brisk cadence toward an adjoining structure built of squared logs. It looked like a woodcutter's cabin, but inside it sparkled as brightly as any ballroom in Petersburg. Tables had been set in long rows with tablecloths and dishes, silverware, candles and flowers, as though we were the kind of guests for whom only the best was good enough.

Surrounded by comrades from a dozen other units, I was struck by the rich variety of Jews, and how many dialects of Yiddish or Hebrew they spoke. Mountain Jews from Kurdistan and Georgia, who looked as though they could uproot trees with their bare hands, were seated beside scholarly men from Carpathia and dark-skinned warriors from Bokhara, Samarkand and other exotic parts of Asia. There were also some more familiar-looking Jews from Poland, Lithuania and the Ukraine, including some whose Yiddish sounded more like professorial German.

But even as we ate and drank and our voices overlapped in songs from every corner of the Czar's domain, I continued to peer in all directions for a glimpse of our mysterious hostess. How could I propose marriage to a woman I had never seen?

A few drinks later, I began to speculate why our hostess remained hidden from our eyes. Could it be that she bore some terrible disfigurement that she was ashamed to display to the world? I refused to believe it. A woman of such holy dedication could not help but radiate an inner beauty that would outshine any physical blemish.

I asked the 'general,' "Where is our hostess so we can thank her in person?"

He smiled, and said she was away on business. Possibly she would return the following day. Or the one after. Or maybe next week.

I plucked up my courage to ask, "Is she as beautiful as people say?"

I saw it was a question he was weary of answering. "Why not judge for yourself?"

"But we may leave any day."

He shrugged. "Then I suppose you will never know."

Somewhat rashly, I wondered aloud, "How is it that such a woman has not yet found another husband?"

His smile mocked my question. "Are you volunteering for the job?"

My face burned with confusion. It was suddenly obvious to me that he, himself, was in love with her. Hopelessly, of course. And if she would rebuff even a 'general,' what chance was there for an unwashed ruffian like me?

Nevertheless, I was determined to return the next day, and the following day, and the day after that, until I met this extraordinary woman, even if our train left without me, even at the risk of being shot as a deserter. I would not have been the first man to die for love.

That evening, my fantasy tormented me with schemes for achieving a meeting face to face so that I could introduce myself in some way that would mark me in her eyes as not just another grateful soldier, but a man supremely qualified to end her widowed loneliness. While fumbling for the right words in which to clothe my proposal, I fell asleep.

When I awoke, I remembered that, in my dream, I had been on the very verge of delivering a speech guaranteed to win any woman's heart. The trouble was, I couldn't remember a single word of it. But before I had time to fret about it, we were all herded back onto the train and headed home.

Drifting in and out of sleep, I felt our train clank to an unscheduled halt. The rain-blinded windows offered no clue, but in the darkness someone guessed that we had reached Tomsk. But beyond our windows lay no glimmer of a city, large or small, or even a railroad station.

Packed together like herrings, we fretted and grumbled and waited for the engine to pull into the depot. Nothing moved. With all the authority of my corporal's insignia, I accosted a conductor. Being a civilian, he was not afraid to reveal why we could see no station. The engine driver was instructed, for the sake of "maintaining order," to halt in an open field at a "safe" distance from the city. How far? He shrugged.

This bit of news infuriated even the most docile among us, stranded as we were in the midst of a wilderness churned up by an exploding sky. Meanwhile, several fine coaches had arrived from town to transport our officers to a hotel suited to their delicate tastes, leaving us half mad with sleeplessness and thirst.

I looked at Glasnik. No discussion was necessary. If Tomsk were reachable on foot, nothing would stop us from stretching our legs on civilized wooden sidewalks, gaping in wonder at the shop windows of a modern metropolis, and maybe even learning to smile at passing ladies once again. In short, to feel for a brief spell like human beings. We also planned to get a decent night's sleep, whether by a warm stove in the railroad station or, if we were lucky, at the home of a fellow Jew able to give us a hot meal and a dry floor to sleep on.

As raindrops rattled like stones upon our roof, we jumped down into mud that sucked at our feet like some diabolic magnet bent on pulling us straight down into the earth. I looked at my friend and couldn't help laughing. We looked like escapees from a lunatic asylum, what with our crudely patched uniforms, gray, collapsed skin, lusterless eyes and such stubble on our jaws as you might find sprouting on a corpse. How did scarecrows like us ever manage to keep the Japanese from chasing us all the way back to Petersburg, or even Warsaw?

The rain had blotted out the moon and the stars, and there was no road to speak of, so Glasnik and I set out to follow the track. For a good hour, while the rain kept up a steady drumbeat upon our heads, we stumbled toward the invisible station.

Glasnik found it difficult to maintain a cheerful spirit. He cursed not only the Czar's army, but demanded to know why the station was not getting any closer, and what I, as his superior in rank, proposed to do about it.

"You want to turn back?" I asked. He did not.

By the time we were able to make out blurred lights of the station less than a kilometer in front of us, it was three or four o'clock in the morning. Once we reached the depot, I understood why our train had been ordered not to pull in to the station: the platform was packed with soldiers left behind by a previous train for Heaven-only-knows what excellent reason. Had our train suddenly materialized in front of them, they would have tried to force their way into our cars, which might have led to some fraternal bloodshed.

At the far corner of the platform, I noticed a man in a European-style suit deep in conversation with the stationmaster. His animated way of speaking reminded me of something I had not seen in almost two years – a Jew in civilian clothes.

I drew closer simply to stare. He looked at me in my Russian uniform and what I assumed to be my brutalized features, and (a miracle!) addressed me in Yiddish. "You're alone?"

"We're two Jewish soldiers looking for a place to sleep."

"So come." Without another word, he led the way. It was as if he had been waiting for us.

Outside the terminal, our rescuer's son was drowsing in his coach. Yawning, he blinked at Glasnik and me, then blinked again as though seeing double.

We introduced ourselves, and learned that our hosts' surname was Grodner. To judge by their vehicle's upholstery, they weren't in need of charity.

But what were they doing at the railroad station at that unlikely hour? With a touch of vexation, the father explained that they had come to pick up a young man from Odessa who had been recommended as a bridegroom for his daughter. The Candidate had sent a telegram announcing that night as his date of arrival. But no one at the station seemed to know why the train had not turned up, or even when the next train from Europe was due.

As our coach raced through torrents of mud, I fell into a deep sleep, which ended all too soon.

When we arrived, Grodner's house was dancing with lights. Friends and neighbors overflowed the parlor, all eager for a first glimpse of the visitor from Odessa. Each had brought something to eat or drink, as one would back home ... after a funeral. Either Siberian Jews, isolated by time and distance, had evolved strange new practices, or their view of marriage was a great deal more somber than ours.

The guests became abruptly silent at the sight of their friend hauling in not one but two strapping, if slightly soiled, young Jewish soldiers. In their eyes, we were not a pack of beaten and exhausted men who had just lost a war, but veritable statues of conquering heroes cast in bronze.

The prospective bride had made a commendable effort to stay awake. Her name was Sonya, and although I could feel my heart begin to pound at the mere sight of a civilized female, she was, in truth, simply a plump, pleasant-looking young woman with a nervous voice. But after not having set eyes on a Jewish girl in almost two years, and especially after a drink or two, I found myself fully prepared to overlook her small nose and placid personality and offer her my heart.

But Glasnik, the scoundrel, pushed himself ahead of me. It had taken only a few drops of high-proof vodka to transform this diffident tailor's apprentice into a well-spoken military strategist ready to explain how, contrary to the common impression, Russia had actually won the war. It was thanks, in no small measure, to the bravery of "ordinary Jewish boys" like Yankel[51] Marateck, he added, flaunting his generosity of spirit toward his lesser comrade.

Without regard for the clock, we sat down to celebrate as though the Candidate from Odessa had arrived and already declared himself. Even

51 Yiddish: Nickname for Jacob, or Yakov

Sonya entered into the spirit of things, serving and laughing and treating us to a very pretty Siberian song before she put her cheek on the table and fell asleep with her thumb in her mouth.

After an hour or two of such merriment, with platters of food descending upon us like waves of infantry, our host took me aside and asked my opinion of Glasnik as a husband for his daughter. In Siberia, a Jewish father was in no position to let his daughter waste time on such indulgences as courtship.

Although I was furious with Glasnik for not having given me, his nominal superior, the courtesy of the first pick, I told Grodner that Glasnik, while possibly not very handy with a bayonet, was a fine, solid fellow, a skillful tailor, and unquestionably able to support a wife.

Grodner assured me that in peacetime, even in Siberia, there was not ordinarily a great demand for expertise with a bayonet. And he revealed that he was prepared to give Sonya and her groom a dowry adequate, at minimum, for Glasnik to open a tailor shop right there in Tomsk. I glanced at Sonya and saw that she was as smitten with my friend as he was with her. Having no language in common, they primarily stared at each other; she, who had grown up in Siberia, had never learned her father's Yiddish, while Glasnik had made a point, throughout the war, of not learning Russian, the better to deny the occupation of his beloved Poland that would end, with God's will, during his lifetime.

As Glasnik was in no condition to think clearly, I tried to cool things down. My friend seemed to have forgotten that his father, widowed only a year earlier, had surely died a thousand deaths awaiting his son's safe return from the war. Who knew how long Glasnik would want to stay home, both to comfort his father and to recuperate from his own ordeals in Manchuria?

What's more, who could say whether, once back in Vishogrod, my friend might not develop a sudden passion for another, more familiar type of girl? Someone with whom he had at least one language in common. And what if the missing Candidate arrived on the next train from Moscow, and Sonya decided she would rather have *him*, after all?

With a grudging look, Grodner admitted my reservations had some merit. But seeing the look in his daughter's eyes and the sheep-like adoration in Glasnik's, and since our train might leave again at any moment, he wanted the engagement papers drawn up as quickly as possible. True, the city had no rabbi at the present, nor had it had one for the past twenty or thirty years. But one of Grodner's friends had once been a lawyer and could draw up a suitable document, although not in pure Aramaic.

Meanwhile, he invited both of us to stay at his home, and even suggested that we consider taking a later train that, he assured me, would expose us to very little risk. How could he be so sure? Our host smiled. He played cards every Monday night with the district's Military Governor to whom, each time, he was careful to lose a reasonable sum of money. By now, surely he had bought himself enough credit to fix a small matter like that.

Glasnik pulled me aside. He wanted my opinion of the girl. "The girl," mind you. He did not yet feel at ease even pronouncing her name. From the depth of my own innocence with women, what possible advice could I give him?

Since I knew what he wanted to hear, and had nobly already decided that I was not in love with Sonya, I told my friend that she was a fine girl, which I wholeheartedly believed, and that he would not be sorry, which no man could ever know for certain.

But what about Glasnik's father? Shouldn't he, at least, cable him and solicit his advice, in fact ask him to come here before anything was decided and meet the family? Not a day went by that I didn't think about my parents and how cruelly they had suffered while my brothers and I were subjected to the anonymous malice of Japanese shells and bullets, not to mention having mourned, already, over each of our mistakenly reported deaths.

With some annoyance, my friend let me know that his father was a simple man, who had never before received a telegram or set foot on a train, and that receiving one might be too great a shock for his grief-weary heart.

By ten o'clock in the morning, as the sun struggled to rise from behind a wall of rain, our host departed to call on the Military Governor to see what could be done to have Glasnik mustered out in Tomsk and save him the long, needless trip to Europe and back.

Grodner returned some time before noon with a sagging face. The Governor called to his attention that Glasnik's files were in Petersburg. Without them, what proof was there that he had ever been a soldier? And if he had never been a soldier, how could he be mustered out? In that case, Grodner shrewdly asked, what would happen if Glasnik simply took off his uniform and stayed in Tomsk, willingly forfeiting his mustering-out pay? Ah, that question was more easily answered: he would be shot as a deserter. So much for influence in high places.

At the time, I didn't realize what a risk our host had taken to make even this casual inquiry. Only two years earlier, there had been a pogrom in Tomsk, if only a modest one by the standards of Kishinev,[52] Bialystock or Siedlce. But to the Government's outrage, the city's small Jewish community had had the effrontery to defend itself and, in the general commotion, had been unable to avoid inflicting some casualties on their attackers.

In consequence, a whole series of laws and decrees had been promptly passed that restricted Jewish settlement in the area, particularly that of discharged Jewish soldiers. While, in practice, those laws were not strictly enforced, the Governor had jestingly reminded Grodner that he could, at his whim, expel him and confiscate his property. In short, whatever cash our host had lost seemed not to have been quite enough.

Glasnik and I wallowed in the Grodners' hospitality for three more days until word came that our train was due to leave at five o'clock the next morning. As we bid long and tearful goodbyes to our hosts, I saw that my friend looked powerfully tempted to desert, and damn the consequences.

But Glasnik's future father-in-law, and even Sonya, herself, had the good sense to overrule him. "What good is it to me having a son-in-law with a death sentence hanging over his head?" Grodner said. He told Glasnik, "If you truly love Sonya, you will find some way of returning as quickly as possible, no matter what the obstacles."

We returned to the station that our train had eventually decided to patronize. As I had feared, our already overcrowded car was obliged to make room for some of the soldiers left stranded by the previous, overfilled train. Jammed up against Glasnik without room enough to blow my nose, I watched him write to his beloved day after day. I asked him, "In what language?" Never mind; her father would translate.

52 Spelled, in Moldova (located between Romania and Ukraine): Chișinău

Having watched him fill interminable pages for the better part of a week, I saw Glasnik's growing frustration at the lack of any response. Not that the train had stopped any place where Glasnik could post his growing backlog of letters. It would be weeks, if not months, before he could get a reply. And whatever Sonya wrote would have to be filtered through my voice or that of some other translator, and thus be somewhat lacking in intimacy. My friend had already begun to speculate gloomily that the missing candidate from Odessa had arrived in Tomsk. And, girls being the flighty creatures that they were, who knew whether Sonya had not already transferred her affections?

Nevertheless, Glasnik resumed his one-sided correspondence. But one day a sudden jolt knocked over his bottle of ink. Although it ruined only one page, he stopped writing. And when, a few days later, we paused at a town from which he could mail his letters and have his ink bottle refilled, Glasnik sheepishly admitted that he had already run out of things to write to his beloved. And how could you spend the rest of your life with a woman to whom you had nothing left to say?

15

A BACHELOR IN VISHOGROD

No sooner had we returned home to Vishogrod than the floor began to tremble under the footfall of well-wishers. My hand swelled from all the men who demanded the honor of shaking it. But they also asked questions that I preferred not to answer, as doing so would force me to remember what I had been trying so hard to forget.

More difficult, though, were the shy inquiries of fathers and mothers whose eyes pleaded with me for some word of hope about a son 'officially' declared dead or missing. The grieving fathers and mothers wanted more than my craven words of hope; they wanted me to swear that I had seen their sons alive, if not guarantee that they would positively return home on such-and-such a day. But behind these questions was another, unspoken one: with so many millions of bullets flying around, how was it that I managed to come through alive and their son might not?

What could I say that would not be a cruel deception? I had seen far too many soldiers die in various unpleasant ways to convince myself that all of their sons had managed to survive. Yet, was it not equally cruel to leave them with no hope at all? The Japanese had taken masses of Russian prisoners, and those still alive could hardly have all been freed on the same morning. Who was to say that a lone soldier might not still be trying to find his way out of the vastness of Manchuria? But Jews, ultimately being realists, were under no illusion that my glib optimism would, somehow, bring back their sons.

Then I was presented with a situation that demanded testimony of a different sort.

One morning while my parents were away, a woman and her daughter came to call. The daughter's name was Shayna, and my last memory of her was as a little girl sitting, hunched-over at the river's edge, making "snowballs" out of mud. It took me less than the blink of an eye to notice that Shayna had grown into a truly beautiful young woman. In my vanity, my heart leapt with anticipation.

But I was terribly wrong about their intentions, as I should have realized immediately from the kerchief that modestly covered her hair. Shayna was a married woman. Married to Berel, a husky fellow from a nearby village whom I remember as being blessed with more stubbornness than sense.

They shyly asked if I might have encountered him in Manchuria, as though all of China were no larger than Vishogrod's Market Square.

However, as it happened I *had* seen him. For a while, he had even been in my platoon. What I couldn't, and didn't, tell them was the rest. How eight of us, including Berel, found ourselves, on a night of paralyzing darkness, huddled in the cellar of a ruined hut in the midst of a snow-covered forest, surrounded by a Japanese unit that had not yet pinpointed our location. Throughout the night, machine guns raked and shattered the trees, and men and animals cried out in their death agonies.

Braced, at any moment, for the enemy to charge our position and impale us upon their bayonets, none of us closed an eye that night. But morning came and, for reasons that no one understood, the firing stopped. The strange silence unnerved us even more than the shooting, but no one wanted to make the first move. No one except for Berel who, after a while, could stand the uncertainty no longer. He whispered to me, "I'm going out to look around."

As his superior, I ordered him to keep his head down; there were still enemy soldiers close by. He shook off my hand and crawled out. Nothing happened for a moment or two, and then we heard machine-gun fire for one long, terrible moment. Then silence. Hours of silence.

Two of us finally crawled out of the hut to look for Berel's body. Almost immediately, machine-gun fire plowed up the ground in front of us and drove us back. Later, under the wings of darkness, we escaped. Of the original eight, only three of us were left.

Once back with my unit, I reported Berel "missing." Although I had no way of proving it, there was no question in my mind that he was dead, but I hadn't the heart to make it official: that would have made me an instrument in the death of a fellow I had once known.

But now Berel's pale widow asked when I had last seen her husband.

I looked at my feet. "Almost a year ago."

"You saw him killed?" her mother continued.

I couldn't bring myself to tell the beautiful young widow that her husband, while remarkably courageous, had also been a fool, and that it had been his folly that killed him. Instead, I mumbled something about the thousands of Russian soldiers who had been captured by the Japanese, or might be in hospitals recuperating from their injuries ...

"But the war has long since ended," her mother said.

I agreed that it had been over for some months but who was to say that all the prisoners had been released on the same day? As we knew from our own experience, neither false nor accurate rumors reached every unit at the same time. Perhaps, as we spoke, a lone soldier was still trying to find his way out of the vastness of Manchuria.

When Shayna and her mother left, I felt chilled by their look of reproach. It was clear they suspected I knew more than I was willing to say. In fact, I was beginning to feel cursed for having survived, and my punishment was having to answer these same unpleasant questions over and over again.

Only a few hours later, I was summoned by Reb Henoch, the town rabbi, a descendant of the original Gerer Rebbe. I was startled by how much he had aged in two years. (I was told later that when he learned under what conditions his former students lived at the front, he had vowed to eat no meat nor sleep in his bed until the survivors returned to a normal life.)

I felt his eyes pierce me to the soul. He got right to the point, "You and Berel were in the same company?" he said. I admitted that we had been.

"You are quite certain you did not see him die?" I couldn't dislodge my tongue, which clung to my teeth, to respond, though what could I say? The Rabbi pointed to a chair and made for me to sit.

"As a student, did you ever learn the laws of *aguna*, the 'tied' woman?" he asked, though he knew that I had not stayed in *yeshiva* long enough to learn the volumes of the *Talmud* that governed marriage and divorce. Yet, I knew the word, knew its awful meaning.

Reb Henoch continued: "Unless there is reliable evidence of the husband's death, Shayna can never remarry. Until the grave, she remains tied to him."

Avoiding the rabbi's eyes, I said, "Berel is dead. He couldn't possibly still be alive."

"Did you see him die? You swear to it?" The words congealed in my throat. "Why didn't you say that to his widow?"

"I *couldn't*."

"Then how am I to believe you when you say it to me?"

"What does it matter? Don't there have to be two witnesses?"

"When there is a question of a woman being an *aguna*, everything possible is done to release her. At the same time, everything must be done to uphold the sanctity of marriage. If a single witness can swear that he either buried the body or recognized it, without a doubt, after death, that alone is enough. Or if he has evidence of something happening that no man could survive, such as falling into a pit of poisonous snakes, that too would suffice."

Was that not what I had said, that Berel could not possibly have survived the interlaced threads of gunfire? But as I had not seen the body, was it possible that he had been merely wounded and crawled off somewhere? No, of course not. We had tried to go out to look for him but gunfire drove us back. As the snipers remained focused on their position, had Berel so much as moved, he would have been shot, again.

"In times of war," Reb Henoch said, "we have to be very careful, because people make assumptions of what another man could, and could not, survive." This I knew to be true because of how many times my brothers and I had been reported killed to our poor parents, who sat *shiva* for us each time.

"If no single person can provide this testimony," Reb Henoch continued, "then we need two witnesses. One man may make an assumption, but it is less likely that two would make the same mistake."

My heart pounded with remorse. In my ignorance, and maybe cowardice, too, I had thrown away Shayna's only chance to marry, again.

"You understand," the Rabbi confided in me, "what a terrible thing this is for a woman. Should she marry again, while her husband may or may not still be alive, and her first husband returned ..." I opened my mouth in a vain attempt to interrupt. "She would be forbidden to live with either man." I saw the pain etched in his face. He shook his head. "It's too dreadful to think about."

The more Reb Henoch mused aloud, the more determined I was that Shayna not remain in her intolerable state of uncertainty. Briefly, I even entertained a fantasy of myself as her heroic rescuer, whatever the consequences in Heaven or on Earth.

But Reb Henoch he had not given up on me. "Who else was there?"

My breath caught in my throat as I thought of one boy in my platoon who lived not far from Vishogrod. It would not take long to get a message to— Then I remembered that he had been killed a few weeks later.

"Glasnik was not there?" Reb Henoch asked.

I started to shake my head, and then caught myself. Was the rabbi prompting me?

"He *might* have been," I stuttered. "In all the confusion, I'm not sure any more." My palms sweated, my ears felt crimson with hellfire heat. Impossible to think he had not read my mind.

"I will send for him," Reb Henoch said. "If there was any chance at all that Glasnik might have some direct knowledge of Berel's death, even if he had heard about what happened without seeing it, himself ..."

I felt a breeze blow through a window of hope, although I didn't know what the Rabbi meant by "direct knowledge," other than Glasnik seeing the corpse, himself. But if a witness was permitted to testify based on what he heard from another ...

My words trembled as I forced them to ask what I hoped sounded like an innocent question: "Would that be acceptable testimony?"

"So long as the witness draws his own conclusion."

I couldn't trust myself not to smile, so I lowered my head. Surely, if I told Glasnik the story of Berel crawling into a barrage of gunfire, he would agree that no one could have survived such a terrible onslaught.

But the rabbi added. "Remember, your friend must not lie, not even from the highest of motives." I nodded a bit sullenly.

Despite the stern warning, I decided to seek out Glasnik. Not to tell him what to say, but merely to … merely to … I raced to find him, and laid out the situation.

Quite unnecessarily, Glasnik reminded me, "But I wasn't there."

"But *I* was there! Isn't that good enough? And I swear to you, the man is dead. It happened almost in front of my eyes, but in my ignorance of the law, my testimony, alone, is not sufficient to release Shayna. Unless you're willing to give the same oath, Berel's widow will be alone and childless for the rest of her life."

Glasnik brooded on it a while. "She is a pretty girl."

I was furious to be so misunderstood. "That's neither here nor there."

"Shall I tell you what I'm going to say?"

"I don't want to know."

And Glasnik did me the kindness of never telling me.

I heard later that Shayna married again and had seven children. And if a violation was committed, I was prepared to believe that Reb Henoch took it upon his own soul.

16

A MESS OF MATCHMAKERS

Ever since we returned from the war, Glasnik had been living at my house. After all we'd been through, I didn't have the heart to ask him why. At first I was happy to demonstrate that I would still honor our pre-war pledge that my home would be his home, and his father would be my father, even though our noble arrangement had been meant to apply only if one of us had been orphaned, or killed in combat. But since we'd both returned alive and in full possession of our bodies, I didn't understand why he didn't return to his own home.

It took me a while to realize that there was no 'home' for him to go back to. Glasnik's mother had died during the fifth week of his military service (and my friend never ceased grieving for her). On that day his father, a man already in his forties, utterly lost his grip on day-to-day existence. Not only could he not cook his own meals or sweep his floors or wash his clothes, he had even sunk so far as to discontinue his daily attendance at the House of Study.

Worse yet, Glasnik's father's irregular earnings as a porter had no longer been enough to pay his rent. And although his landlord did not press him, pride obliged the old man to move out of his little house, sell his wife's clothing along with furniture and pots, and move in as a boarder with another family where, like any orphaned bachelor, he had his meals and slept in the kitchen.

What pained Glasnik was not only the way his father had come down in the world – it was that he seemed not to feel deserving of such a miracle as having his son return alive. And when Glasnik returned, not just alive but fully intact, his father seemed to look upon him like a ghost risen from a mass grave to whom he was afraid to express either relief or affection.

I invited Glasnik and his father to spend the first night of Passover with us. Glasnik trotted off to relay the invitation to his father; minutes later, he was back. His father refused to hear of it. How could a man whose clothes and shoes were barely held together by a few threads inflict his gloomy presence on a home as respectable as mine?

What I couldn't understand was why Glasnik was grinning when he delivered this message. Seizing my arm, he reminded me that since our brief excursion to the Chinese Opera, he had spent hardly a kopek of his money. Now he had enough left to outfit his father in a suitable wardrobe, and wanted my help in selecting it.

We hiked over to Simcha Neches the Clothier who lived on the other side of the hill. His shop was a room in which he and his family also ate and slept. We ordered two suits, two shirts and assorted underclothing in what Glasnik guessed to be his father's measurements. We also bought him a pair of warm boots and two pairs of festive white socks to wear on *Shabbos*.

Before taking the bewildered old man to try on his new clothes, we led him to the barbershop. Here, in less than ten minutes, Glasnik's father was transformed into a new person.

On the way out, people ambushed us, determined to have us reveal what the war was "really like." Was it true that my friend and I had actually tasted forbidden meats, and other foods from *Vanya's* unclean pots, without dying of sheer disgust? I disappointed them all by saying that my head was not yet clear enough to talk about the war, even to my own father.

Glasnik was also not immune to nightmares from our experiences. However, so many young tailors had been killed in the war that employers pursued him like wolves, enticing him with offers of as much as three rubles, four, even four-and-a-half rubles a week. But within days of accepting the best offer, he told me, "I can't work. My mind isn't on it. Today, I sewed a right sleeve on the left side of a customer's coat. My master told me no self-respecting tailor had done such a thing since the Creation of the World."

"He threw you out?"

"He can't afford to. But I don't want to go back. I can't get the war out of my head. My thoughts are simply not on which is the right sleeve and which the left."

In the end, he decided to quit his job and stay with his married sister until either his mind settled down or he found someone to marry. "And you?" he asked.

I confessed that my head was also still full of the war. Of how the Czar and his flunkies had thrown away hundreds of thousands of young lives. And for what? But I had vowed long ago that if, by some miracle, I made it home alive, I would devote my energies to making sure the Czar could never do that, again.

Glasnik looked appalled and whispered, "You want to overthrow the Czar?"

"Why not?"

"What would your parents say?"

"I'm not asking them."

"You think a new Czar would be any better?"

"Who says it has to be a Czar? Maybe, like the Americans, we could have a President, someone elected by the people."

Glasnik gave me a pitying look. "I thought I was going crazy. But if you believe Russia will ever become like America, you're crazier than I am."

"And what do you know about America?"

Here we both sighed and fell silent. We knew about America about as much as we knew about the "Other World." Except that, while no one I knew had ever returned from the dead, those who went to America at least wrote letters and sent packages. Sometimes they even returned for a visit, wearing hats made of straw, and speaking in loud voices like gentiles. Some even brought their American wives, women with painted-on smiles, whose laughter was like the bray of a trumpet. If you believed these visitors, New York was a cauldron of haste and violence and noise and anxiety, a world ruled by money and corruption. But it was obvious that they were lying. Otherwise, why would they have been in such a hurry to go back?

Saturday night, only minutes after my father doused the braided candle that plunged us from the sanctity of *Shabbos* back into the frantic world of the profane, an impatient knock rattled our door. It sounded like the rap of a mounted messenger delivering a dispatch from the Czar.

In fact, the knock portended something equally ominous. Planted on our doorstep was a man I remembered as the most persistent, and least successful, of our town's matchmakers, Koppel the Dairy, so called because his daytime occupation, whenever his horse felt up to standing, was delivering milk and butter. Judging by the state of his coat and boots, he had not become a great success at either profession.

What did he want? Nothing at all. He just happened to be passing by. But now that he was here, if he could have the honor of a glimpsing the "war hero" ...

My father was ready, politely, to close the door but Koppel stayed him with the dire prediction that while I may, for the moment, enjoy the glamour of a man who has returned alive from a great war, I also ran the risk, quicker than they might think, of turning into a crabbed, chronic bachelor, a figure of general ridicule, obsessed with his bowels and teeth, the kind of leftover whom no self-respecting Jewish daughter would look at twice.

My mother pleaded that I had just gotten back from China. "Let him enjoy a few months of freedom." My instincts tore me in both directions. It had been a long time since I had seen as many Jewish girls as Koppel was prepared to present to me, but I was much too young, too unschooled, to take up the awesome yoke of marriage. Not to mention that the only trade for which I had expressed a preference was that of overthrowing the Czar.

Like a good general, Koppel shifted his ground. All he came for, he reminded my parents, was to see what a "hero" looked like at close range. Besides, "What means 'too young?' He doesn't want the girl, he has a mouth to say 'No.'"

Somewhat intrigued, I persuaded my parents to let him sit down. It was true; I knew nothing of how to be a married man, or even by what steps one arrived at such an enviable and terrifying state. But I had had no trouble learning how to lead a platoon into battle, which I also had never done before. How much more difficult could it be to learn how to live with a wife?

My mother served tea and some leftover cake, and tactfully drew my father into the other room. Koppel and I chatted cautiously about topics of general, if not mutual, interest. I learned that a nearby town already had gotten gaslights while Vishogrod, as usual, lagged behind. And that two neighbors were feuding over the ownership of some lumber cast up by the river.

In passing, Koppel mentioned that a certain local girl, whom I would probably remember only as a little terror, had blossomed overnight into a beauty, although she was not for me, her parents having no money at all.

Although we were not rich, either, I assured him that a dowry was the least of my concerns, at which point my father put his head into the room to remind Koppel, "I thought you only came to look."

Koppel favored my father with a benign smile. "Any fool can match up rich with rich or poor with poor. But a beautiful girl and a treasure like your Yakov? Now that could be a match made forty days before he came into the world."[53]

"What girl are you talking about?" my father asked.

The matchmaker rose to leave. "No, no. I totally agree with you. It is far too soon for your son to think of marriage. I only wanted to see how he had turned out."

"And what is your professional opinion, if I may ask?"

"Who am I to draw conclusions about such a fine young man?"

"What, he's not good enough?"

"Heaven forbid. After what he's been through, it's a miracle he still knows how to pronounce a blessing."

"You are telling me he's not good enough for … whoever she is?"

Koppel twisted and turned like a cornered mouse, but he smiled and declined to be pinned down. "If I say he's not, you'll be angry. And if I say

---

53 According to the Talmud, forty days before birth Heaven calls out the name of a child's soul-mate. It is another way of saying, "A match made in heaven."

he is, you will think I have come to propose a match and that I lied to you." Nose held high, he made for the door.

By this time, not only I but also my parents were furious with curiosity. More or less barring the door, my father demanded outright, "Who is the girl?"

"What girl? It happens that she comes, on her mother's side, from one of the finest Hasidic dynasties. But if she had an inkling that I was sitting here, offering her around like a public towel, she would die of shame." (In later years I learned that, in Columbus' Country, this sort of thing was called 'Psychology,' and that people made a very nice living from it.)

To regain the upper hand, Koppel also reminded my father of the well-known speculation by our sages that, now that the Almighty no longer deemed us worthy of overt miracles, He spent His days as a matchmaker. And His achievements in that field were as miraculous and as difficult to get right as splitting the Red Sea.

Having thus put my father on the defensive, Koppel allowed my mother to pour him a second glass of tea. Sipping carefully to avoid where the rim was chipped, Koppel studied me with mournful admiration, and sighed. What a pity it was that his lips were sealed.

But then, as though some magical ingredient in my mother's tea had loosened his tongue, Koppel dropped one clue too many. And while I was still in the dark, my mother pounced. "Is it that Henya with the pock-marked face?"

"Is it a sin for a girl not to have perfect, white skin like a gentile?" Koppel said heatedly. "Does that mean she doesn't deserve to be married? What of my own wife, Chayah? You've seen the scars on her face; she doesn't hide them. Are you telling me I should not have married her, not have had children with her? Are you saying my children should never have been born?" He rose in such indignation that his chair fell over. "What a fine-looking son you've got," he said darkly. "May no evil eye ever befall him."

To compensate for my mother's bluntness, I walked the matchmaker part way home. In return, he advised me that, until I grew a respectable beard and put in some time at a serious *yeshiva*, I may find it difficult, if not impossible, to be matched up with a first-class girl. But, if I wanted him to put in a word with Henya's parents …

I soon found out that Koppel's warning was not all idle talk. The first sign of this came all too soon as matchmakers, even Koppel, himself, stopped calling at our house. Some of them, when they saw me strutting in the street, ramrod-straight and peacock-proud, not only no longer rushed at me with outstretched arms but turned away to look into shop windows, even where there were no shops.

17

AN AMATEUR'S GUIDE TO THE REVOLUTION

You might have thought that the war furnished me with enough thrills to last a hundred lifetimes, but I felt restless, ready to burst with unspent energy. The time had come for me to either to move on or settle down. Either to head for Warsaw and join my brother, Mordechai, in whatever he was doing to overthrow the Czar or, like most of those who had returned from the war, resign myself to a trade and a wife and, except for the fleeting joys of being a husband and father, bury the rest of my days in honest, soul-destroying drudgery. Even my parents agreed that, married or single, Vishogrod held no future for me. So, for the third time in my young life, I got ready to leave home and taste what the great world had to offer.

In those days, going forth to take part in such a world-shaking enterprise as a revolution was a leisurely business. To begin with, there was a round of farewell visits to be made locally. Then I had to stop off and see my married sister, Malkah, in Stritchev,[54] and my brother, Chayim, in Łódź.

Aaron, Malkah's husband, was said to be the richest man in Stritchev. I took this to mean that he lived in a house with a wooden floor, and his family ate chicken more than once a week. In fact, my brother-in-law owned a small flour-mill, which brought in enough money for his family to live in a brick house and also have gaslight and varnished floors.

---

54 Spelled, in Poland, Szczerców

Malkah had insisted that I buy no civilian clothes but arrive in full dress uniform, medals and all. And though I had rather looked forward to burying my uniform without me in it, I agreed to oblige her.

When my train pulled into the station, half the town seemed to be waiting for me. And this half consisted almost entirely of dark-eyed young beauties, whose uncovered hair made clear to the entire world that they were available for marriage.

But instead of being allowed to embrace my sister, the moment I set foot on the platform with my small bundle of belongings, I was set upon by a mob of shouting and elbowing coachmen, each of them determined to carry off this prize passenger. They filled my ears with claims about the strength of their horse, the roundness of their wheels, the dishonesty and drunkenness of the other drivers, and the amount of grease they packed into their axles that very morning, purely in honor of conveying such an important visitor as me.

I resisted a dozen hands snatching at my luggage, until my sister's husband, Aaron, finally broke through and pacified the lot of them by giving each a small coin. Then he introduced himself, shook my hand, and apologized for not yet possessing a coach of his own. We ended up riding with the one coachman who had not tried to force himself on me, possibly because his horse looked as though it might fall over at any moment and crumble into little pieces. We took the risk because we had only two blocks to travel.

Marriage had given Malkah a whole new, matronly appearance. It had also, I was sorry to discover, turned her into a political conservative. Both she and her husband were convinced that my plan to go to Warsaw and dabble in revolution was a pack of foolishness certain to end badly. For such folly, there was only one time-tested cure. Which was to send for the matchmakers and treat me to my choice of absolutely any young woman in Stritchev.

I will admit that it was no small temptation. Even the few Stritchev girls I had observed at the train station seemed incomparably more beautiful and worldly than those of Vishogrod, most of whom I had played with as a child and who were, thus, somewhat lacking in mystery.

But in the end I said 'no.' The Czar's little war had wrenched two thoroughly unpleasant years out of my life, and if I didn't at least try to carry out what I had sworn to do at the edge of countless graves, what good were all my noble ideals?

The most I allowed Malkah and Aaron to do for me was call in a tailor to measure me for a suit of such daunting respectability that, were I to wear it in Warsaw, any serious revolutionary would turn tail and vanish down the nearest alley. In the process, I was obliged to keep my mouth shut while the tailor insulted me with his comments about my sturdy parade-ground posture that made me look like a gentile.

My suit and I took a train to visit my brother, Chayim, in Łódź, the heart of Poland's textile industry, where, thanks to his father-in-law's generosity, he owned a "department store."

I followed Malkah's directions from the station, and after walking for some time, found my way to a drowsy lane of small, flyblown shops whose windows neither hinted at the merchandise inside nor allowed more than a few stale smudges of light to leak through.

Stopping to peer into one of the listless windows or doors, a passerby might have glimpsed an occasional storekeeper or his faded wife in a frayed apron standing guard over shelves as bare as if they had been looted by an invading mob. Arms folded, they repelled my rude gawking. I suspected that Chayim's place of business would be no better.

When I found the right address, I glanced inside and saw that my brother's store was just large enough to hold a couple of shelves, a counter as wide as a bread board, and maybe two customers, if they stood sideways. His shelves were entirely bare, except for the bottom one that held luxury items such as spices, buttons, cigarettes and soap, all of which looked as if they could use a good dusting.

I did not, immediately, recognize the man behind the counter. The last time I had seen Chayim was nearly ten years earlier in the *yeshiva* from which I had departed rather hastily, but at which he had shown a definite scholarly talent. Barely in his mid-twenties, Chayim's ashen face now was wreathed by an untamed beard. My brother looked so worn, so ghostly, so transparent that for a moment I felt almost moved to thank the Czar for having saved me from a fate like that.

Tucked into a shapeless overcoat, Chayim sat bowed over a ledger his eyes could not possibly decipher in the cavernous darkness. A closer look revealed it to be a well-thumbed-through volume of the *Talmud*. He did not trouble to look up at the ugly sound of my boots on his floor. And why would he? Even if Rothschild, himself, came in and bought out the whole store at double the asking price, it would barely have eased Chayim's poverty for more than one or two days.

I demanded a pack of Turkish cigarettes in my most gentile-sounding Russian. He reached behind him, dropped it onto the counter, and scooped my few coppers into a drawer, all without looking up and seeing who had lavished this sudden fortune upon him.

I felt crushed by the weight of his anonymous contempt. I left the store, choking back tears, but stamped back in, slapped the cigarettes on the counter, and demanded a different brand. At last I got a human response. He opened the drawer, tossed my money at me, and told me not to waste his time. My heart broke as I saw what the intervening ten years had done to him.

"Brother, don't be angry," I said in Russian.

"I'm not your brother," he said automatically. Then, as though my voice seemed distantly familiar, he looked up. And for a moment he appeared about to faint. "Yakov?" he whispered.

"Greetings from Mama and Papa."

With a cry, he lunged past the counter, flung his arms around me, and touched my face as though to assure himself I was not some sort of demon.

Before the day was out, I had met his children and his pale, exhausted wife. Rather than hurt his feelings by going to a hotel, I accepted his offer to sleep on a bench in the kitchen. At dinner time, two elderly women – matchmakers, each – came calling. I allowed them to look me over but declined to listen to their offerings. In truth, what I saw in that house made me wonder if I would ever feel ready for the yoke of marriage.

Unable to convince the matchmakers that my mind was on more serious matters, I informed them, with all possible delicacy, that a certain wound acquired in battle had ruined my … appetites.

At this, they sighed with pity and advised me not to despair but to go to Warsaw and seek out a "suitable" wife, that is, one safely past childbearing age.

When I reached Warsaw, Mordechai met me on the platform. In his stained gray suit and hat, my older brother looked so respectable that I almost walked right past him, but he grabbed my arm and embraced me.

Our tearful greetings out of the way, I pressed him to take me, at once, to meet my new comrades. He demurred, saying there would be time for that later. He thought I looked hungry, and wanted to feed me.

Thanks to the war, I was well acquainted with hunger so I didn't want to waste time eating. I wanted to get on with the business of anarchy, the reason I had returned to Warsaw. But Mordechai insisted on taking me to a café where he treated me to a bowl of hot, thick and peppery potato soup. With the air of a man to whom money was dirt, he added a generous chunk of bread covered with prune jam, and a mug of boiling black tea with four lumps of sugar. While I chewed the moist brown bread, Mordechai wistfully eyed each crumb that tumbled from my lips. When I offered him some of my food, he assured me that he had already eaten.

While I ate, I discovered that he had not been leading what I imagined to be the romantic life of an anarchist. He had even gone back to work at the same bakery where, before the war, we had put in twenty-hour days, six days a week. Worse yet, he had hoped to get me a job there but, he said apologetically, his boss seemed to remember me as a troublemaking "union agitator" and wanted no part of me.

Sensing my impatience for action, Mordechai assured me, but with no visible urgency, that we would go around together and get acquainted with the various movements. Then we could decide calmly whose philosophy appealed to us most. With the patience of an older brother who recalled his own youthful and foolish ideals, he explained that things were no longer as I remembered them from those innocent years before the war. Choosing a party was a serious business, not something to be rushed into. Warsaw was swarming with radical organizations, and there was good and bad to be said about each. Some of the more professional ones advocated a Polish nationalism of such grim purity that they planned to exclude not only Russians and Germans but also Jews.

I pointed out to my intellectual brother that, since all radical organizations were illegal, if people saw us browsing from one to the other, like a housewife shopping for a chicken, they might get the impression we were agents of the *Okhranka*,[55] the Czar's secret police. (As it was, we were having this heated discussion in a crowded Jewish restaurant where anyone with ears could have overheard us. Mordechai kept trying to silence me, or at least get me to lower my voice, but his efforts, which felt like attempts to quell my revolutionary passion, only made those urges stronger, and louder.)

In spite of my insistence to the contrary, Mordechai concluded that the long journey had left me tired and grumpy, and took me back to his lodgings, a one-room garret that he shared with three other bachelors. The plan had been to squeeze in a bed for me. Only no one had thought to take measurements. Now they saw that no matter how ingeniously we rearranged the furniture, even if we put the table and washstand out on the stairs, no more than two legs of my bed would ever touch the ground at the same time.

After a night spent rocking back and forth like a shipwrecked sailor, I left to seek a place of my own. I found a storage cellar on Wolynska Street beneath the shop of an old friend who dealt in spices. My bed there consisted of a wonderfully aromatic mattress made of sacks that once had held dried mushrooms, black peppercorns, tea leaves and paprika. The shop's location had the added benefit of lying well within the bosom of the "Thieves Quarter" where the police, wisely, did not set foot more often than was absolutely necessary.

For some days, I rattled around the old neighborhoods, hoping to run into former comrades from my days with the *Bund*. In the two years I had been away, Warsaw had become a modern city, in which many shops and offices had electric lights and telephones, and motor-cars sped by like bullets, tossing up waves of mud behind them.

The only one of my comrades I ran into was Meyer, my former superior at the *Bund*, a knobby, hardheaded northerner with a lion's head of wiry,

55 Russian: The Russian secret police

white hair. He was not only pleased to see me but promptly offered me back my old job as a union organizer. As long as I understood that there was no money to pay me.

And where was everyone else?

Some of them, Meyer glumly reported, were doing time, either in local jails or in Siberia. Others were on the run from the police and would not be eager to associate with someone who had just left the Czar's service. Still others were dead, not always from natural causes. And, human nature being what it was, a few had let themselves be acquired by wives, and promptly lost all interest in changing the world.

Mordechai was horrified to learn of my new "job." According to him, the *Bund* was no longer a tightly knit labor union run by worldly people. Its current leadership was a pack of rattle-headed theorists, inept disciples of Kropotkin and Bakunin and, if I would forgive his mentioning it, young women of impure morals. Furthermore, my brother made the insulting suggestion that they probably wanted me only because I had a working revolver.

I asked Meyer about this. Warsaw being a gossipy city, he knew about the little souvenir I had brought home from the war. But he assured me that, at the moment, they had absolutely no one they wanted me to shoot. Still, as long as I was on friendly terms with firearms and our enemies were not ashamed to resort to violence, he suggested that I keep my Browning close at hand.

Thus equipped, I was sent on various, strange errands. To keep them properly cloaked in secrecy, each mission was organized in a manner so melodramatic that any policeman with half a brain should have collared the lot of us within the first half hour.

One morning, I was summoned to the Bristol Hotel, a place ordinarily out of my class. I saw from a distance that its lobby was densely populated with Czarist agents.

My assignment was to make contact with someone holding one end of a broken match; I was to carry the other half. After confirming that our pieces fit together, the man would say to me in Polish, "Excuse me, sir, can you give me a light?" To which I would reply, "What brand of cigarettes, sir, do you smoke?"

149

It did no good to point out that such a dialogue would be hard to mistake for a casual exchange between two normal human beings. To make things worse, I was given a piece of the wrong match, meaning that each of us would arrive carrying half a match without a head. My handler agreed there may have been a slipup, but it was too late now to alter the arrangements.

Picture, if you will, two shabbily dressed strangers circulating in the crowded lobby of this elegant hotel, stooping over from time to time to gaze at what each other person may be holding between his fingers. After sweating through I don't know how many minutes of this little minuet, my contact and I finally noticed each other's peculiar behavior and sheepishly flaunted our headless matches. We then recited our stilted passphrases and managed to walk out together, all without arousing the suspicions of our excellent police force.

In the street, my fellow plotter, a jittery, young man with bad skin, kept looking over his shoulder. Half a block away, when he finally felt it was safe to talk, he asked, "Are you prepared to go on a mission?"

"What kind of mission?"

He yanked me into a doorway. "I can't tell you."

"Then I'm not going."

"All right," he said grudgingly. "Delivering supplies."

"Supplies of what?"

Scowling with annoyance, he mumbled, "Ammunition." His tone let me know I had no business asking such an idiotic question.

While the task sounded harmless enough for someone of my background, I knew of several comrades who had been arrested while transporting such goods and, with very little fuss, sentenced and shot.

But my contact allowed me no time for reflection, snapping, "Wait here," as he vanished across the street.

Trapped, I loitered in plain sight of the Bristol, straining to look invisible and braced, at any moment, for a heavy hand to fall on my shoulder.

Instead, I saw a tall young woman make her way daintily through traffic. Flustered, she headed in my direction and looked around. This, I assumed, was my same contact since one would have had to be blind not to have recognized her instantly as a man in a poorly fitted horsehair wig. Nor was he too cleanly shaven. I tried to lose myself among the passing pedestrians, hoping this person in a pavement-trailing skirt and high-heeled boots would not be able to follow me.

But the creature caught up with me. Smiling through smudged lips, he motioned coquettishly with his finger. Resigned, I allowed him to capture my elbow and summon a *drozhky*.[56] We climbed in, and he directed the driver to a certain number on Shliska Street. The driver cracked his whip, giving no sign of having noticed that his orders came from a woman with a rather hairy voice.

We pulled up at a shoemaker's cellar where my contact, with the nonchalance of a commercial traveler on an expense account, ordered the *drozhky* to wait, as if we had not been warned repeatedly that some cab drivers also served as police informants.

I staggered out of the *drozhky* hauling two valises so heavy that one of the handles promptly came off in my hand. My load crashed to the pavement.

At this, the shoemaker turned white, and then became hysterical. Hopping up and down, he cursed my clumsiness and consigned me to the seven depths of hell. I realized that I was not carrying mere bullets but a more nervous kind of merchandise, like dynamite or homemade bombs, the kind we cozily called 'dumplings,' some of which had been known to go off at inconvenient times.

Still in his wig and padded dress, my contact ordered our driver to take us to a windowless shack deep in the woods outside the city where, to my relief, a refreshingly businesslike couple accepted delivery of the supplies.

After weeks of playing at being a revolutionary, hauling high explosives all over Warsaw without drawing so much as an unfriendly look from the police, my luck ran out.

It happened one evening when, in all innocence, I crossed the Praga Bridge. A gang of uniformed thugs came running out of the fog shouting, blowing whistles, waving guns, and more or less making it plain they desired to attract my attention.

There was nowhere to run. And if I jumped into the water, they could put enough bullets into me to sink me like a stone. So I stopped and, in all

56 Russian: An open carriage

innocence, waited with raised hands, and inquired politely what the fuss was all about.

After searching me from top to bottom, the officer condescended to let me know that, a few minutes earlier, a policeman had been shot coming out of the Smocza Street station house.

And what did this have to do with me?

An obliging eyewitness had given them a description of the assassin that may or may not have fitted me exactly. Meaning, I suppose, that the perpetrator also had a head, two arms and two legs.

Not only was my conscience spotless, but my emptied pockets revealed that I was not even carrying a revolver. This, to my captor, was added proof that I was their man. Why else would I have been strolling on the bridge if not to dump my guilty weapon into the water?

With all possible tact, I pointed out that people were also known to use bridges as a means of crossing a river. For this, the policeman slapped my face and told me not to be insolent as he hauled me in to the police station.

I spent nine cold and miserable days in a cell at the Smocza Street station before a lawyer hired by the Party attained my release by showing the police a week-old newspaper noting that the actual killer had been caught almost immediately and, in fact, had already been executed. But as the culprit had been taken to a different police station, no one at Smocza felt obligated to know anything about it.

Back home in my cellar, I dropped onto my mattress like a stone. Almost at once, a fist hammered on the door. It was Krinsky, a messenger from the Party, who had come to express delight that I was free again and, by the way, to let me know I was due to take part in an "action" at five o'clock the next morning. Our target was a certain gang of pimps and strong-armed men with whom we occasionally had a "shoot-out." He thought I'd be happy to know that the leader of this mob was Left-handed Stepan, whom I had long suspected of being a police informant.

But, starved for nine days' sleep, I groaned, "Can't it wait a day or two?"

In a day or two, Krinsky pointed out, I might be back in jail as the police now knew my face. All I was being asked to do, with the help of an assistant, was lay siege to the police station on Smocza, the very one whose cells were still raw in my memory. Anticipating that it might occur to the police to telephone for help, we were to cut the wires.

Eyes sticky with broken sleep, I showed up at our post with my assistant. We saw at once that the phone lines were out of our reach. Neither of us had been told to bring a ladder.

While we tried to work out who should stand on whose shoulders, an unpleasant voice at my back ordered us to put up our hands. Without a moment's hesitation, we both ran.

In the awakening street, not a soul turned his head, this being a neighborhood clearly accustomed to seeing men running from the police.

My partner, out of breath, ducked into an apartment house, but I felt confident I could outrun my pursuer. What I didn't count on was his readiness to fire his rifle on a street crowded with innocent people.

Even before I heard the shot, I felt a stinging slap against my leg. I managed to keep running, but my heart hammered with fear.

I dodged into a courtyard, vaulted over a fence, and stumbled through an unlocked door and down a steep flight of steps that led to a wine cellar. Feverish with exhaustion and drugged by the wine's sweet aroma, I huddled behind a stack of barrels, and gratefully lost consciousness.

When the shooting stopped, the streets were once again flooded with pedestrians. My bones felt brittle as eggshells, but I knew it would not be smart to remain in the cellar. Too many of my comrades had been arrested in their sleep, taken to The Citadel's[57] dreaded "Tenth Pavilion,"[58] and were never heard from again.

I waited until after dark to emerge from hiding, and tried to blend in with those citizens who took leisurely strolls after dinner. But it was difficult not to draw attention to myself when I was limping, and an occasional tributary of blood slid down my leg and into my shoe. I only hoped I wasn't leaving a bloody trail to my apartment.

57 Originally built as a fortress, The Citadel later became an infamous prison

58 The "Tenth Pavilion" was where political prisoners and revolutionaries were held prior to execution

Although I tried to look unobtrusive, I suddenly felt an angry hand grab my arm. Before I could reach for my revolver, I found Meyer's soured features scowling at me. Outraged to find me walking the streets wearing my own face, he shoved me into the nearest barbershop and ordered the pitiless removal of my lovingly grown mustache.

Next he hauled me up three unlit flights of stairs to an apartment where another comrade instructed me to take off my clothes and put on a dress, a blond wig smelling of camphor, and a pair of ladies' shoes that could only have fit a ballerina. To make me feel more comfortable about such idiocy, he also smeared some womanly paint on my face.

Luckily, the apartment had no mirror or I would have put a quick end to this clown show before they could tell me the news: My name was on a new list of people the *Okhranka* considered dangerous enough to arrest on sight. Furthermore, if the source was to be believed, I had, in fact, already been condemned to death.

To me, this could only mean that I'd been "whistled out." I demanded to know by whom, though I suspected that I knew. My comrades pleaded ignorance. I kept pressing until they admitted that they didn't want to tell me. And why not? Because they knew I would go and "Have a word with him." And why shouldn't I? As I was sternly reminded, we were a workers' party with ideals and standards, not a pack of hooligans like some of our more radical competitors.

It didn't take a Sherlock Holmes to figure out that the informant was none other than Left-handed Stepan. Bowing to Party discipline, I applied for permission to kill him. Permission denied. Incensed, I threatened to behave like an "anarchist" – a label they loathed – and do the job without their approval.

This moved them sufficiently to acknowledge that the Party had already passed sentence on Stepan, but owing to its lofty ideals, it felt obliged to follow a certain "protocol." To keep things "businesslike," two professional assassins had been brought in from Odessa to do the job. In consolation for not being allowed to shoot the man who'd gotten me arrested, I was allowed to go along, but only as a lookout.

As I watched one of the assassins execute his assignment, I could only surmise that the laws of physics must have been different in Odessa than they were in Warsaw, because our imported experts seemed surprised to discover that revolver shots made noise, and noise tended to attract attention. As we scattered in different directions, one of the shooters, blinded by panic, headed straight into the arms of the police.

Before I could shout a warning, someone clubbed me from behind.

18

THE INTERROGATION

opened my eyes to an abyss of darkness. My head felt like a balloon about to burst. Pressing in on all four sides of me were the icy walls of a windowless cell. If the objective was to make a strong impression, it succeeded. That night I didn't close an eye.

In the morning, with wrists and ankles chained, I was led into a small room with a barred window. It was furnished with little more than two chairs and a cigarette-scarred table. After being kept waiting long enough to imagine the worst, a tall, bitter-faced man in civilian clothes joined me.

He did not trouble to introduce himself, but vanity prompted me to assume it was the dreaded Konstantinov, himself, the local head of the *Okhranka* who, thus far, had survived three well-deserved attempts on his life.

My inquisitor offered me a cigarette. I didn't care for his brand but, given the circumstances, thought it best not to be choosy. He lit a match for me and sat back with the comfortable air of a man who had all the time in world. Then, as though it had just occurred to him, he inquired whether I would like to go home.

I confessed that I had no objection.

"And where is that?"

"Where is what?"

"Where you live?"

"Vishogrod."

"I mean in Warsaw?"

"I just arrived."

He chilled me with his skull's-head grin. "Very well. You may go."

I offered my wrists to him to unshackle.

"As soon as you answer a few questions." I settled back with a look of eager stupidity.

"To begin with, why are you here?"

"Don't you know?"

He shifted to a more direct approach. "Who sent you?"

"Where?"

"To kill."

"Kill? I heard shooting, and I ran the other way."

"We caught the other two men, you know. Tell me their names, so I'll know you're telling the truth."

"I saw two men running. Who knows who they were?"

He leaned in toward me, spraying saliva onto my face. "Who is the leader of your Party?"

"What 'Party?'"

So it went for several days. Konstantinov was furious, but in truth he did not physically mistreat me. Could it be that those attempts on his life had shaken his confidence? Or was he unsure whether I was the man they wanted?

Without warning, on the tenth day of my imprisonment, I was brought before a three-man military court. My judges were two retired colonels and a mummified general whose nose could have been mistaken for a raw carrot.

To my surprise, there was also a lawyer to represent me, a well-spoken civilian who told the court that he was hired by my parents. I distrusted him immediately; my family had no idea where I was. Later, the lawyer whispered to me that the Party had sent him.

This, too, may have been a lie, a trap. Especially when, during the few minutes they allowed us for consultation, my advocate comforted me with the forecast that I was almost certain to be sentenced to death. Therefore, the only thing worth doing was pleading, in view of my military record and my obvious youthful ignorance, to be let off with ten years of hard labor.

I can't say I was charmed by his readiness to bury me alive, although in time I would learn that getting a "tenner" was practically the equivalent of being found "not guilty." But from the moment the trial got under way, I could see that my lawyer had been, if anything, overoptimistic.

My three judges put on their spectacles to study the charges. Wasting no time on what I might have had to say for myself, they retired to consider their verdict.

After a leisurely five minutes, they returned and pronounced sentence. The blood raced in my ears, but I had no trouble hearing the words, "firing squad."

Rather than dawdle about it for months or years as the courts did in Columbus' Country, the appeal my lawyer had wisely prepared in advance was already scheduled to be heard the following day.

Late the next morning, I was marched back into the courtroom, this time attached to three other prisoners who were also appealing their death sentences. Not a good sign.

One look at the bench and my heart sank. The judges who would rule on my appeal were the same three antiques who, only yesterday, had sentenced me to death. It would have surprised me very much if, overnight, each of them had had a miraculous change of heart.

What's more, there was no sign of my lawyer. Instead, I was furnished with a military advocate, a pudgy-handed captain whose middle bulged like a pregnant barmaid. Barely glancing in my direction, he explained to the judges that he had not had time to study my file and asked for a recess for a quick consultation with me.

He took me to the adjacent room where he favored me with a well-fed smile, and said, "To defend you against these terrible accusations, I must have the full truth, you understand?"

Since I had no idea who this man was or which side he was working for, I was not quite ready to take him at his word.

"How many men have you killed?"

I did not find this a very encouraging question. Still, I answered as best I could. "Probably dozens." His eyes brightened. "In combat," I added, "it's difficult to keep an accurate count."

"Fool, I meant in Warsaw. On orders from the Party."

"What 'Party?'"

He raised his voice. "Do you or don't you want me to defend you?"

"Against what?"

"Don't you know you've been sentenced to death?"

"What has that to do with you?"

"I'm your lawyer. I want the truth. All of it."

"I told the truth. Yesterday. And look at where it got me."

"You're a damned Jew-faced liar!"

This, I confess, provoked me. "I want nothing to do with you. If they won't let me have a proper lawyer, I'll defend myself."

My defender sucked in his breath and apologized for having, perhaps, expressed himself a little too heartily. What he would not do was admit that his only job was to extract a confession from me so that the judges could put away my comrades, too.

Sulking, he delivered me back into the courtroom where things had begun without us. Of the prisoners to whom I had been chained, two had already had their death sentences confirmed and were weeping. My turn was next.

The clerk read the charges against me once more. This time I listened more attentively to his monotonic recital of killings, robberies and such, each listed according to date and location.

It took me some moments to realize that nearly all of these charges dealt with crimes committed long before I arrived in Warsaw.

I tried to interrupt and point this out, but the clerk told me to be silent. It was my lawyer's job to speak for me. I looked at my defender, who was goggling at a fly that had settled on his briefcase.

I called out to the court, "I don't accept the man you have assigned to me. I want a civilian lawyer."

"This is a military court. Here you can only be defended by an officer."

"What happened to the lawyer I had yesterday?"

"That was a mistake. The man had no right to defend you. He will be severely punished for misrepresenting himself."

While my doomed fellow prisoners looked greatly impressed by the depth of my depravity, my alleged lawyer went through the motions of pleading with the court to show some leniency to a man who had, in battle, repeatedly proven his love for, and loyalty to, the Czar.

True, he admitted in the same breath, I might have murdered some people in Warsaw, although perhaps not as many as the honorable Court had been led to believe. But surely the real criminals were the Party leaders who distorted my young mind and sent me out to commit these deeds without my fully understanding their seriousness.

He driveled on like this for I don't know how long while the judges listened with all the patience of old men whose bladders were about to burst. The moment he was done, they scurried out to confer.

A few eternal minutes later, about as long as it would have taken each one to have had his turn at the urinal, they were back. The general, himself, read the verdict. It confirmed yesterday's sentence – death by firing squad – to be carried out on the twenty-fifth of May, 1907, a date that has somehow stuck in my memory.

Much as I hated to give them the satisfaction, I staggered for a moment and nearly lost consciousness.

19

~~THREE~~ TWO DAYS TILL "THE CITADEL"

Morning. Chained to 22 other bloodless ghosts, I was marched into a hall of vaulted brick. Seated on freshly disinfected benches, we learned we were about to have publicly read to us the one letter each prisoner was entitled to receive each month. To my total bewilderment, there was one for me.

"Dear Child," it began. "Since your arrest, none of us closed an eye. First, because we know you are innocent. And secondly, because Aunt Reva, after a difficult labor, gave birth to a boy. Luckily, we were able to bring in two of the greatest specialists, and we feel confident that, with their help, she will soon be able to walk around again."

Not one word of this made sense. I was, by no means, indifferent to the news of "Aunt Reva's" troubled health; it was just that my only relative with that name was at least eighty years old, which most people would have considered well past childbearing age.

Therefore, I assumed that the letter was the Party's way of letting me know I had not been forgotten. It might even mean that the Party had hired two "specialists" to defend me. But what could even the greatest lawyers do for me now?

My correspondent had also sent me a book of Psalms in Russian, presumably so I could pray for "Aunt Reva's" recovery.

I was not greatly comforted to find that my comrades, so devoutly un-religious on principle, were suddenly concerned with my spiritual welfare. To be honest, I would have much preferred something a little more secular, like a warm blanket or a bar of chocolate, to ease the few days I had left.

Back in the blindness of my own four walls, my fingertips leafed irritably through the book and I found that the Party had not deserted its principles, after all. One of the endpapers felt poorly glued. Carefully peeling it back, I found five rubles, along with a note I barely had time to read in the dribble of light reflected off my morning bowl of black chicory.

It read, "COMRADE, DON'T DESPAIR. YOU ARE SAVED."

I would have liked nothing better than to believe this excellent news. But their forecast seemed to me less a prediction than a flight of fantasy.

"Amateurs!" I raged.

Or perhaps I should have been grateful that the Party, at least, knew where my family could claim my body.

But being suddenly five rubles better off than I had been the day before, I decided that all was not yet lost.

One of my guards was a Slovak named Anton. Unlike the other dull brutes who looked after me, he, at least, had the decency not to gloat. Which, under the circumstances, was enough for me to trust him with my life.

To break the ice, I tipped him a ruble, the equivalent of half a week's pay. He promptly wanted to know what he could do for me, either now or after my execution.

Still somewhat leery, I asked him to find out how much longer I would be in that prison. The next morning I got my answer. I was to be transferred to The Citadel in three days. I knew what that meant.

I handed over another ruble and asked Anton to get me a pencil and a piece of paper. This made him uneasy. He was smart enough to know that writing implements were dangerous. I hastened to explain how, in the modern world, when men of substance were faced with death, they wrote something called a "testament." This was to avoid quarrels over dividing their property among the next of kin.

Impressed by such foresight, Anton returned the next morning with a torn sheet of schoolboy paper and a broken piece of a pencil.

In total darkness, I drafted my message to Mordechai: "Brother, sell everything and get me the best criminal lawyer in Warsaw, or in three days I'll be dead!"

To add a bit of urgency, I crossed out "three" and made it "two." I folded my note, and wrote Mordechai's address on the outside.

The question then became who would deliver such an incendiary document? Did I have the right to endanger Anton? For that matter, what if he took it to the commandant, instead? There was little more that could be done to me, but what about my brother?

I agonized until I heard the stony echo of Anton's limp. His metal teeth glinted at my offer of yet another ruble. But when I asked him to deliver the note, he vigorously shook his head, and offered to return the last ruble I had paid him. The previous year, a comrade of his was caught trying to smuggle out a letter. He was still in jail.

The hard fact was that the only thing that might save my life was a letter I couldn't get delivered.

It pained Anton to see my frustration. He tried to comfort me with the reminder that my earthly sufferings would soon be over. In fact, rather than two days from now, I was being transferred to The Citadel tomorrow. One day less to live.

The following morning, before they chained my wrists, I slipped the letter into my sleeve.

We stumbled out into the blinding sparkle of a warm, Warsaw day. There was velvet sunshine, the thick perfume of lilacs, the merry clang of electric trams, and the curious glances of clean-faced pedestrians strolling by without a care in the world, their minds untroubled by such follies as Polish independence or the steely rattle of 28 doomed prisoners.

Some pedestrians peeked at us, furtively sympathetic, while others stared with cud-chewing indifference. A few actually shrank back as though we carried a contagious disease. Which, I suppose, we did.

I hadn't had much time to decide where to drop my letter. The muddy road under my feet seemed paved with bits of dirty paper. How would mine stand out? It would take a miracle for anyone to notice it, pick it up and read it, let alone deliver this particular scrap of paper with my futile message on it.

En route to The Citadel, we clanked past the railroad station from which a trainload of provincials poured out, stunned, as usual, by the noise and vitality of the great city. Among them, only one, a dark-eyed girl, barely more than a child, seemed to look at us with open pity.

My theatrical cough caught her attention. Pleading mutely for her not to look away, I fluttered my iron-bound hands like a pigeon's wings and let my folded note drift to the pavement. Our column clattered on, and I dared not look back, dreading to see the heavy boot of the man behind me grinding it into the mud.

The iron gates of The Citadel fell shut behind us. Their crash vibrated in my bones, making me think of the handful of earth dropped onto the lid of a coffin. Not that any us would be buried in such luxury as a box.

We were counted off twice, and then taken straight to the Tenth Pavilion. Crossing the yard, we got a good look at the Execution Wall, which was peppered with bullet holes and streaked with eloquent dark smears.

The ceiling of my new cell glistened with black sweat. It seemed to bear the crushing weight of the Vistula's waters only a few meters above me. My heart raced in its cage. I suppose reality had sunk in, at last. I had entered the last room I would occupy in this world.

A volley of muffled shots blasted through my sleep. I sat up, startled. My blood was still pounding with the residue of an ugly dream. Gratefully, I had forgotten what it was.

A slot opened in my door. I accepted a tin plate with a chunk of bread, and a cup of something hot. I gulped down my breakfast standing up. Outside, the whip-crack of rifle fire came to a halt. Another day of 'life.'

A sluggish afternoon, followed by a restless night and another dawn. Then footsteps echoed in the corridor. The door opened on only one guard, not the two I assumed custom, or practicality, called for to lead, or drag, a man to his encounter with the wall.

With a grin at my bloodless look of fear, the guard motioned me out. Barely breathing, I was made to precede him through a labyrinth of stone passages that ended in a fine staircase of polished wood.

Once upstairs, my escort deposited me in an office with an electric light blazing into my eyes. Three men in dark suits looked at me as though puzzled by what right I was squandering their costly time. The parchment face of the one behind the desk must have been that of the commandant of The Citadel. But who were the other two?

Cheeks puckered with disgust, the commandant muttered, "These gentlemen are lawyers. They claim to represent you. This is totally irregular."

I had been introduced before to lawyers who supposedly represented me. I wondered how these two would try to convince me to confess – perhaps by promising that my guards would aim for my heart so as to spare me an agonizingly slow death?

I felt faint as the lawyers, still unsmiling, introduced themselves. I was too nervous to catch the name of the first one, a Russian in a frock coat and celluloid collar. But I recognized the name of the second: Noah Prilutzky. A stooped man with glowing eyes and disheveled hair, he was a famous criminal lawyer. I didn't understand how I had earned this cruel moment of renewed hope.

Prilutzky's tobacco-yellowed fingers ruffled through a stack of files thick enough to tell me that I was only one of many hopeless customers that unkind fate had laid at his door.

Although not in the best position to be choosy, I asked, "Who hired you?"

"You have no right to ask questions," the commandant said.

But Prilutsky had already begun to answer in Yiddish. By the time his associate snapped at him to speak Russian, I had learned that he was hired by my sister, Malkah, who had "somehow" gotten word of my imprisonment.

Switching to Russian, Prilutsky introduced his gloomy associate as a brilliant trial lawyer hired by certain "friends" of mine.

Did this mean I was to receive a civilian trial? Unfortunately not.

They looked at the commandant in quest of a little privacy. He sulked, but removed his cadaverous self to an adjoining room, leaving the door half open.

I began, with great enthusiasm, to discuss elements of my defense: my alibi, my military record and, above all, the laughable inaccuracy of the charges.

The Russian lawyer cut off my babbling with an impatient gesture. That morning, Prilutzky explained, while I had been idling in my cell, waiting to be taken out and shot, my "appeal" had been settled.

"And what was the outcome?" I asked, and why I hadn't been invited, being what you might call 'an interested party?'

But I had already taken up too much of my defenders' time. They were halfway to the door before replying, "Of what?"

"The appeal!"

The Russian lawyer sighed at the foolishness of my question. "Ten years. Hard labor. Followed by permanent exile in Siberia." He appeared well-satisfied with himself. As I suppose I should have been, too.

That afternoon, a guard escorted me to a smithy. Not being a horse, I couldn't imagine what business I had with a blacksmith. But the stocky, silent Pole with coal black arms handed me two rags of heavy canvas to put around my shins. Proud and unhurried, he welded leg irons around each of my ankles. The canvas fabric was mine only for the few minutes it took to hammer and melt the iron into a closed ring, and for the red-hot metal to cool a little. The shackles were then attached to a thirty-pound chain.

The word "gangrene" was not in my guard's vocabulary. Perhaps having found me a good listener, he favored me with a detailed account of how those leg irons caused some prisoners' legs to breed a kind of ulceration that inflated the foot until it had to be sawn off. People like that, he said, counted themselves lucky. If they survived the operation, they got to work in offices and kitchens, making it quite possible that they would live out their ten-year terms.

I asked a guard how long I would be obliged to wear these things. He laughed. "Brother, you will wear them all your life, all the way to Siberia, at least. It saves from having so many guards."

"Even on the train?"

"Train?" He almost choked on his laughter. "You think you're going on vacation? You'll be walking most of the way. Take care no one steals your boots. They have to last you at least a year."

I looked at my tattered footgear and knew that I would be barefooted in two weeks, at most.

20

FAREWELL TO WARSAW

Early the following morning, raindrops thick as pebbles beat on our skulls as our column straggled along. On the damp pavement of the sleeping city, the echo of iron links on cobblestones buried all other human sounds.

Here and there, a window brightened, flew open and someone gaped down at us. But the few citizens who troubled to witness our shambling parade from the comfort of their nightclothes, soon locked us out of their sleep, again, with a little slam. Otherwise, not a soul seemed to know of our departure. By the time word got out, we would be long gone.

Our column reached the dock at around four o'clock in the morning. Shaking off the rain like dogs coming out of the river, we stood to be counted, again.

But it seems that news of our departure had spread, after all. *Drozhkys* pulled up, their passengers waving and shouting as they descended into the pounding rain and, with cries of grief, splashed as close to us as our guards' leveled bayonets would let them.

I twisted my neck, hoping for a glimpse of at least one familiar face. Where was *my* family, where were *my* comrades? How could anything have stopped Mordechai from being here, from saying goodbye to me, perhaps forever?

All around me, prisoners talked and gestured excitedly with relatives or friends. Some even managed a quick embrace while accepting a package slipped under their shirts. I, alone, had been forgotten.

Crushed and bitter, I was about to turn away when I saw my brother loping toward me through sheets of rain. More irritating yet, all he had brought for me was a roast chicken. Why not a sausage that might have lasted me for a week? Had he not been a soldier like me? And why had he not been able to guess how badly I would need a blanket, a coat, and a pair of strong boots?

I stood in the rain, tearing off slippery handfuls of chicken and stuffing them into my mouth while shouting at my poor brother for having over-slept. Only when my jaws were briefly silenced by chewing did he tell me that a messenger from the Party had awakened him in the night with the news of my departure. At which point, he ran to a neighbor to phone for a cab, and borrowed a roast chicken. He had been about to leave when he heard footsteps laboring up the stairs.

Our mother!

Tormented with anxiety after so many months without mail from me, and little reassured by the evasive tone of Mordechai's letters, she had taken the train to Warsaw to find out for herself what had become of me. Now, seeing Mordechai dressed to go out in the rain, she naturally demanded, "Where are you going this time of night?"

What could he do: tell her the truth? Instead, he explained that I had not been able to write home because, like many other young idealists, I was in trouble with the police. And though innocent of any crime, I had thought it prudent to escape to a small town near the German border where I was hiding at the home of an old comrade from the Army.

And what, my mother asked, was Mordechai doing fully dressed at three o'clock in the morning?

Having by now regained his wits, he explained that he was on his way to Łódź for the funeral of a fellow baker who left behind a wife and six children.

My mother was so moved that she insisted on accompanying him to the funeral. Mordechai had been able to dissuade her only by explaining that the cab he ordered had space left for just one more passenger. If he tried, now, to get another, he would miss both the train and the funeral.

The Cossacks began parting us roughly from our weeping visitors as the barge put out its gangplank. In the few moments we had left, I asked Mordechai if he had received my note.

He nodded in annoyance. "I couldn't make out half the words. Do me a favor, the next time you write—"

"Fool," I shouted at him. "I wrote it in the dark. But how did you get it? Did someone pick it up and bring it to you?"

"Yes, of course. Wouldn't you?"

Not for the first time, I suspected that my brother lacked curiosity. "A girl?" I asked.

"What girl?"

"The one who brought the letter. Was it a—?"

"A girl, a boy, what's the difference? You're alive, aren't you?"

"Was it a girl?" I shouted.

"A girl, I think. So?"

"A pretty girl? Dark hair?"

"And if she were ugly, you wouldn't have let her save your life?"

"A young girl? About sixteen?"

"You think I asked for her birth certificate?"

"Did you get her name?"

"A strange girl knocks on the door. With a note, an important message. Do I care about her name?"

Shabby and soaked, he returned to his waiting cab, mumbling, "He has to know the name?"

Leaving me with greasy cheeks and all the benefits of my superior imagination.

21

THE "KING OF THIEVES"

Still short of sunrise, under a cloud of fog as thick as snow, our barge inched away from the dock. With a consumptive cough, the engine pushed us upriver, or possibly downriver – there was no way to tell, either by the flow of the water's oily skin or by the shoreline that remained invisible.

I asked a crewman where we were being taken. His shrug could have meant either that he didn't know or didn't feel it was worth his effort to tell me.

A more talkative crew member let on that, in the early days of steam, our particular barge had carried coal for the Imperial Navy. Having outlived its seaworthiness, it was renamed, "Little Russia," and set to earning its upkeep for a few more voyages. Although it was no longer trusted to carry coal, it was still healthy enough to haul lower-value cargo, such as prisoners, on the first installment of their trek to Siberia.

That is, he whispered with a foolish grin, until the barge crumbled under our feet and was sucked down into the icy black waters. Although the crew treaded the same rotted decks as us, they seemed unaware or unconcerned that they were doomed to go under with the rest of us. Or perhaps they were more optimistic about their chances for survival as they weren't weighted down by thirty pounds of chain.

In the evening, as I elbowed my way toward the railing, hoping to bask in a last glimpse of the expiring sun, I found myself beside a man who, even in a metropolis like Warsaw, would have stood out in any crowd. Tall, broad shouldered, and with penetrating eyes that appeared to look down from a great height, he had managed, even in that welter of filthy and ragged convicts, to remain dressed and groomed like someone about to preside over a court of law or lecture at a University.

In the soiled half-light, his face wore an amused kind of serenity, the look of someone who might have joined our transport purely as a lark, or as a scholarly observer of our misery, collecting anecdotes with which to regale his colleagues tomorrow over cigars and wine. He struck me as a man who could, any time he chose, order our barge to halt and put out its gangplank so he could board a waiting *troika*[59] that, piled high with fur blankets, would whisk him back to his mansion in Petersburg, or even Vienna.

I spent hours of my worthless time trying to guess what a person of such quality was doing among riff-raff like us. He looked far too shrewd and self-assured to be a revolutionary. And if he was, indeed, a criminal, where in all the Russias had there been a policeman smart enough to capture him?

While the rest of us fell upon the hot, slime-coated cauldrons of cabbage soup or kasha with our tin bowls and grimy bare hands, I never saw him shove or be shoved, curse or be cursed. Yet by some effortless authority, he never failed to come away with a full bowl while the food was still hot, and without a sleek, red hair out of place. Truly a man born for leadership.

I spent several days covertly studying him like some rare specimen. In time, I felt his steady gaze pin me, too. I begin to think of him as the Prophet Elijah, or one of the legendary "Thirty-Six"[60] mystical beings known to appear incognito, from time to time, to comfort or rescue some deserving soul.

At other times, fascinated by the copper gleam of his hair and beard, I saw him as a Satanic emissary who walked the earth in one seductive

59 Russian: Carriage or sled drawn by three horses

60 According to the *gemara* (rabbinical commentaries on the Talmud), in every generation there are 36 individuals who greet the Divine's presence daily. Later literature suggests that they sustain the world.

guise or another, the better to plot the downfall of some unsuspecting innocent. Such as myself.

I finally made his acquaintance under unusual circumstances. Among us was a fiery young revolutionary I had known in Warsaw, a Russian named Volodya whose iron fists he never hesitated to use in a good cause.

One day, one of the less appetizing of our legitimate criminals suggested that Volodya, "like all revolutionaries," was "no better than a damned Jew." And Volodya, too simple-hearted to recognize the accusation as a compliment, unleashed his fist on the ruffian with such force that the sound was heard at the opposite end of the deck.

I was surprised to see the other criminals take Volodya's little burst of temper with apparent good grace. But the following morning, no matter where I looked, there was no sign of my revolutionary comrade. After a while, someone advised me to stop searching because, during the night, Volodya had been quietly surrounded by half a dozen shadowy men, one of whom inserted a knife between his ribs while another shoved a rag into his mouth. His body had been gently heaved over the side. If a guard or a member of the ship's crew heard the muffled splash, none had been foolhardy enough to wake the captain and suggest that he stop the boat to investigate.

With a little shiver of prudence, I decided that, while aboard this floating prison, I would try to avoid fights, at least until I was better acquainted with my fellow travelers and knew who was armed and who, if anyone, would be prepared to back me in a brawl to the death.

That evening, as I dozed under the shabby moonlight, the subject of my speculations materialized. He bent over so close to me that, after blinking the sleep out of my eyes, I could almost count each silken hair in his fine, cavalry mustache and lovingly trimmed beard. Meanwhile, his spotless vest seemed to have retained the odors of pungent Cologne water and tropical cigars. I recalled thinking that this was surely no prisoner, unless he was a criminal so wealthy that he could even buy an aura of respectability.

"Apparently, it is not wise in a place like this, to make enemies," he said.

I was stunned by the banality of his remark, although he had only echoed my own thoughts. Could his words have masked layers of meaning that I was too drowsy to appreciate? His voice had a curiously nasal, unphilosophical quality to it. He sounded like a man so abruptly stripped of his worldly authority that he had not yet found a new tone in which to address his inferiors.

All I could think of replying was, "If you're a convict, I'm Count Pototzky."[61] He nodded modestly, and I could almost hear him blush.

"I suppose I am a little different than the others." With a touch of kindly authority in his voice, he asked, "Is there anything I can help you obtain? A loaf of bread, a warmer coat, a pair of boots?"

I considered his offer as solemnly as I did any other bad joke. "You own a department store below deck?"

He only smiled. "You mistrust me. In your place, so would I. But you may take my word for it; I am a criminal like you." That avowal was invested with all the humility that only a truly great man could have summoned. "In fact, I have far more cause than you to be here."

Making no effort to defend my well-earned right to be on a Siberia-bound transport, I waited for him to explain.

"A man gets lonely all by himself," he confided, as though pressed to justify taking up with a non-entity like me. I had already noticed that he was not on speaking terms with anyone on board.

"Even with money?"

"I don't buy friendship," he said scornfully. "As you should know, money is not an unmixed blessing among men who would slit your throat for the nails in your boots."

I controlled my urge to ask why, then, he allowed himself to look so conspicuous, or how he expected to buy me such a costly item as a warm overcoat without exposing at least some fraction of his wealth.

"I took you to be a man of some learning," he said, "as am I."

---

61 I have come across two possible Pototskys (also spelled Potocki) to whom this might refer: Count Valentin Potocki, an 18th century Polish nobleman, renounced Catholicism and converted to Judaism. For this heresy, he was burned at the stake in 1749, though it is unclear whether this story is factual or legend. Alternatively, this may be a reference to Count Felix Pototsky, who was one of the richest men of the 18th century. He is remembered for having built Sofiyivka *Park* in Uman, Ukraine, in honor of his wife, Sofia of Greece. (It is unclear whether Valentin and Felix were related). Although my grandfather might have been aware of both of these individuals' by reputation, the context of the comment above suggests that he was referring to Felix Pototsky.

This struck me as curious coming from the mouth of a criminal, however distinguished he was. Only the tilt of his homburg and the elaborate knot in his cravat detracted from his aspect of professorial wisdom.

But 'learning,' where I came from, had only one meaning: the study of serious subjects like the *Talmud* and its commentaries, not the cluttering of one's mind with the kind of paltry, secular information acquired at a university.

Before I could ask what he meant, or confess that my formal education of both kinds stopped before I turned thirteen, he demanded with a flare of contempt, "What have I in common with them? Murderers, drunkards, wife-beaters, wild-eyed revolutionaries?"

I was both amused and incensed at the way he lumped my social activism with the brutish crimes of violent gangsters and assassins.

Not without a little jab of sarcasm, I inquired, "Then what kind of misunderstanding brought you here, brother?"

I felt ashamed the moment the words left my mouth. It was not sort of question one asked of a new acquaintance, especially in a place like this. Not only on social grounds, but with our poor country liberally infested with Czarist spies, how could I be certain that he was not one of them?

My new friend, however, was not offended. "A bit of bad luck," he said, as offhandedly as an English lord witnessing his yacht go down in a storm. "Some swine turned me in."

At this, he smiled and granted me the knowledge of his name. (Out of respect for any descendants he may have, let us call him 'Pyavka.') I recognized it, at once, from all the months I spent submerged in Warsaw's underworld, as that of the man respectfully known in certain sections of that great city as "The King of Thieves."

Just one example of his renown: Some years back, the saintly Amshinover[62] Rebbe had come on one of his rare visits to Warsaw. During the few steps he took between the railroad station and a waiting *drozhky*, some insolent thief stole his fur-lined coat right off his back. The crime had shocked even a city as hardened to villainy as Warsaw. What's more, it had been

---

62 Pertaining to the Hasidic dynasty originating in Mszczonów, Poland; Amshinover takes its name from the Yiddish name for the town of Mszczonów

perpetrated in bitterest mid-winter so that the Rebbe's hosts were justly concerned not only for his health but his very life.

At the synagogue the following morning, the Rebbe preached so powerfully that the very walls were said to have glistened with tears. But as it was *Shabbos*, the rabbi had forbidden the board to discuss, or even think about, worldly matters until after sundown. The instant *Shabbos* ended, the board went, as a body, to call upon "The King of Thieves" to plead with him to intercede in a crime that had, after all, taken place in his jurisdiction.

Since criminals were assumed to love money at least as much as did bureaucrats and policemen, the delegation had been authorized to offer a 100-ruble reward for the return of the coat, no questions asked.

Unfortunately, the board happened to intrude upon the King's palatial home at the very hour he was giving a dinner party for some of his distinguished friends. Worse yet, these included several high Polish officials and even – the Devil take them – a couple of Russian officers in glittering dress uniform, none of whom a Warsaw Jew would lightly disturb at his pleasures.

But the moment the board's spokesman stuttered out the reason for the intrusion, Pyavka excused himself from his astonished guests, without whose tolerance he could not have reigned for even an hour. He led the intruders into his paneled study, carefully closed the door, passed around a box of cigars and sat down to listen to every known detail of the outrage. He then instructed the delegation to go back and tell the Rebbe not to worry. Not only would he, Pyavka, exert his best efforts to recover the stolen coat, but he also all but guaranteed its return before the rabbi needed to leave the following dawn.

The King was as good as his word. As for the 100-ruble reward, he ordered that it be given to a charity of the Rebbe's choice.

No doubt, you will have suspected that the Rebbe's warm overcoat had been hanging in Pyavka's cupboard, all along. The thought had occurred to me, as well. Nevertheless, in my present circumstances, the very idea of meeting this living legend left me as awed as a modern American boy who'd been granted an audience with Al Capone.

"And you," Pyavka demanded with a lordly wink. "What sort of thievery did they get you for?"

It surprised me that he had not instantly realized that I was not a member of his odious profession. I also didn't take well to his patronizing tone. But he awaited my answer with such genuine benevolence that I hadn't the heart to disappoint him. Even less did I want to endanger our still-green friendship by confessing that I was there precisely for certain types of activities that would, if successful, put an end to parasites like Pyavka and his high-born Russian protectors.

So I made up a story about how I had recently met a beautiful girl from a fine family, and under her tender influence had forsworn my thievish ways. But, alas, my past had caught up with me. An informer who had seen me in a coffee house with my fiancée summoned a policeman. As I carried a revolver, I could have saved myself by putting a bullet through the arresting officer's heart. But I simply could not commit such a cold-blooded act before the eyes of this very pure and noble creature. Thus, I ended up clapped in irons while she looked on, her face streaming with maidenly pity. And now who knew if I would ever see her again?

I was so moved by my own recital, not only did I have tears in my eyes, but if you had handed me pencil I could have drawn a perfect likeness of the girl.

Pyavka, for his part, was so affected that he encircled my shoulders with his arm and declared, "Soon you will be reunited with her. You have my word. Why do I say this? Because at the first opportunity I intend to escape."

I didn't have time to react to his ludicrous statement because he continued directly: "Before taking you into my confidence, I spent several days observing you. I wanted to be certain you were one of us and not some fool of a political firebrand. But I judged by your eyes that you were far too intelligent to be anything but a thief."

I acknowledged the compliment and awaited further revelations. Not that I believed, for a moment, he had the slightest chance of escaping. Granted, Russian guards were not famous for their hatred of money. But rather than take a mere portion of Pyavka's wealth and let him run away, why not simply kill him and take it all?

"And I have decided to take you with me." Pyavka looked deeply into my eyes, and I exerted myself to make a proper show of gratitude for his preposterous offer. I wanted to hear more, if only to keep alive some spark of hope in my own heart. It also pleased me to be able, as the greater realist, to feel superior to him in something.

But as though he had already said too much, Pyavka volunteered nothing further. Instead, he solemnly began to reminisce about the tangled motives that compelled him, *him*, the brilliant son of a fine Jewish family, to take up his perilous and unconventional trade.

As I might have known, he viewed himself as anything but a common thief. What he saw in the glittering mirror of his self-esteem was a social reformer, a zealot who daily risked his freedom and reputation, indeed his very life, in order to redistribute other men's ill-gotten wealth. "I am what the English call a 'Robin Hood.'"

Moreover, he had convinced himself that it was he, and not the *Bundists* or Socialists or other such hollow-headed rabble, who was the true revolutionary, treading, until his cruel downfall, in the very footsteps of the great Hebrew prophets.

In the face of such impregnable delusion, there was little to do but keep silent.

I lost count of how long our vessel drifted helplessly in the embrace of a fogbank that enveloped us like a shroud. But one morning, a small, pale echo of the sun broke through. Its sparse light and shriveled dimensions might have led one to believe it was the moon or some impossibly distant star not visible from Warsaw. Then, just as suddenly, a gray sliver of land appeared before us.

My fellow prisoners broke into cheers. Escaping drowning in a sea of eternal darkness was grounds enough for celebration. But the weeks of doing nothing other than eat, sleep, fight, curse and rake their hair for hard-shelled lice had made them forget that this period of cozy idleness would soon come to an end. That we were still bound for Siberia, half a world away, not merely to die there but, on our way to the grave, to pay for our own upkeep with months or years of crushing labor.

That afternoon, our barge rubbed its flank against a creaking dock. We struggled to our feet, lumpy from disuse, no longer to enjoy the luxury of traveling by boat. Our destination, to which we would travel by foot, was a fortified camp, the first of many transit stations awaiting us in the months to come or, as the case may be, not awaiting us at all.

All at once, we were being shouted at, buffeted, counted and menaced by rows of guards who, with rifle butts and blank bayonets, did their best to pay us back for the discomfort they had been forced to endure for our sake.

Just as in *Vanya's* army, there was the usual hysteria and rage arising from the traditional Russian failure to plan ahead and anticipate that a barge would soon deliver hundreds of starved and savage prisoners, and maybe somebody should have given a moment's thought to how and where they were to be housed and fed.

Mad with exhaustion, we milled around on the drill field waiting to be noticed.

It wasn't until near dark that a passing officer stopped and demanded to know what the devil we were doing there. We leapt to our feet and eagerly confided that we had arrived that very day and had not yet been given a meal or a place to sleep.

Consulting a folded sheet of paper, the officer satisfied himself that we were not due until the following week and, therefore, he was not responsible for us.

We pointed to a row of sturdy-looking barracks at the far end of the field and wondered if we might sleep there tonight.

Foolish question. How could we not know those buildings were already occupied by a work brigade sent the previous year to enlarge the camp's capacity? Only, having not yet been supplied with lumber, nails, bricks or cement, not to mention tools, they were believed to be somewhat behind schedule.

As usual in such places, it was the hardened criminals who ran the show. To get your share of food it was necessary to be on good terms with them, a talent not all of us possessed in equal measure.

This, I thought, was an ideal place for someone like Pyavka to demonstrate his mastery over his fellow thieves. But mysteriously, from the moment of our debarkation, I had seen no trace of him. And at roll call the next morning, twelve prisoners were listed as missing. Despite Pyavka's not exactly shrinking appearance, I had no idea whether he was somewhere in the vast camp or had already found an officer he could bribe to send him back home. And without a word to me! So much for a thief's loyalty.

Given that there was no earthly place for him or anyone else to go, no one doubted that the fugitives would be back before dark. But with good Russian logic, we who had made no effort to escape were punished with a four-week loss of "privileges."

By afternoon, three of the missing were properly accounted for, having died during the night. I volunteered to help bury the corpses, one of whom had a fairly decent pair of felt-lined boots, and seemed not to mind my making a trade.

We remained in this camp for several weeks, watching as ancient vessels with decks as long as the Jewish Exile continued groaning up to the dock, ready to take yet another load of men to some dark and distant region of eternal ice. It seemed as if the ships grew older and more decrepit with each visit.

When it was our turn to depart, we were marched in single file onto another sea-going barge whose decks made you hesitant to put your foot down too heavily. The way some of those vessels managed to stay afloat, I wondered if it might have been safer to swim to Siberia. But, to be truthful, I was in no hurry to find out.

Before the boat could leave, the guards lined us up once more and tried, four or five times with rapidly decreasing patience, to count us and make sure that each name had a likeness or a body attached to it.

Once again, I heard no mention of Pyavka's name, and he was nowhere to be found. Suddenly I wondered whether some fellow prisoner, fed up with his aristocratic airs, might not have stuck a knife into him – whether for the money he carried or as a simple outlet for irritation.

Although I might have lost confidence in Pyavka as a friend, I had not been ready to give up looking for him. I missed the encouragement I had gotten from his fantastic notions for escape.

Later that day, just as mysteriously as he had disappeared, Pyavka reappeared. I asked him where he had been, and what he had been doing.

"Negotiating," he said.

"For what?"

With an air of deep mystery, he let on that it was best I didn't know.

Under a steady, sullen downpour, the guards finally allowed us to make our way down a ladder into the cargo hold. Most of us were shivering, but still in reasonably good spirits. That is, no knives had yet been drawn in a threatening manner.

A few slivers of daylight leaked into the hold. Enough for me to see a skin of greenish slime that corroded the bulkheads, which I fervently hoped were above the water line.

The deck under our feet was slippery as ice, and no one had thought to provide facilities for us to sit or lie down, not to mention relieve ourselves. Some of the men began, in blind panic, to gasp for air and try to struggle back up the ladder. But they discovered that someone had thoughtfully locked the hatch. We were not allowed back on deck until summoned for our evening soup. Afterwards, most of us decided, despite the cold and damp, to spend the night under the black sky rather than return to the hold, even if it meant sleeping standing up.

Increasingly, on those moonless nights, a prisoner might sling one leg over the railing and, deaf to the amused shouts of the guards from their warm cabins on the quarterdeck, mutter a farewell prayer before flinging himself, headlong, into the water. None of his comrades showed any inclination to intervene. In fact, should someone bent on suicide prove too weak or too frozen to make this small climb, there was no shortage of brotherly hands ready to give him a hearty boost.

All around me, people were so numbed with boredom and hunger that their only entertainment seemed to be dredging up old scores, ranging from the division of loot from a long-ago robbery to the disputed income of some shameless female walking the streets. Once ignited, these little squabbles burst into flame so quickly that they often left one or both parties expiring of stab wounds or screaming in pain. Some convicts averted their eyes, while others looked on as raptly as a child in the circus.

There were, I regret to admit, also familiar rumblings of how the Jews were responsible for the way things were going, both aboard the ship and back in the miraculous world of civilian life. Fortunately, I was able to get my hands on a knife from one of the bodies waiting to be thrown overboard. Since I couldn't sleep with my eyes open, this was no guarantee of absolute safety. But it made me feel that, should I need to defend myself during daylight hours, I would not die without a fight.

One day, a minor encounter left me with a set of teeth marks in my fist. I knew our vessel had a small room set aside as a dispensary. I knocked and entered, surprised to see an actual doctor in a white coat standing hunched over a guard who complained of a sore throat. Having squirted something from a rubber bulb into the man's mouth, the doctor sent him on his way, "cured" and grateful.

With a sigh of impatience, the doctor rinsed off the tongue depressor and asked what the devil I wanted. The voice was startlingly familiar. Provoked by my silence, he turned around. For a moment, we stared at each other. I said, not very pleasantly, "Are you also The King of Doctors?"

My friend's, or former friend's, face had already brazened out its look of embarrassment. Without a word of apology, he assured me, "I did actually have some medical training. In fact, I might still, one day, go back and finish my studies. There's something fascinating about medicine, don't you think?"

I ignored his question. "How did you convince them?"

He laughed. "They had a doctor, but he came down with the cholera and they needed someone right away. To take care of the guards, not the prisoners. Eventually, they're bound to find me out. But meanwhile, I have a bed to myself, and there's plenty of food."

"Do you need an orderly?" I asked half-jokingly.

"I have one. In fact, he knows more about medicine than I do. But I keep him so busy, he doesn't have time to notice."

My friend painted some fiery stuff over the teeth marks in my hand. He then stuffed several biscuits into my pocket, and swore to me, once again, that he would not escape without me.

22

GOLD MINE AT THE END OF THE EARTH

Days later, our barge docked, again. While guards shouted, we staggered down the gangplank under a rusty sun, our legs struggling to adjust to a ground no longer moving. Unlike the previous barge cruise, after which we were relieved to be on solid ground, what awaited us this time would make us regret not having fully appreciated our previous voyage.

We were immediately formed into a *konvoi* and told to start walking. Before us lay a six-month trek. Provided that we walked briskly and avoided dying on the way.

It was clear that my new boots would not last through the winter. Not unless, like the old-timers, I walked barefoot. At least until the road iced over. So I slept with the boots under my head, and advised Pyavka to do the same. He gave me the pitying smile of a man who had no plans to winter in Siberia.

For days and weeks, and still more days, we trudged toward an unchanging horizon. Some of us had learned to walk with our eyes closed, asleep from the waist up, until we stumbled and fell upon our faces, to the great merriment of those who lacked this useful talent.

It was August, or maybe September, when we lurched to a halt near an old Cossack settlement. At such rest stops, women often came to the road with baskets of bread, milk, fish pies, and even eggs, sometimes for money, sometimes out of pure charity. This time we were disappointed. Even the women who ordinarily worked the fields were nowhere in sight.

But shortly after nightfall, a handful of our guards came back from the village with the news that, for those who still had money, 'arrangements' could be made for female companionship.

Although by now I was hardened to depravity, the only thing that shocked me was that the money went not to the women but to their husbands.

Midnight came and went without a sign of the expected visitors. Some of the men began voicing ugly suspicions. In response, we heard the nervous click of bolts, as our guards made sure each rifle had a bullet ready in its chamber. All, however, was instantly forgiven at the cry, "They're coming!"

Men jumped and rushed to the road to observe the shy approach of a remarkably small woman. On closer inspection, she turned out to be a goat.

In the morning, the cheated prisoners complained bitterly to their procurers who, for their part, insisted heatedly that the women did show up. "But when they saw how many of you were waiting, they got frightened and ran away. So you see it's entirely your own fault."

To avert an outright mutiny, our commandant agreed to let us rest there one more night. Some of the men demanded their money back. This, they were told, was impossible, because the Cossack husbands had drunk it all up.

But one of the guards shrewdly guessed that Pyavka still had some money. He took him aside and offered, for a mere ten rubles, to furnish him with the exclusive use of a "beautiful young Cossack maiden."

While Pyavka weighed this proposition with the solemnity he might once have devoted to, say, a cartload of smuggled tobacco, I took the liberty of reminding him, with all possible tact, of the heartbroken wife he had told me awaited him in Warsaw.

Pyavka's wintry expression made it clear that I had overstepped myself. No man ever had a wife so loyal, so devoted, he confirmed angrily. "A woman who is more angel than mortal. And yet, the fact is, she and my lawyer control all of my bank accounts. And women, after all, being weak creatures and easily misled, and in a city like Warsaw, where temptation springs from the very cracks in the pavement, who could truly say … ?"

Overcome with emotion, he covered his eyes for a moment. Then looked around for the guard to hear more details. Rebuffed in my appeal to his finer feelings, I addressed myself to his commercial sense, pointing out that, as any worldly person knew, ten rubles was well above the going rate for a "young Cossack maiden," even in an expensive city like Petersburg. Besides, "Tomorrow we'll be moving on. So if they don't come through tonight, you know what they say in Warsaw: 'No refund on perishable goods.'"

Being, essentially, a capitalist, Pyavka took this to heart. He told the guard that for the fee he was charging, the only acceptable terms were cash on delivery. This so deeply affronted our intermediary that he turned his back on us, muttering indignantly about tight-fisted Jews.

Around midnight, there was a fresh uproar. Some prisoners had managed to slip their fetters and run away. Or more likely, had gone to the village to collect, by force, what they felt was owed to them.

Awakened, our Commander flew into a rage and concluded that he had been too lenient with us. Orders were shouted for us to line up and, in utter darkness, continue our march.

By the time we were ready to move out, all but one of the escapees had returned from the village, some with scratched and bloodied faces, but mostly looking well pleased with themselves.

This, however, did not settle the matter. Cossack discipline demanded that for the one prisoner still missing, one of our guards was to be held responsible. His punishment consisted of having his horse taken from him. While this may not seem very tragic, a Cossack's horse was more precious than his wife. To be 'unhorsed' was the height of humiliation. Indeed, when a thief was caught stealing a Cossack's horse, even women and children participated in his execution.

Our escort of 55 Cossacks was compelled now to ride on 54 horses. We prisoners walked with carefully averted faces. It was obvious that our guardians were only itching for their chance to settle accounts.

Before the night was out, one convict, unable to resist the same fatal curiosity as Lot's wife,[63] turned his head to see which of the guards was traveling on foot. For this, he got a bullet in the back, and was left unburied by the side of the road. This made a distinct impression on the rest of us.

Our commandant obliged us to walk all that night and halfway through the next morning with no break even to relieve our bladders. Yet, having seen a man shot just for looking behind him, no one breathed a word of protest. We could hope only that, sooner or later, the horses would need a rest.

Around midmorning, a general in a coach descended upon us in a cloud of red dust. We lurched to a halt, and then turned, finally permitted to urinate. Every last one of us collapsed where he stood, not even troubling to choose a dry spot.

Puzzled by our quaint manner of greeting him, the general questioned our commanding officer, who assured him fervently that everything was in perfect order. None of us was insane enough to contradict him.

The general strolled past our row of sprawling bodies and demanded to know how we were. No one said a word. Impatiently, the general ordered us to rise to attention. He marched up and down once more, looked deep into our faces and insisted that we tell him, truthfully, how we felt.

Dead silence.

By now feeling somewhat provoked, the general ordered anyone who spoke Russian to take three steps forward. Long drilled in instant obedience to generals, my feet responded without consulting my brain.

He asked me how I felt. I tossed him a vigorous salute and answered, as he expected, "Very well, your nobility."

Pleased with my intelligent response, the general asked me to translate his words into Polish, as follows: "Brothers, you are indeed prisoners. But you still remain the beloved children of your Little Father, the Czar. And I demand to know whether you are receiving adequate food at least once a day."

63 Reference sources give various explanations for why Lot's wife might have turned back to see the destruction of Sodom and Gomorrah, but all generally agree that her sin was disobeying God's admonition not to do so. Her punishment was to be turned into a pillar of salt because, during her lifetime, she had "sinned through salt," that is, she was stingy toward the needy by being reluctant to share that precious commodity.

Still no one opened his mouth. The general glowered at me, and I sweated with remorse at having volunteered.

"I see by your posture you were once a soldier." I admitted as much. "Then you know what happens to a man who fails to respond to a direct question from a superior officer."

I assured him vigorously that I did, indeed. But I also knew, if I answered truthfully, what would happen to me after he left.

At this, the general, beet-faced, summoned our commandant and warned him that he would hold him personally responsible for my safety.

Our terrified commandant insisted that all of us, not just I, alone, were free to speak our minds. But I didn't see anyone else jump forward to take him up on this offer.

The general looked at me as though all this were my fault. And so, standing at strict attention, I reported to him that one of our group was shot during the night. And for all I knew, his body still lay where it fell.

I said, "Either we are all under sentence of death, or we are not. And if we're not, does any guard have the right to kill a man merely for turning his head?"

Having heard me out with some impatience, the general confronted our guards and demanded, in a terrible voice, to know precisely what had happened.

They assured him, to a man, that the only rifle discharged during the night had fired no more than a warning shot over our heads to frighten some prisoners poised to run away. If anyone was actually struck by this errant bullet, of which there was not the slightest proof, it was his fellow convicts who were guilty of not having reported it until now.

Not being a total fool, the general demanded a head count. For two long hours, we stood in a ragged line while his Adjutant checked off each name against the roster. Nearly ten percent of the names on the list were unaccounted for. All of us, prisoners and guards alike, professed to be mystified.

Pyavka singed me with a look of reproach. Why, his eyes demanded, had he been such a fool as to listen to me, a man habituated to slavish, soldierly obedience, when he should long ago have realized how easy it was to run away?

The general sent an aide back to where I told him the body had been left. I could only hope that the villagers had not, with unaccustomed neatness, already buried it.

Some hours later, the aide returned. He carried a bloodless corpse lashed down in front of his saddle. The victim was someone who, from my perspective, fully deserved to come to a bad end. But given a choice, I would have preferred to settle our differences with my own hands.

At the sight of the body, hardened murderers wept rivers of tears. Even the general dabbed at his eyes. An immediate investigation was ordered to identify the killer. Too late. A shot echoed from the nearby woods, and the guards followed the sound. Presently, they produced what was left of the guilty party – one of their fellow guards. Clearly familiar with Czarist justice, the shooter had decided to cheat his own fate.

Unfortunately for the rest of us, this investigation had so distracted our general that he drove off in his coach without ever finding out whether we received enough to eat.

Pyavka no longer spoke of escape. In fact, he hardly spoke at all. Over the weeks, his lordly personality had leaked out of him, like straw from an old mattress. In the words of the Psalmist, the water had reached the edge of his soul. Even his once-majestic features had shrunk to little more than a freestanding nose with barely enough room around the edges for a haunted pair of pinpoint eyes, and a wormhole of a mouth that expanded only at feeding time. While once he had treated me as a disciple on whom he might deign, out of sheer caprice, to shower a few crumbs of royal benevolence, he now clung to me like a child to his mother's skirt.

We came to a place with a more permanent look. It was, in fact, less a camp than the kind of log-walled "fort" seen in a Western film beset by the flaming arrows of encircling Indians. Most of my fellow criminals assumed, with great joy, that we had reached our destination, and eagerly agreed that "Siberia" was not nearly as bad as they had feared.

For those of a trusting nature, the fort even boasted a charlatan in a medical coat who was prepared, for a modest price, to paint a few strokes of foul-smelling ointment on the ulcerous sores caused by our leg irons. He was also available to perform surgery and cut hair.

While Pyavka darted like a crab in all directions, gathering crumbs of information on where we were and how far it was to the railroad – assuming one managed to escape – I, like any soldier, concentrated on being first in line at the cookhouse.

The sludge ladled into our bowls had a raw green color that, for the next two days, was reflected in our urine.

My belly filled and warmed, never mind with what, I found a sheltered space and devoted myself to some serious sleeping.

Agitated, Pyavka shook my shoulders. He had just learned what most of us knew from the day we arrived. Where we were was simply another transit camp. Our final destination was a gold mine in the "real" Siberia, a walk of three or four months which, by my calculations, should get us there at a fairly cold time of year, a season when daylight lasted about as long as a cigarette.

Why did I need to be awakened with this wonderful news? "It means I don't have much time," Pyavka confided rather more loudly than necessary. "The guards here can still be bribed with money. At the mine, they will accept nothing but gold, and I'll be left with a pocketful of worthless rubles."

Still scraping the sleep out of my eyes, I tried, but failed, to follow his reasoning.

"Don't you understand? My only hope is to escape now while my money is still worth something."

"And then what?"

"I'm trying to tell you. From here it's only a five-day walk to the railroad."

I was interested, but not excited. And even less so, when Pyavka, with a smirk of pride, disclosed that he had already made a deal: "One hundred rubles to let out twenty men, each with a loaf of bread and a bottle of water."

My jaw dropped. Having walked and slept at this man's side for the past ten or twelve weeks, I couldn't imagine when he had suddenly acquired eighteen other intimate friends. And what mad excess of generosity was it that moved him to treat a pack of cutthroats and bandits to the honor of taking part in an escape that might be a little bit conspicuous?

He waited patiently for me to ask, "Why twenty?"

"In a mass escape, the commandant, himself, is held accountable. Which will make him eager to cover up the whole business."

"And the other guards will just sit there and scratch themselves?"

"Oh, they'll come after us all right. And Heaven help anyone they catch."

"But you believe you can outrun them. Chains and all? You can outrun Cossacks on horseback?"

"I've taken care of that, too," he said, testy at what he took to be my unceasing tendency to find fault. Pyavka then favored me with his most irritating smile. "Haven't you ever wondered why, all along, someone didn't simply kill me and take all my money?"

"Frankly, yes."

"It's because they know about you."

"*Me?*" My heart did a hop and a skip. "What do they know about me?"

"Only that you were a famous terrorist whom I employ as my bodyguard. And that you are so devoted to me, you would give your life to keep me from harm."

"Thank you very much," I said. "So any time they want to rob you, all they have to do is kill me, first."

"No one needs to kill anyone. I told you, it's all fixed. The guard is even drawing us a map of how to get to the railroad."

He had not, in so many words, invited me to take part in this mad excursion of his. Nor was I at all sure I would accept. But it crushed my spirits to know that the man had, entirely on his own, made these dangerous plans. And used my name to frighten people.

I was not, by nature, what you would call a pessimist. But I could suddenly think of a million obstacles. To begin with: "A five-day walk with shackles on your legs? Just how far do you think you will get? The guards will take your money and open the gates. And then they'll sit and laugh until you all come limping back, begging to be let in."

"You think I haven't thought of that?"

"Being let back in?"

"How to get rid of our chains. One of the old-timers explained what to do. Of course, we can't actually test it until we're outside." But he illustrated how, with a flat rock, one could *possibly* pound rings into an oval that *might* allow one's foot to slip through.

One didn't need to be an engineer to see the flaw in that, too. Even assuming the iron was soft enough to shape with a rock, what if you hit it a little bit too hard? How would you then, without a blacksmith's help, widen it again? Because if you couldn't, within hours your foot would turn black, and then …

One look at the naked desperation in Pyavka's eyes and I said no more.

A moment later, he acted again as though he had no further need for me. This annoyed me enough to mention one or two other small details he might have overlooked. "What about the guard dogs?"

"There aren't any. The prisoners ate them last year."

"If the wolves or bounty hunters don't get you first, you'll lose your way and die of hunger or walk in circles until you go mad."

Once again, I regretted my harsh words. A moment ago, I was angry because, in sheer panic, he had saddled me with a killer's reputation. Why, then, should I have gotten angry once he assumed he could do without me?

Pyavka's features collapsed in despair. "All right. It's off."

"What? What's off?"

"If you don't think it's possible, then it's off. I told the others right from the start that I wouldn't go without you. They growled and grumbled, but I wouldn't give in. I know I wouldn't last one day out there on my own."

In an instant, I was appeased. How could I have spoken so cruelly to my only friend? Schemes and ideas erupted from me like fireworks. Of *course*, it was possible.

"Then you will come with us?"

At the point of saying 'yes,' I asked how much money he would have left after bribing our way out.

"Thirty-seven rubles," he said sheepishly.

I knew this was not the best time to bring it up, but didn't he know a ticket to Warsaw would cost at least ten times that much for him, alone?

His eyes glazed over with tears. "Why are you trying to crush my spirit? You've been a soldier. You're used to rough living. Ten years from now, you will still be thriving. But me, I've always lived in comfort. If I don't get out of here, I'll croak like a dog!"

Even as I fumbled for some way to reassure him, he added, "Once I'm free, I can always earn my way. Not every village needs a lawyer or a doctor. But there is never a time when a good thief cannot find work for his hands."

I admitted that this was the first halfway intelligent thing I'd heard him say in some time. Yet, I was still uneasy. Not only about the villains who would be flying out on my friend's coat tails. But what made him so certain he could trust our guards even as far as the gate?

He flashed a rueful smile. "I didn't want to worry you, but let me explain why I believe they are being truthful with me. The fact is they had one condition. The Cossacks never forgave you for your complaint to the general, which led one of their men to kill himself. So when I told them I would not leave without you, the truest friend I have in all the world, they made it clear that they were ready to pass up the 100 rubles sooner than let you escape.

"So you see," he continued cheerfully, "If they intended to swindle me, why would they object to your name?"

There was good, crooked logic in what he said. Our guards may have been corrupt, but clearly they were men of principle. I felt a sudden chill of loneliness. Once Pyavka was gone, I would have lost my only ally. The guards would be able to exact their revenge on me any time it suited them. I swallowed my bitterness. "When are you leaving?"

"I'm not."

"What?"

"I told you. Not without you."

"Then you're a fool. You're twice as old as I am. You have a family waiting for you. And how long do you think you will last in those mines?"

"I will not go without you," he repeated doggedly. "Not from friendship. I'm a thief; I spit on friendship. But you're quite right. I am a city man. I never dealt in violence. Without you at my side, they would slit my throat without a knife."

"But if the guards won't let me out ..."

Pyavka interrupted, smiling again. "I'm on my way to meet with one of the officers. To offer him an extra 25 rubles for you, alone."

And off he went, not, alas, in the brisk, balanced stride of a man who knew how to get things done, but placing one foot daintily in front of the other, like the kind of person whose dreams lasted longer than his sleep.

Not for the first time, I marveled at how this man, in a hard city like Warsaw, could ever have ruled over a kingdom of thieves.

Ten minutes later he was back with a face like a rained-out funeral. "Not a chance. In fact, the Cossacks are so angry with you that I fear for your life."

Trying to keep the tremor out of my voice, I asked, "What time is the escape?"

"Two o'clock in the morning. But there will be no escape. I told you as I told the guard: I will not go without you."

I seized his arm. "You *will* go. And so will I. There is no moon, and once the gates open and twenty men burst through, who will notice one extra body? And if they try to shoot the extra man, I'll make sure it's not me."

Pyavka slung his arms around me. "I knew you would think of something!"

"You realize I could be endangering the rest of you."

He shrugged. "Tonight, either 21 men will get out or no one will escape."

Back in our barracks, I lay down and tried to sleep. But the blood thumped in my ears the way it used to on the eve of a military attack. Hours later, I was still awake when I saw men arise from their shelves, like specters out of their muddy graves.

Outside, in the not-quite-moonless fog, ragged shadows flitted toward the assembly point behind the tool shed. From the few faces I recognized in the darkness, it was plain that my poor friend was a lamb among wolves. No wonder he refused to go without at least one person on whom it was safe to turn his back.

Huddled against the blind wall of a guardhouse filled with snoring bodies, I watched twenty men being carefully counted twice, and again once more, and the 100 rubles being paid out and counted with at least as much care. I smudged my face with lampblack, but no one seemed to notice.

Four guards, including one officer, seemed to be in on it. The gate was quietly unlocked, and a bird cry sounded the signal. Half expecting a bullet in the back, I timed my moves so that, with twenty other sets of chains clanking like sleigh bells in heavy traffic on Nevsky Prospekt, I reached the open gate at a dead run among the first half-dozen. No one was intent on anything but running as fast as his fetters would allow.

The plan was for Pyavka and I to meet near a stack of freshly cut timber less than two kilometers from the gate. This meant Pyvka had to break away from the others almost at once. But an hour passed with no sign of him. Meanwhile, all around me, the forest rang with the insolent peal of shackles being hammered. To my ears, each blow echoed like a rifle shot. How could the camp commander sleep through all this racket?

I was about to give up on Pyavka and drag my feet to a deserted part of the forest when he showed up, panting and drenched in sweat.

"Why didn't you wait for me?" he moaned.

"I did wait for you," I said, without mentioning that I had been about to abandon him, the very instrument of my freedom.

"I looked for you at the trees outside the gate."

"Not trees – timber," I said. "And far from the gate. Why would we meet somewhere close to—?"

"Trees, timber," he said with a wide grin. "What does it matter now that we're together again?"

I was about to explain the subtle differences between my words and Pyavka's interpretation, but we were still too close to the camp to engage in such lighthearted argument. At any moment, we might hear horses' hooves, furious commands, and a burst of machine gun fire.

I stooped for a rock, two rocks, and pulled Pyavka into a dense thicket of trees. Handing him one rock, I wrapped my footrag around my stone, which Pyavka copied, and we each pounded at our fetters, hammering rock against steel until, at the cost of some skin, I was able to wrench mine off. Once the clanking stopped echoing in my ears, the only sound I heard was the clean breeze moaning in the treetops.

After seven months and sixteen different prisons, way stations and transit camps, I was finally free.

23

WHICH WAY TO THE NORTH POLE?

y unchained feet felt feather-light, as if they barely touched the earth. Surprisingly, although he wheezed like a milkman's horse, Pyavka was able to keep up with me. But I suppose the first thing a thief must learn how to do is run.

Which reminded me. "Where is the map?"

"What map?"

Then it came back to him. Stricken, he admitted that in all the confusion he had failed to notice who, if anyone held onto that priceless piece of paper.

It took some effort, but I controlled myself. A map without a compass would have been of little use, anyway, surrounded as we were by trees that were identical in height and girth, giving us no signpost by which to orient ourselves.

But as we had put some distance between us and the camp, whether in the right direction or not, I suggested that we stop and rest while deep in the bowels of a forest that may not have been touched by human feet since the Six Days of Creation.

When we settled in for the remainder of the night, enveloped by curious noises, I made the innocent suggestion that we arm ourselves.

"Against what?"

"Bears, wolves, bounty hunters. Your nineteen friends."

With a tolerant smile, Pyavka shook his head at my timidity. "Even in Warsaw, I never felt the need to go around armed like a hooligan."

"You didn't have bodyguards?"

"Bodyguards, of course I had. Two fine young lads. Followed me everywhere. Looked up to me like a father."

"And where were they when the police came for you?"

His mouth twisted into a pained smile. "Would you believe it was they who turned me in? Of course, they had been handsomely paid. But I could swear there were tears in their eyes when the police hauled me off." Even all these months later, his eyes dampened at the memory.

Mostly to occupy my hands, I broke off two straight branches and fashioned them into spears whose points I hardened over a small, smokeless flame.

"In which *yeshiva* did you learn that?" my partner scoffed.

"Never mind that."

"Wouldn't it be better to build a fire to frighten off a wild beast that might attack you in your sleep?"

It was true; if we built a fire, we wouldn't have to worry about wolves because the Cossacks would be here long before them.

"Then where is it safe to sleep!" he inquired in the usual tone of a spoiled English tourist.

I pointed to a nearby tree.

"How can a human being sleep in a tree?"

It took me a moment to realize that he was serious. His parents must have strongly impressed upon him that climbing trees was not respectable. Only how, I wondered, having grown up with such a noble inhibition, had he achieved his eminence as a master criminal?

"I grew up on the city streets. By the time I saw my first tree, I was already too well-dressed to think of climbing it. But just you watch me go up the bare facade of a house."

I promised him that, should we both live long enough to make it back to Warsaw, I would be glad to have him give me a demonstration of his talent. Meanwhile, I tried to teach him one of the useful skills I picked up in the army, which was how to sleep in the natural hammock formed by the branches of a tree.

Hours later, from a nearby roost, I saw my comrade still clinging to the trunk like an exhausted wrestler, noisily thrashing and reassembling his limbs from one contortion to another. Until, without warning, he fell asleep, almost in mid-air.

In shameful contrast, I couldn't close an eye. Unsure how far we were from the camp, I felt that at least one of us should stay alert. Since Pyavka's snores might as well have come from the depths of a feather bed, and I would not have had much trust in his watchfulness, anyway, the watch might as well be me.

Scarcely had I arrived at this noble decision when I was seized by the kind of drugged sleep from which, less than a year earlier, only a cluster of incoming artillery could have shaken me.

In the end, what ruptured my sleep was not the cold glare of the dawning sun but the nightmare of a monstrous shadow flapping its wings above my face. In a fierce rush of air, the Creature burst at me like a cannonball, intent on pecking out my eyes.

I rolled sideways, trying to convince myself that it was only a dream, no worse than most, while its beak slashed at my arms and eyes and shoulders. Only the sharp stick in my hand hindered my attacker from taking more substantial bites out of my flesh.

What did that bird want from me? Only then did I notice that I had made my bed right next to a nest of large speckled eggs of a type that weren't meant to be eaten. Holding on to the tree with one hand, I ducked and parried with my primitive spear as the winged beast, attended now by a squadron of relatives, friends and neighbors, tore through a cloud of dry leaves to get at me for the kill. Already it had shredded my sleeve. Blood spurted out of my arm, but I was too excited to be conscious of the pain.

In all the commotion, Pyavka had rather slipped my mind until I felt his bulk drop past me, snapping branches and nearly pulling me down with him. He slammed into the ground and remained sprawled, silent as snow.

The giant birds, awed by the violence of his fall, gleefully wheeled off into the sky.

With thumping heart, I jumped down to see if my friend was still alive. As I drew back one of his lids, he groaned with annoyance at being awakened. Only then did I notice that my forearm was losing blood. Pyavka, exercising his medical skills, peeled off a soiled strip of cloth and bandaged the spot where the bird had taken a nip out of my flesh.

At this point, neither of us was eager to climb back into the tree to finish our night's sleep. So we sat together, dozing intermittently, until a smear of pearly gray light revealed the horizon, although not from the direction I had thought was east. Which left me to wonder whether, up here, more or less next door to the North Pole, "east" meant something different than it did in Poland.

Pyavka sat up abruptly. "Where is our bread?" His voice carried a scowl of accusation, and he dropped to his knees. His frantic fingers groped for the shallow hole in which we had hidden our rations. I wanted to be helpful, but faced with a sun rising from the wrong end of the sky, I was no longer sure in which tree we had slept.

"A soldier you call yourself?" Pyavka grumbled. Then he cried out, in triumph, or rage. He had tripped over our water bottle and almost broken it. But there was our bread, fully intact, except for what resembled a set of teethmarks. To avoid any strain on our friendship, we hastily attributed them to some species of animal not burdened with our human sense of ethics.

Although a drizzle of sunlight filtered through the trees, the frost under my naked soles was sharp as splintered glass. It weakened my resolve to hold off wearing the shoes I had saved from traveling to the bottom of the river with their owner. I reached into the bag, and my heart sank into my bowels. Some scoundrel in our barracks had exchanged them for a different pair that fell apart the moment I tried to walk in them.

Pyavka found this to be a good moment for irony. "My friend, you forget; among the noble souls our Little Father banished to Siberia, there may have been one or two actual thieves."

I started to laugh, which was just as well since it did me no less good than a sputter of curses.

We examined our diminished loaf of bread from every angle, and comforted each other with the lie that, by exercising a bit of self-control, we might stretch it to last four more days.

What I didn't reveal to Pyavka, who was depressed enough already, was that I hadn't a clue where we were or in which direction we were headed.

Nor did I dare guess what would happen when our bread ran out. Which, no matter how bravely we talked, was certain to be by tomorrow.

Shoulders propped against the rugged skin of an ancient tree, we shared our day's ration. But the bread only stimulated our hunger more cruelly. To divert ourselves from the tormenting images of food, we let our fantasies roam. Assuming that we made it as far as the railroad, by some miracle got our hands on "good papers" and even came up with money for tickets, in which direction should we travel – toward Europe, home? Or through the unmapped vastness of China, Korea, Japan? Pyavka, in his ignorance, pictured a coastline crowded with steamers waiting to depart for the Golden Land, non-stop to Chicago or wherever. Surely, at least one of those ships would have space for two more bodies, whether as crewmen, passengers or stowaways.

As he saw it, once safely in America we would simply cable our families to pack up and join us, money being no object as Chicago, all the world knew, was a city made for thieves.

That evening, under a vanishing sky, my partner and I vowed, once again, to take turns standing watch. As before, we only had trouble agreeing who would take the second shift.

With the shameless eloquence of a born lawyer, Pyavka reminded me that in Warsaw he was, like most rich men, accustomed to staying up late and sleeping late. Whereas I, having spent my adult years in unskilled trades such as soldiering and baking bread, ought to be well used to going without sleep. Worn down by his logic, I capitulated.

"You gave in too easily," he charged. "You are planning to wait until I'm asleep, and then eat my share of the bread."

"How do I know you wouldn't do the same?"

"Ha! An honest man wouldn't have such thoughts."

"And what about you?"

"I am a thief. For me it's natural to think that way."

I knew this circular wrangling could go on for hours. I don't know how his wife put up with it. Like me, I suppose, she had no choice.

Sometime during this conversation, Pyavka fell asleep. I watched him snore, his cheeks glowing with contentment born of a spotless conscience.

Soon I was tormented by aromatic visions of our common chunk of bread. Especially since Pyavka had placed it squarely under his head, which I found insulting. Was his skull so soft that he needed bread for a pillow? Or did he not trust me? In which case, would it not serve him right if I paid back his ugly suspicion by stealing a piece, a mere sliver, the thickness of a fingernail, purely on principle?

While engaged in these dark speculations, I, too, dozed off. And by the time I could think of awakening Pyavka for his turn to stand watch, the sun had long since shed its blood across the sky. With aching bones, I lay back down to snatch a few minutes of rest, while my partner, refreshed, booted and impatient, grumbled that my "sleeping disease" was costing him valuable time.

24
INTO THE WOODS

Dawn rose, heavy as lead. After days of walking without seeing any evidence of human ingenuity, I climbed a tree, hoping to get a fresh perspective on the world. Moments later, I jumped back down and shook my partner out of his sleep. What I had seen bore every sign of a man-made path.

We hiked for some hours without finding so much as an empty vodka bottle, let alone a human footprint.

Pyavka sat down and announced he could not go one more step. I reminded him that he had been saying that almost hourly for as long as we'd been walking. But this time, as proof he really meant it, he offered me his money, his boots and his tearful blessings.

In no mood for sentimental gestures, I told him that if he really wanted to give me his boots, I'd be glad to help him remove them.

At which heartless response my partner looked up and decided I was joking. So instead of giving me his shoes, he draped his face in a broad smile, groaned back to his feet, and proclaimed to all the world that by not abandoning him to die here, I, Yakov Marateck, proved that I was one of the saintly "Thirty Six", just as I had once naively suspected of him. Pyavka then grabbed my hand and overwhelmed it with kisses. It was only because I didn't have the strength to make a fist that I was able to keep from hitting him.

Suddenly, he said, "Do you hear it?"

"Hear what?" But, a moment later, the shriek of the whistle was unmistakable. In an instant, hunger, thirst, exhaustion, and pain were forgotten as we ran and lurched and limped in the direction of that life-restoring shriek.

Within the hour, we glimpsed telegraph wires, followed by the blessed sight of iron tracks. Pyavka flung himself across the rails and embraced them, while I looked in both directions, hoping to spot a depot or some other form of human habitation. This brought us up sharply against the delicate question of where, assuming we managed to reach a depot, we would get enough money for two tickets home.

Pyavka gave me a pitying look. Was he not "The King of Thieves?" Just turn him loose among the passengers, and before the conductor even knew we were on board, he would have "earned" enough to take us both, not just to Warsaw but, if we wanted, all the way to Berlin, Paris, even New York, traveling first class all the way.

I had no reason to doubt his felonious skills. I wondered only if he had already forgotten that even those who had tickets also needed to produce such treasures as a passport and a travel permit

He glowered and shook his head. "Always the pessimist."

We had been walking along the tracks since early that morning without seeing or hearing any sign of human life. By this time, the sun had shriveled to a flat white circle, no brighter and no warmer than a small coin.

At the very edge of darkness, I spotted something that made me mistrust my eyes. Of course, I was hungry, Pyavka's and my inability to trust each other had resulted in our consuming our bread rations well ahead of schedule. But seeing my partner's gaze fixed in the direction of my mirage, I blinked again and saw a prettily built cottage surrounded by a wilderness of dwarf pines. The very existence of this image was so fantastic that its walls might as well have been made of gingerbread.

Clutching my ridiculous spear, I scouted ahead. As in the fairy tale, all seemed improbably inviting. All except for a neatly painted sign whose message, deciphered by the light of a match, advised in blunt military terms that trespassers would be severely dealt with.

Lightheaded with hunger yet afraid to knock, I stood on an upturned pail and peered through half-drawn curtains into an old-fashioned sitting room aglow in the halo of an oil lamp. A sharp elbow nearly threw me off my perch. Crowding my ear, Pyavka declared that, in his experience, lamps didn't light themselves. Therefore—

We debated in a fierce whisper how dangerous it would be to knock on the door. Pyavka held that, since I spoke Russian and looked, to his eyes, more like a typical *Vanya*, I ought to be the one to introduce myself.

"As what? An escaped convict?"

Nose pressed to the cold glass, I gawked once more into a room equipped with good furniture, a gleaming samovar, and a table covered with a lace cloth. A young woman's face suddenly broke into my line of vision. Captivated, I stared at her pale, gaunt features until she caught sight of my flattened nose and bulging eyes, and cried out in alarm.

I jumped off the pail and blindly ran. Back among the trees, I paused and cowered, breathlessly waiting to see if anyone was pursuing us. To my astonishment, the Lady stood in her open door and, betraying no fear, motioned us to approach.

Pyavka vigorously shook his head. I shared his mistrust. But after so many days without bread, my brief sprint had drained my strength and my caution. "She invited us in," I said.

"Maybe you she invited."

"I'm hungry."

"So am I. But I'm not stupid."

Denied my sympathy, he grumbled as though I were Moses navigating the horizonless desert under direct guidance from the One Above, and all I needed to do was to let Him know our exact map coordinates for where to drop the manna.

In no mood to listen, I dropped my spear and approached the door, gliding on its outflow of light and warmth until I came face to face with a woman whose long, black hair was streaked with white. I bowed my head in greeting. She responded with a smile of such piercing sadness that I was mute with confusion.

Once inside the cottage, I noticed that the rough-hewn walls gleamed with delicate gilt paintings of an infant being cradled in the arms of what looked like a somewhat inexperienced mother. I knew what icons were, but I had never seen one at close range.

A knock jolted me out of my trance. I turned to see Pyavka enter the cottage. I saw at once that he knew far better than I how to conduct himself with ladies of breeding. Dumb with envy, I watched the courtly tilt of his body as, clearly back in his element, he bowed to kiss the knuckles of her hand.

The Lady smiled at his Varsovian[64] manners, but her eyes included me in her question, "Where are you from?"

Pyavka looked to me for enlightenment. I explained, "He is a Pole; he doesn't speak Russian."

"Ah, a Pole. With that beard, I took him for a Jew."

What I found odd about that remark was that she would comment on his beard and not on the more obvious feature of our convict clothing.

"You're not Russian either, are you?" she said to me. "Although no one would know it from the way you speak."

"I was a soldier."

"And now?"

It was futile to lie. "We're from a labor camp. We ran away to save our lives. But, I swear, we are quite harmless. I'm 'political,' and my friend is," I hesitated a moment, "also political."

She smiled at my transparent untruth.

"Neither of us has eaten in four days," I said. "I beg you to have pity on us."

She appeared neither surprised nor alarmed by my confession. She merely nodded, and called to a stout servant woman who burst in so quickly that she must have been waiting at the keyhole.

In her arms was a pitcher of freshly drawn milk. A few moments later, she delivered a loaf of bread no smaller than a millstone, a great lump of butter, and a basin heaped with hard-boiled eggs. Pyavka and I exchanged a glance. We knew that we dared not drop our guard. But even if she had already dispatched a servant to the nearest village for help, surely we had time for a small bite.

64 Pertaining to someone from Warsaw

Addled by hunger, we fell upon the food. We hadn't the strength or the patience to shell the eggs. Soon, to our hostess' polite amusement, the room crackled with the sound of eggshells being ground between our teeth.

We concluded our feast with a flood of black, sugared tea until, gloriously bloated, we set our glasses upside down on the table to signify that we'd had enough. To further establish that, despite our somewhat irregular appearance, we were still Polish gentlemen, Pyavka took out two crumpled ruble notes and offered to pay for the food. The lady smiled and pushed back the money.

Reinvigorated by the strong tea, I had the nerve to ask, "Is there a place we can sleep tonight?" I also made an offer of payment, counting on our hostess to reject it, too, as I had no resources to back it up.

She said, "I cannot let you stay in the house. But there is hay in the barn, and the servant will give you blankets and pillows."

Blankets and pillows! Could there ever have been a time when I took such luxuries for granted? My alertness briefly restored I tried, to Pyavka's yawning disgust, to behave like a guest by engaging our hostess in refined conversation. I began with the obvious question. "How is it that a lady of your quality lives in such isolation?"

Compared with the "real" Siberia, she said, this was quite a tolerable place, other than the lack of cultural opportunities. I suppressed the impulse to flaunt my refined views on the Chinese Opera in Harbin. But the lady soon steered our conversation to more practical matters.

Like all fugitives, it was obvious we were blindly headed for home. She made us understand that so many escaped prisoners tried to steal aboard westbound trains that even business travelers in first class were forced to undergo an endless ordeal of searches and inspections at almost every station.

"Without proper documents, you would be mad to try it."

But how would criminals like us ever attain such precious documents?

Here she surprised me. "Would you be willing to travel for some days in the opposite direction?"

"Where to?" I asked.

"Irkutsk. It might take as much as a week. But eastbound trains are not watched so closely. After all, who would go to Asia except on serious business?"

"And what is there for us in Irkutsk?" I said. Other than "Queen Esther" who, even in her absence, had captured my heart that for the few days we stopped there on our way home from the war.

"I have heard of a printer who is renowned for making passports of the highest quality. Of course, he will take such a risk only for honest revolutionaries, not for common criminals."

I translated this for Pyavka, who was visibly offended by the man's scruples and was, therefore, inclined to be skeptical. He asked me to translate, "When was the last time she had any news of this great artist?"

"Three years ago, maybe longer," she admitted.

"And you believe that he's still alive and at liberty, just waiting for us?" he asked me in Polish.

If I said 'yes,' it was only because, having no other hope, I needed to believe he existed.

"What if he'll do it for you but not for me?"

With a cruel shrug, I told him, "At least in Irkutsk you'll be that much closer to America."

This earned me a deep sigh of disappointment. Following which, my partner begged our hostess' pardon and went outside to relieve himself.

A good fifteen minutes had ticked away since Pyavka had left us flagrantly alone in the room.[65] While my eyes burned with fatigue, my partner, I assumed, had found his way to the barn and sensibly bedded down. And yet I couldn't tear myself away.

To dissolve the lump of silence between us, I lamely asked how our hostess came to live in such a wilderness.

"My husband is stationed not far from here. And both of us enjoy the solitude and silence."

My pulse drummed a little note of caution. "He's a soldier?"

"A colonel of cavalry."

---

65 Under the laws of Orthodox Judaism, a man and a woman are not permitted to be in the same room, behind closed doors, unless they are married.

My voice quivering, I asked, "What would he say if he knew you were sheltering two escaped convicts?"

She shrugged. "We all know the revolution is coming. And it is obvious that you, at least, are not a common criminal."

Again, that look of utter melancholy. In the humid silence of a Siberian autumn night, her ghostly beauty frightened me. I obliged myself not to forget I was a fugitive and she the wife of a high Russian officer. Who, for all I knew, could walk in at any moment.

Nor was I at ease with the trusting, almost intimate turn our conversation had taken. Still, I felt some obligation, as a guest, to make myself agreeable for as long as it suited my hostess.

She startled me by saying, "You are a Jew, are you not?"

I sagged with resignation. "Do you want us to leave?"

"What are you saying?" Motioning me to keep my voice down, she began, in educated, schoolgirl Yiddish, to tell me her story. I lost the need to sleep, so totally caught up was I in her tale, related without drama or any attempt to claim sympathy.

Her name was Evgenia. An only child, she had grown up in a serene and prosperous household in Brest-Litovsk.

"When I was fourteen, my mother went to the Ukraine to visit her father and mother. The day before Passover, my mother and my grandparents were butchered in a pogrom." That had marked the end of her childhood.

"It left me so enraged against the God of the Jews, I felt the only way I could settle scores with Him was to have myself baptized." For the first time in her life, her father slapped her face.

That night, she packed a few belongings and left her father's house forever. For some months, she lived at the home of her mother's younger brother, who was kind to her and even offered to pay for her education.

But again fate was cruel. Her uncle's wife was a jealous woman who suspected her husband of being in love with his niece, and accused both of them of trying to poison her.

Once more, life became ugly. And so, at the age of fifteen, Evgenia accepted the proposal of a dashing young Russian lieutenant who, shortly after their marriage, was posted to Siberia. And there they had lived ever since.

As though the question were written on my face, she said, "I know what you must be thinking. But I have never had a moment's regret. Admittedly, my husband and I have almost nothing in common. But he trusts me, and I trust him, and to me that means infinitely more than what people call 'love.'"

She saw me glance at the icons on the wall. "Yes. We were married in a church. They poured some water on me, but it never entered my heart.

"I have had more than enough time to see the cruel irony in what I did. In order to avenge my mother's murder, I embraced the religion of her killers."

The lamp had grown dim. I felt chilled to the bone. Yet my face was on fire. I was afraid that too many more moments alone with this sad lady would begin to stir emotions that neither of us could afford to indulge. I knew that I should get up and look for my partner. But my feet were no-where to be found.

In the barn, amidst the spicy dust of hay and manure, Pyavka slumbered, complacent as a corpse. Only his nose was alive, glowing and honking in rhythmic triumph

I gathered an armful of straw and tried to bury myself in sleep, but my mind was racing and my eyelids would not close. One thought, in particu-lar, left me chilled. If our luck held up, we were about to re-enter the civi-lized world. I dared not forget that my fate was shackled to that of a man for whom stealing was second nature. Until now, the worst Pyavka could steal was a mouthful of bread. But how would I control him from here on?

Pyavka, ignorant of my fears, slept as though he were already back in Warsaw; that is, until noon.

Eager to share our hostess' history, I waited for him to rub the film out of his eyes. I started talking, but he cut me short.

"You're so innocent," he said almost indignantly. "Think, for a minute. If you were a woman living in the wilderness, and two desperate fugitives turned up on your doorstep, wouldn't you treat them nicely until help ar-rived? And her husband a Russian officer? Mark my words, the moment he appears we will be looking into a loaded rifle and off on a long march back to prison."

Then how had he been able to sleep so long and peacefully?

He shrugged. "After all that food, I was tired."

I shook my head in pity. My partner may have had far more exposure than I to the full range of human treachery, but surely I was still able to recognize true kindness. "And what, exactly, do you suggest?"

"I'll tell you what. While you two were entertaining one another with fairy tales and Heaven-only-knows what else under the table, I was hard at work."

"At work!"

"I climbed into their bedroom and took a look around." I stared at him in total horror.

"There was a locked iron chest in the corner. It had a fairly primitive lock and I tickled it open. It's packed with money. Far beyond the honest wages of a colonel. And if we borrowed just enough to—"

Clawing the front of Pyavka's shirt, I lifted him off his feet. It was the closest I had ever come to killing a man with my bare hands. "This woman has shown us nothing but kindness. If you steal so much as one kopek from her, you will never see me again."

Somewhat shaken, my colleague swore to me he would forego all acts of thievery until he was safely back in Warsaw. Unless, of course, I directed him otherwise. A moment later he wanted to know. "And what if her husband turns us over to the police?"

"Then the 'borrowed' money in your pocket will, no doubt, convince him of our innocence."

Pyavka rewarded me with a twisted smile. "When it comes to crooked thinking, I see you're not so hopeless after all."

Our hostess emerged from the house. With her was an equally tall man in a *polkovnik's* uniform. His eyes were hidden in pools of shadow, but his mouth was tight with authority.

Coming out of the barn, my gray convict shirt feathered with straw, I tried to put some military snap into my posture. But my feet were so swollen that my steps became a parody of a small boy playing soldier. The colonel watched me, unamused.

Shoulders braced, I stumbled to a halt, barely suppressing the impulse to salute. The colonel's eyes measured me inch by inch. Then, pointedly ignoring Pyavka, he motioned to me to follow him into the house. Leaving his wife outside, he shut the door and said, "Which party?"

It was futile to play dumb. "You've heard of the *Bund*?"

He nodded curtly. "What is your sign?"

My party's secret emblem had been sewn on the inside of my waistband. Months of sweat and harsh soaps had largely erased it. But, from long habit, I hesitated before showing the patch to someone I didn't know.

The colonel's lips curled in an amiable sneer. "Good brother, do you think if I meant you ill I would have let you and your friend sleep peacefully until now? I asked for the sign only because, these days, too many thieves and murderers and other scum try to pass themselves off as revolutionaries."

I folded back the upper edge of my trousers and showed him the residue of my secret emblem. The colonel nodded, satisfied. "There is a train tomorrow to Irkutsk."

Although that was where we had already decided to head, I was not charmed by the abrupt way this man took charge of our lives. Officers, as I well knew, were used to giving orders and gave little thought to their cost in human suffering. But what choice did I have?

With the same brusqueness, he ordered my 'companion' and me to remain in the barn. Then he called for his horse and, without a word of explanation even to his wife, rode off.

Pyavka cornered me. "I see what's being cooked here. You, as a fellow soldier, he will help escape. And me he will send back in chains."

"That's ridiculous."

"You didn't notice how he never once looked me in the eye? At least he had that much shame. What if I'm right? What will you do then? Get on a train and wave goodbye to me?"

Frankly, I could understand his fear. But even assuming he was correct, what did he expect me to do? Insist on going back to prison with him?

"All I want," Pyavka said, "is no more than what any honest friend would do for another."

"Which is what?"

"If you don't know, there's no use our talking."

We continued this circular conversation until, toward evening, the servant woman summoned us to take dinner with the colonel and his lady.

While my friend squirmed with suspicion at the dinner table, the colonel ate sparingly and said not a word about what, if anything, he had arranged for us. Only when the maid had cleared the table did he casually mention that a certain "connection" of his was due the next day with "arrangements" for us to travel to Irkutsk.

The following day, our "connection" greeted us with an Asiatic smile. His eyes remained as blank as buttons. I didn't know whether to interpret this as discretion or simple-mindedness.

Pyavka was sulking, but I was still annoyed with him and didn't bother to translate our guide's casual estimate of the train's arrival time.

We hid until dusk when the train made its thunderous approach to the station.

Our guide mounted the ladder to the locomotive. Out of our sight, he held a long conversation with the engineer, and then climbed down to inform us we had been "hired" as stokers, giving the regular crew a few welcome days of vacation in an empty first-class compartment.

Feeling a little foolish, I asked if he was certain that the train was facing the right way. He clapped me on the shoulder with a bark of laughter at my dainty European sense of direction.

With its boiler filled by its two new stokers, the train limped back into motion. Our guide stayed on the train with us, and twice a day brought us food and water.

Stripped to the waist, we fought to keep up with the furnace's insatiable appetite. Scorched, half-blinded by sweat, I felt as though I were back at the infernal ovens of the Warsaw bakery. But then I had been at the height of my youthful vigor.

Barely aware whether it was day or night, I kept battling to transfer a mountain of coal into the furnace's roaring belly, with Pyavka seizing my arm now and then when, drugged with exhaustion, I had been about to pitch headfirst onto the blur of tracks.

While the engine growled with hunger and the muscles in my back and shoulders screamed in protest, I soon found myself reduced to making little bayonet-thrusts with my shovel. But my partner's spectacular suffering was worse.

Once, in irritation at one of his lesser complaints, I snapped, "If you can't even bear the hot breath of this feeble old furnace, how will you stand it in the Other World in whatever hellfires are reserved for professional thieves?"

He repaid me with such a pained look that I instantly regretted the cruelty of my remark.

After a few days during which we received neither food nor water, we began to suspect that our guide was no longer on the train. And, as far as I could tell, no arrangements had been made for anyone to relieve us, either.

On the morning of the fourth day, a mirage of golden domes loomed out of the mist. We were coming to a city. Could this possibly be Irkutsk? Had we been on the train for a week, already, and in our exhaustion lost track of the days?

As the engine slowed on its approach to the station, we dropped our shovels and poised ourselves to jump ship. That is, I jumped, while Pyavka clung to a handrail and stared at the moving ground in frozen terror.

I ran alongside to coax him down, in growing fear of being spotted, either from the train or by people waiting on the platform. In the end, to solve my partner's indecision, I leapt and seized his arm. He landed on top of me, and together we rolled down the embankment until we fetched up in a comfortably muddy ditch.

25

DOWN AND OUT IN CHELYABINSK

t was some hours before I realized that I should have trusted my quaint European notions of east and west. The city in which we had landed was not Irkutsk but Chelyabinsk. All that furious coal shoveling had taken us several days in the wrong direction.

I shared my discovery with Pyavka, expecting him, once more, to laugh at my 'military ineptitude.' But all he said was, "Now, what can we eat?"

I recommended that we look for a synagogue.

With a theatrical look of astonishment, Pyavka demanded to know what had brought on this sudden seizure of piety.

"Because," I said, "among Jews you can always get something to eat." This struck him as not unreasonable, and we set out to look in all the more obvious places, that is, down muddy lanes and sunless back alleys whose suffocating rows of wooden houses seemed barely able to support a vertical line. But all we found were grimy flour mills and breweries, disappointed shops and homes that were as flimsy as summer cottages, and shabby police posts from which swine-faced men in uniform issued forth each morning to fill their jail cells with the likes of us.

It took barely an hour to conclude that if there were such a thing as a synagogue in Chelyabinsk, it would take greater explorers than we to find it.

Pyavka announced that his feet hurt. Before I could stop him, he boldly entered a store and squandered a fair portion of his remaining wealth on a modish pair of shoes.

Apparently moved by my shameless look of envy, he allowed me to keep his old boots. Then, swept away by the momentum of his generosity, he went on to treat us each to a fur hat with earflaps that still smelled of rabbit. Thus respectably attired from head to toe, we made our way to a shallow lake in which we washed our shirts and as much of our bodies as we could bear to expose to water chilled by melted snow. To cap off this orgy of cleanliness, we visited a barbershop from which we emerged feeling fully the equal of any honest man in town.

With the approach of darkness, unsure whether it was safe to close our eyes, we retreated to the tangled edges of a forest and bedded down. After two days and nights in the stoker's cabin, singed almost hairless by the hellish breath of the furnace, I fell asleep immediately and was immersed in the felony of dreaming.

Late the next morning, we ventured cautiously back into the city. Our sense of smell drew us to an eating place grandly called "Cafe Łódź." Given the history of that fine Polish city, we took this to indicate that Jews would not be unwelcome there.

But even by our undemanding standards, "Łódź" was not an actual 'cafe,' nor what might generously be called a restaurant. Lodged in a building that clung to the edge of a ravine at the city's outer extremity, it was merely the windowless ruin of an abandoned warehouse. Abandoned, I presumed, because its builders had failed to allow for the sudden flood of melting snow that must have rushed through it every spring with the force of an avalanche.

Presiding over what passed for a kitchen was a small, nearsighted woman with a face so modeled in the image of a chicken that you expected her, at any moment, to aim her beak at the ground and peck for grains of corn. In contrast, her husband was a meek, blubbery giant with a barrel-like chest. He welcomed us with the uncertain smile of a newly-honest merchant.

The owners acknowledged with pride that all the vessels and utensils employed in that establishment had been derived from the city dump. Even the meat had been salvaged, collected at night from the pits into which the city's butchers tossed bones and scraps and other such offal. From these amputations, shreds of actual meat that could still be scraped off the bone were plunged into a perpetually boiling cauldron that was never allowed to cool off long enough to be cleaned.

The table and the seating were equally modest. But to Pyavka and me, after more than six months of prison, exile and flight, it was a place of sheer luxury that awakened fond memories of Warsaw, itself.

Best of all, they served a decent portion for only five kopeks. And when Pyavka yelped that he had been scalded by the soup because his wooden bowl had a large crack in it, the owner's wife calmed him with the gift of an extra bone, much as she might have offered to appease a creature of a different sort.

As we were about to tuck into our meal, Pyavka and I noticed that the other customers did not sit at the common table but carried their food outside where they ate standing up or squatting on the ground. I asked one of them why.

He flicked a black thumbnail at the ceiling, which I noticed consisted of moldering straw in which spiders and other creatures had built their nests and webs. And since the roof had, for some Siberian reason, been designed to capture every passing gust of wind, a sudden rain of stubble and spiders could erupt upon the table and into the food at any time, presumably offending those of more sensitive appetites.

Duly warned, my partner and I took our bowls outside and joined a group eating at the edge of the ravine. None of our fellow diners showed much inclination to chat. I knew from my days as a prisoner that this marked them as traditional criminals: surly, brutish, hard-drinking louts, ragged and unshorn, whose silence was no great loss to the world's accumulated wisdom.

But among his fellow outlaws, Pyavka was instantly transformed. He clearly felt as he had in Warsaw where he had been a man of consequence, a diplomat, an arbitrator, a "King."

Meanwhile, the lacerating September winds served notice of a Siberian winter drawing close with all the ferocity of an invading army. I was racked with sudden nostalgia for my old life.

I asked Pyavka to calculate for us the number of days until *Rosh Hashanah*,[66] two days on which our clouded destiny would, or would not, be inscribed in the Book of Life for the year to come.

Pyavka, however, focused on a calculation of a different sort. If I insisted upon our accepting nothing but so-called honest work, assuming that we miraculously found such employment, it would take a good year and a half to earn the price of two tickets to Warsaw, all the while in danger of arrest, fearful even to notify our grieving families that we were still alive.

"You have a better solution?" An unnecessary question. Had he not already assailed me with his envy for the practicing criminals, gentile and Jew, who scattered each night throughout the city, stealing with both hands? Instead, we squandered our days walking the streets, smoking cheap cigarettes, spinning impossible plans, and trembling in fear of every thug in uniform.

"I am a man with a profession," he said. "All I lack is a trustworthy accomplice." He fixed me with an accusing look.

"There is a shortage of thieves at the Cafe Łódź?"

"They're criminals!" he shouted in exasperation. "Lowlifes! The scum of the earth! How could I trust any of them?"

I laughed heartlessly. "So, only an honest man makes a good thief?"

"I am trying," he said with teeth-gritting patience, "to induct you into a trade that will never let you down, no matter where fate may cast you."

"I have a trade," I reminded him, although without much conviction.

"Organizing bakery apprentices to overthrow the Czar? On that you expect to support a wife and family?

Which may have been true. But I was also the son of Shloime Zalman Marateck of Vishogrod, whom, I assumed, would not do cartwheels at the news that his son had entered into a career of crime.

Pyavka raised his voice. "It is exactly blockheads like you that are keeping the Czar in power!"

"Like me?!"

"The ordinary *Vanya* – what does he care about Revolution? All he wants is to be left alone to sleep in his bed, drink his vodka and beat his wife. Tell him he has no 'freedom' and he will look at you like an ox at a circumcision.

66 Hebrew: The Jewish New Year (literally the "head" of the year)

218

Get his wife to run away with you, and he will grumble at having no one to serve him his dinner. But let somebody steal his boots or his cow and just watch him curse the Czar and his corrupt police. *That's* when he'll be ready to talk Revolution!"

I had to admit that Pyavka's regrettable philosophy was not far from the truth. But if thievery was what it took to bring on the dawn of a Just New Society, then I would never amount to anything more than a baker's apprentice. My glum silence must have persuaded Pyavka that I was softened up enough to hear his plan.

He had heard that Chelyabinsk also had a master forger who could create the passports and travel documents we needed. But, being a businessman and not a crazy radical, he expected to be paid for his services. The amount in question was a mere few hundred rubles, which, in our present state, might as well have been a hundred million.

As far as Pyavka was concerned, the only real problem was that I, his so called friend, chained his hands with pig-headed *Talmudic* scruples and was deaf to the voice of reason, even in a crisis. Especially since we were lucky enough to find ourselves in a civilized city, an ideal site for him to take up his old career. He had, in fact, already earmarked a target.

Having carelessly neglected to put my hands over my ears, I realized that this was an artist possessed by his craft. What could I do? I reached into my hidden pocket, took out our common funds, and started to divide them in half, kopek by kopek. In other words, dissolved our "partnership."

Pyavka was not only shocked, but tears of honest pain rush into his eyes. "After what we've been through together? Would I be here today without you? Would I even be alive today? My dearest friend," he said, "we will either return to Warsaw together or we will perish together."

And having delivered himself of this oration, he forced all the money back into my hands for safekeeping.

More days went by. Paralyzed as we were by my grim notions of right and wrong, our cash reserves had very nearly reached bottom. Meanwhile, Pyavka, quietly confident, bided his time. And when he judged I was demoralized enough, he once again brought up the matter of a small venture that would, in one night, enable us to travel home in dignity and comfort.

This time it was not a matter of my helping him commit an actual "crime," not even a small misdemeanor like breaking into a home or a business. All he needed me to do was something so simple that no man since Noah's Flood could possibly be arrested for it, let alone punished. All I had to do was follow him around until he had targeted some well-dressed victim and then, in some polite manner, distract the man while my accomplice picked his pockets as neatly as a surgeon removing an appendix.

What my good friend failed to consider was that, while he performed his little operation, I would have to look the victim in the eye.

Disappointed once again, yet unwilling to let me condemn him to an existence of idle honesty, Pyavka asked how I would feel about him stealing from other criminals. That could not, on any scale of morality, human or divine, be considered anything but a meting out of deserved justice.

Which, I gently drew to his attention, was also likely to get us knifed or shot.

Barely a day or so later, Pyavka came up with another proposal. This time, he had his eyes on a factory not far away, a place that turned out agricultural tools. Tomorrow was the day it paid its workers their miserable, weekly pittance. Which meant that on that very night, and that night, only, the strongbox would be stuffed with cash. On a scouting expedition the previous week, Pyavka determined that the management had such blind confidence in the Germanic precision and hardness of its safe that it did not feel the need to squander a few extra kopeks to hire a night watchman.

"So you see," he said to preempt whatever far-fetched objection I might contrive this time, "you will simply be punishing a Capitalist Exploiter."

My accursed friend began sounding almost tempting. But having had run-ins with members of Warsaw's underworld, and been involved in a couple of Wild West-type shootouts, I also knew that every word spoken by a professional criminal must be weighed, measured and filtered a hundred times before you swallowed it.

But I was half won over and only in need of a small push. In consequence, I forgot to ask one obvious question, which would only occur to me later at precisely the wrong time.

Pyavka woke me at midnight, annoyed to find I was so relaxed that I had fallen soundly asleep.

We fumbled our way out of our wooded dormitory under a moonless sky. As luck would have it, all of the city's fierce guardians of law and order appeared to have been smothered in sleep. We reached the factory without being accosted by so much as a cat.

The tall iron gate presented no serious obstacle. The way Pyavka set to work on its padlock, however, made me wonder why the noise did not wake up every householder on the street.

"We'll go over the top," he proclaimed, as though this had been his strategy all along.

I was about to sling one leg over the spiked gate when a couple of bellowing watchdogs exploded under my feet. *That* was the question I had forgotten to ask. The dogs flashed their avid fangs and fiery tongues at us, and hurled themselves against the bars of the gate as though hoping to tear off at least one of our legs. Before I knew it, I was back outside and running like the wind, with Pyavka panting and trampling behind me.

Back in the forest, I rolled on the ground, laughing with hysterical relief. Pyavka was furious to see me take the matter so lightly. "With anyone competent," he said, "I would, at this moment, be sitting in front of an open safe, stuffing my pockets. Do you realize what you cost me tonight?"

"The question, good brother, is how you would have gotten away on one leg?"

At which Pyavka, not being entirely without humor, allowed himself to cough up a lump of dry laughter.

26

EVERYONE COMES TO CAFÉ LÓDZ

As September ran its stormy course and we awoke, mornings, on a bed of frost, my friend announced that he would no longer sleep in the forest. Not when, if not for me and my "womanly" scruples, he might already be home with his wife. Oh yes, it was all well and good for a feather-headed idealist like me to turn up my nose at such a bourgeois trade as common thievery, but what alternative did I propose?

I agreed that we may not be able to sleep under the stars much longer. "But what else can we do?"

"Nothing," Pyavka said bitterly. "We'll live in the woods until we freeze to death. But at least you will die an honest man."

Infected by my comrade's desperation to return home, and eager to encourage what might be a turn toward repentance, I began to think, again, about *Rosh Hashanah*, when Jews in more civilized places assembled and prayed for a good year. The High Holy Days were less than a week away and there I was, in exile within our Exile, a castaway among castaways.

I decided to ask the distinguished owner of the Cafe Łódź whether there might be such a thing as a synagogue in his desolate city. He gave the matter several seconds of his deepest thought, and then referred me to his chicken-wife whom, he confessed, was the 'scholar' in the family.

Busily stripping shreds of meat from a bone of dinosaur dimensions, she could only shrug. "I have a prayer book, if you want it," she allowed, "although it doesn't have all the pages. He," she singed her husband with a scornful look, "used some of them to roll cigarettes. As for a synagogue …" She choked with laughter at the thought. "You can make one right here. My customers will be your congregation."

The husband also laughed and, frankly, I laughed with him. By this time, I had lived, worked, fought and prayed with almost every manner of Jew, from exotic Georgians, fierce as wild Indians, to glum, Russian-style Marranos.[67] But expecting to make up a congregation out of the dregs, Jewish and otherwise, who constituted the clientele of the Cafe Łódź seemed like nothing but a bad joke.

Pyavka, on the other hand, was charmed by the idea. To my surprise, I discovered that he fancied himself a talented cantor and could not wait to demonstrate his skills.

Since we needed a quorum of at least ten adult male Jews, Pyavka canvassed our fellow diners and asked whether they would care to join us for two days of prayer. They didn't exactly jump to their feet. But Pyavka was not discouraged. To him, the criminal mind was an open book. With great dignity, he simply let everyone know what time the service would begin the following day, with or without them.

The next morning at the precisely appointed hour, Pyavka and I arrived to find ourselves the only congregants. (This being a sacred occasion, I refrained from asking my friend when he had suddenly acquired a gold watch.) Even the cafe owner and his wife were nowhere in sight. But they had left us a tattered prayer book and a large gray *tallis* that had been somewhat diminished by moth holes, and not very skillfully patched.

Pyavka mantled himself in the *tallis* and, before my eyes, underwent an astounding transformation. His long-untended copper beard that had lent him the aspect of a low-grade charlatan suddenly framed a profile radiant with other-worldliness. Surely the Gates of Repentance were open even to those who had gone astray on the harsh plains of Siberia. This being the season of forgiveness, I was prepared to accept that no Jewish soul was ever totally lost. No doubt it was only Pyavka's laudable desire to make a comfortable life for his family that had diverted him onto the hard path of criminality.

67 "Secret Jews" who had been forced to convert to Christianity but still practiced Judaism privately

By mid-morning, the congregation had grown to six tentative men and the cafe-owner's wife who, with admirable modesty, had put up a ragged curtain to separate the men's section from the women's. Gradually, more men ambled in, hands in pocket, intending perhaps to scoff or, at best, stay a moment or two. But something in Pyavka's voice seemed to penetrate their souls and most of them, Jew and gentile, stayed on, mute, respectful and only mildly bored.

Intending to save the full power of his voice for the *Musaf*[68] service, Pyavka paused and invited the cafe-owner to take his place for a while. Our host obediently stepped forward, accepted the mantle of the *tallis* and slung the ends of it over his shoulders. He picked up the prayer book, opened his mouth and – silence. He must have suddenly remembered that he could not read Hebrew. But he bravely tried to chant what must have sounded to him like prayers until some of his more knowledgeable customers stood up and tactfully dragged him from our makeshift pulpit.

I looked around. While my back had been turned, our congregation had grown to nearly fifty men, including some I had never seen before. Unfortunately, not one of our new congregants knew a single word of the prayers. In desperation, Pyavka snatched the abandoned *tallis* and draped it around me.

For a moment I felt overwhelmed. Never in my life had I led a congregation. But with a little prompting from my partner, it all came rushing back. The melodies that once had stirred my heart were still capable of extracting tears from my eyes. And so I thanked the Almighty who had (thus far) kept me from stumbling, while I poured out my pleas on behalf of assorted highwaymen, housebreakers and pickpockets. And though I failed to raise any responding echoes from anyone other than Pyavka, the congregation's very silence made me feel a curious kind of solidarity with even those tainted souls. I imagined my words entering the hearts of the congregation's murderers and thieves, gentile and Jew, alike. But I still took care not to let any of my fellow worshippers stand close enough to pick my pockets.

Afterwards, in excellent spirits, we sat down and pounded on the tables, clamoring for our mid-day meal. We cheered as the owner's wife emerged from the kitchen carrying a large, steaming wooden platter almost as heavy as she was.

68 Hebrew: Additional prayer said on Sabbath and holidays

We fell upon our portions, but only for the first mouthful. By then our noses warned us that whatever dark magic she usually worked in the kitchen couldn't disguise the fact that this animal flesh was not merely spoiled but had already begun to putrefy.

Alerted by our mutterings, she popped out of the kitchen, face and apron blackened with wood smoke, and demanded, "Why aren't you eating?"

No one said a word. The silence grew embarrassing. I looked to my friend Pyavka to exercise a bit of diplomacy, but he avoided my eye. I finally opened my mouth and said to our hostess, "It seems we're a little late for this meal."

"Late? What do you mean 'late?' I just served it."

I explained that, for this particular piece of meat we were, in fact, quite a bit late. Seeing her look of dismay, I conceded that, no doubt three months earlier it would have been delicious.

With a look of utter scorn, she padded back into the kitchen, spilled a torrent of abuse upon her bewildered husband, and did not show her face again until evening. We looked at one another in resignation and made a holiday meal out of gray, glutinous chunks of bread and a basket of shriveled Siberian apples.

Purely from the standpoint of attendance, things went about equally well the Second Day of the holiday with more than half of our congregants returning for that day's prayers.

That night, as Pyavka and I returned to the Cafe Łódź for dinner, we were startled to witness a barefaced act of armed robbery. Two of our fiercer-looking cutthroats went from man to man and, at knifepoint, extracted money from each. Should I really have been surprised that neither Pyavka's prayers nor mine had softened their hearts?

But no knife-blade threatened either of us. Perhaps our new status as religious functionaries had earned us some immunity. If so, how long would it last?

As they approached our table, the two cutthroats' faces split open in broken smiles and they dumped their loot in front of us.

"What's this?" I asked.

"For your work these last two days. Divide it between you. Divide it honestly!" they threatened.

It was the first legitimate money I had earned in over six months! Flushed with enthusiasm for my newly discovered aptitude, I leapt up on the bench and assured my fellow diners and idlers that, never in my life, had I prayed in an atmosphere of such broken-hearted remorse. Swept along by my own eloquence, I wished them all a year of good fortune, a short exile and a speedy reunion with their loved ones back in Europe, and assured them that, come the Revolution, there would be a new social order. It would be governed by universal justice that would provide enough work and food for all so that no man ever needed to steal or lift a hand against his neighbor, again.

This last observation did not go over well, and Pyavka tugged me down by my coat before our newfound admirers regretted having spent good money on nothing more than their spiritual betterment.

Comforting as it was to be so warmly accepted by the underworld of Chelyabinsk, this did not free us from having to think about tomorrow. The money we earned would keep us from going hungry for, at most, a week or two. But it did not bring us any closer to the nameless forger in Irkutsk who was our only hope of ever getting back to Poland.

Pyavka, I regretted to see, was back to his old practice of looking on the dark side. "What if it turns out that this printer of yours has been arrested? Or died of old age? Leaving us stranded thousands of miles from home."

After correcting his impression that the man was "my" printer, I pointed out that we were already such a hopeless distance from Warsaw that even a few thousand miles more amounted to barely a blink of an eye. And reaching Irkutsk, I reminded him, would bring us that much closer to America, a country we knew to be so disorderly that anyone who bought a ticket was allowed to ride on a train, and no policeman had the right to demand his passport.

But Pyavka's quarrel was over something more immediate. Bitterly envious of our fellow thieves and outcasts, he pointed out that, while we spent our days in squalor and anxiety, doing nothing more productive than wearing out our shoes and trembling at the sight of copper buttons, the working thieves scattered merrily through the city each night and stole with both hands.

His complaint reminded me that my partner was not your common criminal. He was an artist, driven to maintain certain standards of excellence in his challenging vocation. I was convinced that, even if there were no money to be made from stealing, he would continue to exercise his skills as lovingly as a young prodigy who spent endless hours scraping on his violin with no assurance of worldly recognition.

This was not to say that I had given up hope of reforming him. The only question was what else could a man of his obvious talents do to support his family?

"We could give lessons," I proposed one day.

"In what, stealing?"

"What about tutoring young ladies in French, a language essential for advancement in society, even here?"

"What does it pay?"

"Whatever it pays, at least it's honest work."

"Do you know French?"

"Don't you?"

"Who in Warsaw needed a fourth language?"

"Maybe we could teach Polish?"

"That would help young ladies advance in society?"

Thus ended our first and last discussion of how to support ourselves honestly.

27
OSIP'S TABLE

We had been living in the woods outside the city, creeping in tentatively each day to try to find something to eat and a way to get to Irkutsk when, behind our backs, the non-criminal householders of Chelyabinsk suddenly lost patience with being plucked by every felon who blew into town on the Siberian wind. But instead of merely cursing the plague under their breaths, they petitioned their Military Governor to do something about it. It must have been the first time that the citizens of the town expected this man to perform a useful function and, to their astonishment, he obliged them beyond all expectations.

Thus, early one morning, without a hint of fair warning, the city was flooded with Cossacks, militia and other such riffraff that the law had empowered with its uniform. These good servants of the Czar began combing through each neighborhood, arresting people right and left. Those who had neither documents nor a fixed residence were given a good thrashing and put in chains, to be shipped to some camp whose inmates had been dying faster than the Mother Country could replace them. A dozen of our fellow castaways at the excellent Cafe Łódź had also been shot or severely clubbed. This made for a rather sour atmosphere and left Pyavka and me eager to move on. But how, and with what?

Venturing deeper into the forest in search of shelter, we came upon a decaying lakeside cabin belonging to an elderly fisherman. We didn't have time to consider the wisdom of counting on the goodwill of the owner, but fortunately Osip was a staunch Christian whose grandfather had been banished to Siberia for some unnamable political crime. He needed only to be assured that, despite my villainous appearance, I was not a professional thief. About Pyavka he had no doubt, recognizing him instantly as a born aristocrat.

The old man trapped fish by sitting up all night in his boat, and watching over his nets. It was his ill fortune that, every year, there were not only fewer fish (each of which, he assured us, he knew by name), but fewer people able to afford his merchandise. If not for the few Sabbath-observing Jewish householders in Chelyabinsk (of whose existence we had been ignorant), he would have no customers at all. Because the Russians – "a curse upon them!" – would only buy his fish when it had begun to stink and he was forced to sell it for next to nothing.

My partner and I had just begun to feel secure when, on a treacherously starlit night while Osip was out on the lake, we were roused by the sound of scattered shots and avid hooves heading in our direction. Moments later, stray bullets punched through Osip's hut, obliging us to dive through an unglazed window. Outside, I stuffed Pyavka's ungainly head under a thick patch of sweetbriar and kept a firm hand on his neck to let him know that, should he move or even breathe aloud, I would smother him. Meanwhile, other fugitives raced past, wide-eyed with terror, hunted like rabbits by a column of mounted Cossacks. The horsemen easily caught up with those who had been running, but moved too quickly to spot our shallow conceal-ment. We remained facedown, trying to block out the pitiless cries of the pursuers and pursued.

At the first light of dawn, I risked looking around. In the moisture-heavy stillness of night, I found no trace of Cossacks. Chelyabinsk, itself, seemed to have sunk into a sea of fog up to its glistening domes. But we didn't trust that it was safe to return to town. Thus, much as it pained me to continue burdening his hospitality, we returned to Osip's hut.

Seeing us return, the old man turned white with shock. When he had arrived back from the lake and found that we weren't there, he took for granted that we had been slaughtered. He had even gone to look for us and found several bodies that, he assured us, had not included ours.

Pyavka politely let on that he was not only alive, but hungry. At which Osip, with a shrug of regret, showed us his breadbox. It contained not so much as a crumb. And because of heavy winds, he had been unable to haul in his nets last night. As a result, he had no money with which to buy bread.

I gave Osip one of our remaining rubles and asked if he would buy bread and herring for the three of us. He returned some hours later, loaded down not only with several fat herrings but a five-pound loaf of bread. We fell upon the food and tore it apart with our hands. Osip, gentle soul that he was, looked surprised that we expected him to share "our" meal.

But he spoiled our enjoyment by reporting on last night's toll. Of the convicts who had fled into the forest, eight had been shot, sabered or clubbed to death, and an unknown number had been wounded or captured. The fugitives, though, had fought back with knives and iron bars, leaving one of their pursuers dead of stab wounds and several others with broken bones. This so infuriated the Cossacks that they were rampaging all over town. Finding few criminals left on whom to let out their indignation, they had begun to mistreat the very householders who had most urgently called for their help. These same good citizens now prayed for Chelyabinsk to return to the peaceful state of being robbed by professional thieves, men who at least knew when to stop.

We knew it was not safe to remain so close to the city, but Osip said it would not be possible to board a train to Irkutsk. The city was still so thick with uniforms that we would never get near the station. However, if we were willing to hold out one more day, someone called "Baba" would arrive and guide us to safety.

That night, while we tried to formulate another avenue of escape, a storm whipped the lake into waves that leapt as high as the windows of Osip's hut. The wind threatened to tear off the roof, and I felt as though a hungry wave could fall upon the frail cabin and drag us all into the black depths of the lake.

During a brief lull in the storm, whose purpose I suspected was only to gather more strength, we heard a chilling sound – the whinny of a horse.

Osip peered through a gap in the wall and in a choked whisper reported a Cossack patrol, soaked, and in foul temper, cradling their rifles for instant use.

"Do you know how to row?" Osip asked me.

I was touched by the old man's offer. I had grown up on the banks of a river. But it is one thing to glide along our civilized Vistula and quite another to navigate a raging Siberian lake. If Osip's boat sank or we failed to bring it back, he would be left to starve. And yet he offered it without a second thought.

Pyavka chose that moment to offer his opinion that being shot was a more merciful way to meet his end than drowning.

"Then stay here if you like," I snapped,

"What's on the other side?" Pyavka now asked, sounding like a man deciding where to take his family on holiday.

"Rocks, trees, swamps. But the Cossacks are not likely to follow you," Osip said.

"What if they shoot at us while we're rowing?"

"I thought you preferred a quick death," I said.

"Not without a proper burial."

"Do as you please." With one knee on the windowsill, I prepared to jump. But first I promised Osip that we would bring back the boat as soon as the storm, and the Cossacks, let up. We arranged for a signal by which the old man could let us know when it was safe to return.

The little boat, tethered to a tree, danced at the water's edge, skittish as an untamed colt. Pyavka took one look at it and announced, "I'd rather stay and be shot."

I shouted above the wind that staying with Osip would not only endanger our generous protector, but that he, Pyavka, would sure be dead by morning and his wife would never know the location of his grave.

Mentioning his family was my most compelling argument with Pyavka. Although he wavered, I took him by the neck and threw him into the boat. He took a seat, plainly relieved at not having had to make the decision, himself.

Meanwhile, we heard the Cossack patrol heading our way.

Osip untied the rope and, with his bare feet braced against the slippery clay, gave us a hard shove into the water. Although dense curtains of raindrops hung between the Cossacks and us, we would make a target hard to miss until we were at least halfway across the lake.

Pyavka took the tiller while I tried to row. Mountains of water erupted under our feet, tossing the boat high as a ball, and slamming it back down while snatching playfully at my oars. There was no question of trying to navigate. All our strength and ingenuity went into shifting from side to side to keep from tipping over.

A faint thread of silver gave us a glimpse of the opposite shore on the horizon. Encouraged, Pyavka stood up for a better look and nearly lost his balance. Lurching to pull him back, I dropped one of the oars into the water. I lunged for it, but almost ended up head first in the water, myself. Pyavka seemed to find all this highly entertaining. "If only you could see yourself!"

I admitted that I probably would not want to be looked over by a prospective father-in-law just then. But Pyavka looked so woebegone that it gave me a pang to realize how close I had come to losing my only companion in the world.

By the pale glow of a freshly washed sky, I saw that we were not even halfway across the lake. But ahead of us lay the small, stony ledge of either an island or a peninsula. As I paddled there with a single oar, I was bathed in sweat. Hearing the echo of shots behind us, I shuddered at the thought that Osip might have paid for his hospitality to us. In twisting my head to look behind me, I lost sight of the landing, and heard a harsh scraping beneath my feet. I feared that, in my indecent lust to survive, I had wrecked Osip's only source of livelihood. But I managed to beach the boat safely between two jutting rocks.

We clambered up a shallow cliff on our hands and knees, until we reached a level spot where we waited for the miserly sun to melt the ice in our bones.

The next time I opened my eyes, I judged that it was close to noon. The lake, which last night felt like a turbulent ocean, was less than half a mile across. I squinted, hoping to spot a signal from Osip, but there was neither a warning nor any indication that our friend was still alive.

233

Now that we were safe, Pyavka announced he was in mourning. And with no encouragement from me, proceeded to share his grief. He confessed that, despite his youthful appearance, he was more than fifty years old, which was not the best age to be a fugitive in Siberia. He also claimed remorse for having chosen a profession of which his parents had disapproved. In punishment for which, who knew if he would ever see them, again? In his melancholy, Pyavka vowed that the moment we reached the other side of the lake, he would give Osip the last of his money to buy us a revolver.

I pointed out we were in Siberia, not the Wild West.

Pyavka shook his head. "Not for self-defense. The revolver will be for us to kill each other, as a final act of brotherly friendship."

"You mean, I kill you, and then you kill me?"

He agreed that this would be difficult to do, and almost smiled. "But you can kill me and then yourself."

"And what if, after I've shot you, I don't keep my end of the bargain?"

"I promise, once I'm dead, I will not hold it against you if you change your mind."

Now that we were both able to laugh at the idea, I told Pyavka that he could do as he pleased but I would not give Czar Nicolai the satisfaction of seeing Yakov Marateck do away with himself.

Through the corner of my eye, I picked up a sudden glint of mirrored sunlight. I shouted to Pyavka, who had found a comfortable place for a nap, "We're going back."

"In broad daylight?"

I didn't need him to tell me it would be safer to return after dark. But Osip needed his boat and I had given my word.

"What guarantee do you have that the Cossacks aren't waiting to pick us off?"

"Osip signaled it was safe."

"What if they forced him to signal? What if they held a gun to his head?"

"They're not that smart," I said without complete conviction. Pyavka's professional experience might have given him a deeper insight into villainy than I could claim.

"How many flashes did you see?" he asked.

"Three."

"He said he would flash five times." At that, Pyavka rolled over to go back to sleep.

"I might have counted wrong. I'm tired, too."

"The captain of a ship has no business being tired. Once, when I was on a cruise in the Baltic—"

"Are you coming or not?" I slid down the rock and freed the boat. It took only minutes to row back across last night's tumultuous sea.

When we reached the opposite shore, Osip helped us beach the boat, and told us that, moments after we had left, five rain-soaked, mounted Cossacks entered the clearing, their rifles sniffing at every leaf. As they circled the hut, one recommended riddling it with bullets, and then setting it aflame. But their officer gallantly dismounted and kicked in the door.

The Cossacks hadn't merely searched the cabin; they had torn it apart. Osip's mattress, punctured and slashed by bayonets, had barely any straw left in it. And when they left, Osip heard the officer say, "They can't have gone far. Spread out."

Without a glimmer of reproach, Osip added, "In your place I would not stay here much longer."

Of this we needed no convincing. Only yesterday, near the station, he saw honest travelers with documents and tickets randomly abused, beaten, robbed and arrested if they protested.

The question was how far we could get on the few rubles we had left. Osip agreed our position was difficult.

Hearing this, Pyavka accused me, again, of saving him against his will. "Who appointed you my keeper? The other night, if you had let them shoot me, I would now be out of my misery."

"Who told you to become a thief?"

"Who told you to become a revolutionary?"

"After what I saw in the war, I could not be anything else."

"The same goes for me."

"You were in the war? Since when?"

"I am always at war against injustice and inequality. A thief is the only true revolutionary."

His claim was so outrageous that it stopped my breath. "You are not really a criminal," I said. "You're an impostor, an actor, a charlatan."

This got his attention. "How am I a charlatan?"

"A professional criminal is someone without conscience and without fear. He is not a person who would, the moment any little thing went wrong, rush to kill himself." And once more I threatened to leave without him.

Osip had been carefully attending our circuitous argument. It must have already occurred to him that Jews were crazy, but only then did he fathom the full depth of our madness.

Not feeling safe in Osip's cabin any longer, but having nowhere else to go, Pyavka and I crawled under shrubs at some distance from the hut. For the first time in two days, I allowed myself to lose consciousness.

A burst of sunlight seared my eyelids. Birdsong pierced the air, and treetops swayed, shedding flurries of black autumn leaves. I sat up and rubbed my arms. It felt like a glorious day to be alive. Then I remembered where we were.

We crept back to Osip's hut where we met a small, squarely built woman about half his size and age whom he called "Baba." This failed to make clear whether she was his wife, daughter, aunt or some other kind of female relation. Apparently, he had briefed her that my friend and I were Jews, because she assured us that the pot contained no meat.

What pot? I saw then that, aside from bread and herring, there was a steaming cauldron swaddled in a large rag. I ran to awaken Pyavka, who came in rumpled and surly but, faced with both food and a woman, was at once on his most courtly behavior.

Baba lifted the lid, handed us each a wooden spoon, and urged us to eat. I was so hungry I did not look too closely into the pot. I simply stabbed my spoon into it and filled my mouth repeatedly, moving faster and faster. There was an agreeable taste of kasha and beets and cabbage, and only a hint of machine oil. When we were finished, the pot was so empty that only the most rabid housewife would have felt it needed washing.

Baba told us she had once worked for Jews and learned not only their language but also their customs. Her hope, at one time, had been to marry a Jew. Not any particular Jew, merely someone who lived by the same admirable practices as had her employers.

I asked what had happened with her plans.

She scorched Osip with an accusing smile. "*He* had already made me pregnant." Osip glowed with pride.

Switching to a slangy Yiddish, Baba went on to relate what a bitter thing it was to be married to a Russian although, she admitted, Osip only beat her when he was drunk.

I tried to console her by assuring her that a Russian husband differed from a Jewish husband only in one way: the more a Russian beat his wife, the more he showed he loved her, whereas a Jewish wife was forced to do without such direct proof of her husband's affection.

When we were ready to leave, Baba directed us to the edge of an open field from which we could glimpse the roof of the train station. She advised us to lie down and not move until she returned with our tickets. If it was safe to show ourselves, she would cough three times. If she returned in silence, it meant she was being followed.

"And what do we do then?" Pyavka asked.

She shrugged, which was as good an answer as any.

Hours passed. It was getting close to midnight. I knew there was no reason to be anxious; our train was not due for some hours, and yet …

Shortly before two o'clock in the morning, I heard a single, polite cough as Baba came toward us, smiling. She had not only bought our tickets but, with the money left over, had gone into the city, awakened a shopkeeper, and bought us a bottle of "Red Label" vodka.

Pyavka uncorked the bottle and took a deep pull. I reminded him that our train was due any second, and it might be wise to remain sober until we were safely aboard.

My friend scowled, and accused me of begrudging him one of life's few pleasures. I shrugged, and charged on ahead. When I approached the depot, I circled it and watched. After seeing no men in uniform, I decided to risk going in to find out when the next train was due.

A yawning old man at the window told me that in a few minutes there would be an eastbound train that was not listed on any schedule.

Electrified, I ran back to fetch Pyavka, returning to the station just as the train signaled its departure. Barely keeping pace with the last car, I seized one of the handrails. With the other hand, I grabbed my friend's arm, opened the door, and flung him and then myself into the car.

There were empty benches for us to stretch out upon. Pyavka lay down, and was promptly rocked to blissful sleep by the rhythm of the wheels.

Although I, too, had been known to fall into a stupor at moments when danger wasn't far away, it always impressed me how easily Pyavka could put aside concern for his personal safety when there was an occasion to sleep. He, apparently, had more confidence in my loyalty to him than I had in his to me though, truth be told, he had never given me any reason to suspect that he didn't value my life as much as his own. Whereas I had threatened, and intended, to leave him behind on countless occasions.

28

THE 'PARIS' OF SIBERIA

My bones felt a sudden silence, and I realized that the train had slowed down. I consulted my watch, forgetting that it had stopped working several days earlier, probably for good. It didn't matter. At that time of year, I knew that the Siberian sun didn't rise until at least mid-morning.

I pressed my eye to a gap in the train's wall. This time, the station coming up really was Irkutsk. The last time I had passed through this city, I was a soldier on his way home from war. Not a war in which we had been victorious, but at least my body was intact. This time, however, I was an escaped convict, a revolutionary, a wanted man. Last time, a veritable Queen of charity had fed us and treated us like human beings, in gratitude for which I had wanted to offer her my heart. Now I felt ashamed to do so. The town of Irkutsk, which had once held a magical place in my heart, was now just another burg in which I hoped to obtain forged documents that made it possible for undesirables like Pyavka and me to leave it as soon as possible.

I shook Pyavka's foot. He yawned and stretched and demanded to know for what good reason I had woken him.

"It's Irkutsk. We're getting off."

The notion of once again walking on proper streets seemed to revive Pyavka's spirits. Suddenly, he was impatient to get under way. But then he had second thoughts. Perhaps, he said, owing to my background as a soldier, I ought to take a *drozhky* into the city, alone, and find the printer who could furnish us with passports and travel permits.

The Jewish subdivision of Warsaw's underworld must have been very short of talent if such a model of timidity could rise to be its "King."

I reminded Pyavka that it was still dark. And that between the city and us lay a river. In a region swarming with outlaws, vagrants, exiles and runaways, the bridges were certain to be patrolled. Best to wait for daylight when we might lose ourselves among others headed for the city. But from his long acquaintance with police procedure, Pyavka assured me that, while it was dark and cold outside, any normal policeman would have found himself a warm place to sleep.

We jumped off the train. The gas-lit platform was packed with lost souls, fellow castaways who had no foothold on the world. On tiptoe, we picked our way across the platform, careful not to step on any faces. In the faint light, the huddled, gray bodies looked as though they had been camped there for so long that they wore a fine blanket of dust. From the few scabbed ankles I could see beneath their shredded clothing, I could tell that many of them were fugitives like us. I marveled at their audacity to sleep where, at any moment, a policeman could give a good kick and demand to see their papers.

I soon noticed that my friend's criminal mentality had not deserted him, despite having been forced to abstain. He had begun looking at the litter of inanimate bodies in light of his own regrettable expertise. "A person could pick up a good few rubles right here." He seemed prepared to demonstrate how simple it would be to work one's way along the sooty wall and, without awakening the sleeper, remove what little money he may have hidden in whatever rag he used for a pillow. Not to mention the ease with which one could pick the fat pockets of honest travelers passing through.

"One or two weeks' work," he assured me, "and we'll have enough for train fare back to Warsaw."

I didn't share his easy confidence. "Here I thought you were a true professional," I scolded. "And yet it never occurred to you that if only one of these people catches you at it, the lot of them will tear you to pieces."

"What a pessimist you are! I don't know what possessed me to let you escape with me."

Before I could connect my fist with his face, he flung his arms about me. "Forgive me! You're absolutely right. In a strange city, it is best not to trust anyone."

We took the precaution of dividing what was left of his wealth before we set out. It amounted to three rubles and twenty kopeks. Before letting me go, Pyavka made me swear my most solemn oath that, no matter what temptations or disasters awaited me in this great, unknown city, I would not abandon him at the railway station, leaving him like a shipwrecked sailor clinging to a plank.

We bade each other farewell with enough tears and good wishes to send a regiment of infantry to fight the Turks, until I shouted at him to stop his blubbering because we were drawing attention.

Outside, the ghostly fog had thickened. I asked some of the coachmen who huddled against the station wall how much they proposed to charge to take me into the city. I was greeted with such laughter as would have gratified any comedian. Then it dawned on me that I must not look like someone whose pockets were bulging with small change. But since it was still before dawn and I was the only customer on the horizon, I managed to stir up a shriveled, sullen creature who agreed to take me into town for a mere fifty kopeks.

We rode onto the bridge unchallenged, but halfway across I was jarred back to reality when my yawning *izvoshchik*[69] turned around and demanded, "Where to?"

Foolish question. "Into the city," I shouted back.

"Where in the city?"

It had never occurred to me that my beggarly fifty kopeks entitled me to the luxury of door-to-door service.

I wanted to go to a place where no Jew was ever turned away – a *shul*,[70] a House of Study, what in more elegant corners of the world is called a synagogue. But that was insufficiently precise. Apparently, this old man was not the kind of gentile who counted Jews among his closest friends.

---

69 Russian: Taxi driver

70 Yiddish: Synagogue

While I pondered how to instruct him, we continued clattering along a broad country road lined with tall trees. I could barely detect the city's golden domes beckoning through icy streaks of morning mist.

Above the warped thunder of his wheels, my driver again shouted, "Where to?" this time with less patience.

Ahead of us, the specter of a policeman on horseback trotted sleepily toward the city. As I began to slide down in my seat, the driver, fed up with my silence, slyly suggested that we stop and ask him for directions.

"I know what sort of a place he'll find for me," I said with a coarse wink, as one outcast to another, and instructed the driver to keep going. He laughed, and cracked his whip.

We reached the city's edge, a landscape of log houses, small garden plots and streets paved with lumber and mud. My driver pointed to a raw wooden building I recognized as what Siberians called a 'tea house,' a place not limited to selling bitter Chinese tea. With a compassionate leer, he urged me to dismount and have something to eat. Then, perhaps, it would come back to me what pressing business had brought me to Irkutsk in the first place.

Driven by a sudden, uncontrollable lust for hot, sugared tea, I jumped down. Before I could change my mind, my driver tugged at his reins and raced back to the depot.

I approached the building and took a cautious look inside. It held the customary long, rough tables and benches where, even at that unlikely hour, furry men sat enveloped in such clouds of smoke as would be created by setting fire to fourteen straw mattresses. Between slurps of tea or vodka, some of the denizens added to the cheer by croaking out a gloomy Siberian song that would not have been out of place at a funeral.

I arranged my clothing Cossack-style, with my shirt pulled over my trousers and cinched by a piece of rope, and one pants leg tucked into a boot-top, hoping to be taken for an ordinary *katzap*. And then indulged myself by buying a cube of sugar. By custom, that entitled me to all the hot tea I could drink until the sugar had melted in my mouth.

I slurped the boiling, coal-black water and listened to my fellow drinkers lift each other's spirits with hair-raising tales of demons, devils, Jews and other such unnatural phenomena. I considered it prudent to keep my mouth shut and remember that my freedom, not to mention my friend's, depended upon attracting as little notice as possible.

Once the sugar in my mouth had fully melted away, I decided that tea was not a sufficiently sociable drink to break ice with hardened frontier types. So for five kopcks, I splurged on a glass of vodka.

Within minutes someone asked me if I had come to town to work on the new road being built. I responded with a rude shrug designed to mark me as a man who did not discuss his personal business with strangers. I bought another lump of sugar and thriftily used it to filter several more glasses of tea strong enough to stain furniture.

Feeling my bladder press against my belt, I stepped outside to relieve myself in an explosion of foam. Feeling pleasantly lighthearted, I returned to hear two factions reach a climax in their solemn and circular wrangling about Jews. One side maintained they were all creatures of Satan and, therefore, not fit to live on this earth. To my pleasant surprise, there was a vocal minority that held that since Jews were kept, by law, out of the more respectable ways of making a living, one could not totally blame them for trying to stay alive by whatever devilish means our benevolent Czar had not yet closed off to them.

One of the drinkers pounded me on the shoulder and demanded to know my views on the subject. I cautiously let on that I, too, felt Jews were entitled, like any other living creature, to do what they could to survive.

And, when no one offered to break my nose, I asked with the utmost casualness, "*Are* there any Jews in Irkutsk?"

At this, my new friends exploded with laughter. "Jews in Irkutsk? The Devil himself couldn't find you a Jew on the street. They're all in their Jewish church, begging forgiveness for the sins they'd committed all week. And every Saturday, their God forgives them all over again."

Too late did I wish that, instead of indulging my momentary lust for a glass of scalding tea, I had simply demanded that my driver deliver me to a 'church of the Jews.' Crushed by loneliness, I wanted to go in search, by foot if necessary, of people who might look upon me as a fellow human being, even Queen Esther whose staff, I hoped, would not remember me.

But my feet were nailed to the floor. Had I truly had only one glass of vodka, or had I lost count? Judging by the few coins that remained in my pocket, I must have been drinking for far longer than I thought.

Somehow, in all the merriment, I failed to notice the arrival of a shaggy giant in a bearskin coat, but with the features of a lost child. He pounded on a table for silence, held up a letter and demanded that someone read it to him.

As it passed from hand to hand, each drinker scowled sagely at the scrawl but gave no sign of being able to translate it into a human language. In the end, the barkeep himself snatched the page, squinted at it, frowned and delivered himself of the words, "Dear Parents."

But that was as far as he got. Exhausted, he cried, "To the Devil!" and gave back the letter.

I suddenly found all eyes on me. "Brother, do you know how to read?" I hesitated. I had wanted to be taken for a road-worker, not an educated man. I knew that, in certain parts of the country, a man who knew how to read was automatically suspected of being a revolutionary, a Jew, or a government agent. But the vodka had addled my judgment, and the large man looked so pitiably anxious to know what the letter contained that I agreed to decipher it for him. Heart pounding, I took care to make my efforts look and sound about as easy as splitting rocks with a large hammer.

The news from his son, I announced, was that the pigs were faring well. And that the son's wife was temporarily incapacitated due to a beating the letter-writer had given her for having been found, apparently not for the first time, in the tall wheat with one of the neighbor's boys. Whom he would already have killed except that this particular young man still owed him four rubles. The rest of the news was equally routine. The giant beamed with bleary-eyed joy at the excellent tidings.

My exhausting recital left me the focus of boisterous approval. What cleverness, to have been able to extract such a wealth of information from a few lines of ink scratches! One of the drinkers accused me facetiously of being a Jew, at which I laughed as heartily as the rest.

A wagon with barred windows rattled by outside. Grinning, one of the drinkers said, "Some escaped prisoners are being hauled back to where they came from."

Suddenly feeling the effects of the vodka, I steadied myself against the rough-hewn wood on which my empty glasses were stacked, and asked, "Where were they arrested?" hoping that my voice didn't reveal my anxiety.

"The railroad station."

Everyone found this not only hilarious, but also proof that, despite all appearances, there was still justice in the Czar's domain.

I was oppressed by the thought that my poor bumbling friend, drugged with luxurious sleep, might well be among those rounded up. I dared not speculate how he would get along in prison this time without someone as "worldly" as me looking out for him.

"Poor fellows," I said cautiously.

"To the devil with them. Our Little Father knows what he's doing. Jews and revolutionaries. If he packed them off to prison, he had his reasons. Let them serve out their time like anyone else." No one disagreed.

Despite the storm outside that had formed while I was drinking, I suddenly felt impatient to leave this place.

29

THE IRKUTSK JEWISH BENEVOLENT SOCIETY

Lowering my head like a battering ram, I made for the door and launched myself into a wall of rain. A muddy river raged across my feet, and I felt as if I were drowning in darkness. Black shards of heaven fell on me as I hunched my shoulders within the tatters of my coat. While the turbulent water threatened, with each step, to draw me into its deaths, I remembered some babbler inside the *kretchma*[71] saying that today might be *Shabbos*. Or had it been yesterday? In addition to my dignity, the brief time I spent as a chained prisoner must have also stripped away my consciousness of the Jewish calendar, without which I was no more than a heathen.

Crushed with penitence and longing, I waded through the torrential streets in search of a hospitable face. With each step, one of my boots opened its mouth, the better to collect large gulps of icy mud, while the other, lacking its sole, gleefully danced around my ankle. But there was scarcely a human being to be found. The few I managed to accost to ask where one might find a Jewish 'church' looked at me as though I were mad.

My bones trembled with exhaustion, and I didn't know how long I had been on my feet before I allowed myself to sink onto a bench in a small park to catch my breath. In fact, the feeling was so agreeable that I stretched out to appreciate it more fully.

71 Yiddish: Tavern, or bar

247

A timid hand shook my shoulder. I blinked to find my head lying on the damp, fragrant ground. My eyelids split apart to observe a small man with an intrusively dripping mustache. For some reason, he wanted to know if I was ill.

Irritated by his foolish question since he was plainly not a doctor, I assured him that I was perfectly well. But, pained by his look of disappointment, I allowed him to help me back onto my feet. While he struggled to keep me upright, I explained in my most reasonable tone that, while looking for a synagogue, I had lost my way and merely lain down for a brief rest.

He laughed, and pointed across the street to an unmistakable building that had not been there earlier. Hearing familiar sounds issuing from inside, I headed for the entrance as if I'd been shot out of a cannon. I recognized the slurred cadences of the regular weekday morning service. Although it was, by now, mid-morning, amazingly it was not yet over. Siberian Jews must be late sleepers.

A few heads turned to stare as the new face entering the synagogue. When they didn't immediately turn back to their prayer books, I followed their eyes and saw that my boots had left a trail of slime. I sat on the farthest bench, not even daring to take a prayer book into my muddy hands.

Before I knew it, several men had edged toward me and began asking the types of intrusive questions asked in any *shul* back home: Where was I from, what did I do, was I married, did I have relatives in town … ? I was among my own people, again. In fact, the friendliness around me became so intense that someone pounded on the pulpit to request what in America is called 'decorum.'

When the morning prayers concluded, these same men briskly packed up their gear and, without a glance in my direction, headed for home.

My mouth was still smiling in delusion, when someone put out the lights. I was stunned by how little time it took for the novelty of my presence to wear off. Should I have stopped one of them and confessed that I had no place to eat? Suddenly, I felt oppressed by the loneliness that must be Pyavka's only companion.

But what I had forgotten was that I probably did not strike most people as the sort of guest one fought to bring home. Disappointed by Siberian hospitality, I was about to stumble out when my passage was blocked by a stout man in a top hat.

"You have a place to eat?" he demanded.

I was not sure I liked his tone, but this was not the time to pass judgment on the manners of my betters. So I admitted, humbly, that I had neither a place to eat, nor sleep. "You will," he growled, and with a twist of his hand commanded me to follow him.

Before I could imagine the kind of delicacies that awaited me at his table, he led me outside and pointed toward the bottom of the road where an anxious little house stood surrounded by a moat-like puddle.

"You live there?"

"The Rabbi," he said, and climbed into his waiting coach, which spared me the embarrassment of asking further idiotic questions.

I gathered up my strength and splashed toward the Rabbi's house. A gaunt and sickly young man received me pleasantly enough. He explained why few people were eager to take a stranger home with them. Too many escaped criminals pretended to be Jews, it being well known that, even in this forsaken corner of the Creator's universe, only Jews seemed to know how it felt to be cold and hungry and unwanted. Grateful for his frankness, I saw no point in mentioning the obvious, namely that in some peoples' eyes I, too, might be counted among this brotherhood of undesirables.

Within moments, his wife brought me hot coffee and two buttered rolls, which disappeared in less time than it took to look at them. The Rabbi also handed me some printed coupons good for three nights' lodging and meals at the Jewish community's Guest House.

I asked him for another set of coupons for a friend who was too weak to leave the railroad station. But here, it seemed, I had overdrawn my credit. Possibly, after spending so much time in the society of hardened thieves and murderers, my voice had acquired a timbre of insincerity. Which only shows how careful one must be in choosing one's friends.

Ankle deep in what passed for a street, I didn't feel ready to undertake the long, uncertain trek back to the station. With only a small twinge of guilt, I headed for the Guest House, eager for an empty mattress and the chance of a quiet nap.

The dormitory was a large, bleak but clean-smelling room with twenty beds lined up in two rows. Its caretaker had arms like the blacksmith who had welded my leg irons but keen, compassionate eyes. Far from making a to-do about identification, he smiled and said I was the first person with a legitimate ticket he had seen all week.

I asked, "How often do the police raid this place?"

He smiled mournfully. "About half our budget goes into paying them off. It doesn't leave much for food, but it's easier on everybody's nerves."

I located an empty cot and stretched out luxuriously, for once without fear of being robbed or assaulted. Not only was I among Jews, but I had nothing left worth stealing, other than the meal tickets that I had carefully marked with my name. Ignoring the noise made by the other guests who were playing cards, and the sting of bedbugs feasting on what was left of my blood, I slept like a stone until someone shook me and told me there was dinner on the table.

Deep into my soup, the only thing to cloud my pleasure was the thought of Pyavka abandoned at the railroad station, weak, helpless, starved and wondering, no doubt, whether Yakov Marateck had proved to be only a fair-weather friend, after all.

That is, if the police had not already bagged him.

I resolved to hurry back and look for him – right after dinner. But the street was still seething with rain, and the sky was as dark as the insides of Jonah's whale.

Nevertheless, I asked the four card players the way to the depot. Without hesitation, each pointed in a different direction. None of this, I knew, was reason to forsake my comrade. Yet, on a night like this, a man hobbling on icy roads without proper boots was as useless to himself as a man without feet.

Even as I tried to salve my conscience for wanting only to go back to sleep, the door flew open. All of us froze, either from the wind or a healthy jolt of fear. The card players scrambled to hide their few kopeks. But our three ponderous intruders were not Cossacks; they were respectably dressed Jews. The three, one of whom was Mr. Top Hat, made up the Committee that managed the shelter, and their concern was not with who was playing cards, but with some badly overdue repairs to the leaky roof.

Top Hat's eyes swept over me without a glimmer of recognition. A bit later, he took disapproving notice of my footgear, and was curious to know why I did not wear something better suited to the climate. I confessed that I did not have other footwear.

He cleared his throat in what sounded like a comment on my lack of resourcefulness, and briefly consulted with the other two. From the way they glanced in my direction as they conferred with one another, I gathered that they were far from sure whether a halfwit like me was capable of benefiting from their charity.

But ultimately Top Hat turned to me and ordered, "Come with us. You'll get a pair of boots." My fellow mendicants glared in envy at the way I, an utter novice, already knew the *schnorrer*[72] business better than they did.

---

72 Yiddish: Beggar (implies 'professional' beggar)

30

"BROTHER, WE ARE SAVED! "

utside awaited a carriage with rubber tires and a team of horses as proud and independent as eagles. I struggled up the rungs after my three benefactors, and tried not to let my soggy trousers rest too heavily on the soft leather bench. Within moments, we were soaring under a glistening moon through a broad, tree-lined street studded with such mansions as I had previously only seen in the finest quarters of Warsaw.

Since there was little I judged either safe or interesting to volunteer to my hosts, they must not have found me very stimulating company. Or else, having already judged me to be a little soft in the head, they saw no need to include me in their discussion about community matters, such as the need for a new guesthouse that would be a credit both to the city of Irkutsk and to its Jewish community. It would cost 25,000 rubles, of which 10,000 had already been pledged by a certain *macher*,[73] Divanovsky.

I nearly exploded out of my seat. "Divanovsky!"

"Maybe you've heard of him?" one of the men said, almost kindly.

Had I heard of him? If his first name was Vassily, which I was too ashamed to ask, I not only knew him, but you might say he owed me his life. Or so he

73 Yiddish and German: A person of influence; a big shot

had sworn when his very survival was at risk under the tormenting thumb of Haman as his commanding officer.

Of even greater interest was the fact that Divanovsky also owed me the astronomical sum of 50 rubles that I had never expected to see again. (While I may have been blessed with a miraculous talent for encountering Jews in the most improbable places, I had best bear in mind that the Czar's empire was not a village, and every man's name was likely also to belong to thousands of others.)

So I bit my lip, preferring to let them to go on thinking me an imbecile, rather than bringing up the matter of such a trifling sum and being branded a swindler, an extortionist, or a clumsy charlatan unworthy of having a new pair of boots lavished upon him. And for the remainder of the ride, I merely stared at my feet.

The coach halted in front of a palace that could hold up its head beside Baron Günzburg's[74] mansion in Petersburg. It was surrounded by an iron fence that would have given pause even to someone as nimble as Pyavka. About whose existence I had until that moment, once again, totally forgotten.

A liveried servant ran to unlock the gates so that we might fly through them with a minimum of inconvenience. At the front door, a butler scurried out with an open umbrella. He bowed so deeply, it took him a moment to realize, possibly from a whiff of my disgraceful boots, before whom he was abasing himself.

Top Hat ordered the coachman to wait, so he could return me to where I had come from as quickly as possible.

I trotted humbly at the heels of the three men into a warm, well-lit foyer that could have been mistaken for a museum. I ignored the sardonic looks on the faces of the servants.

My benefactors filed into a study the size of a ballroom. Given no instructions to the contrary, I was about to straggle in after them when Top Hat said, "Wait here." The door shut in my face, leaving me to gape at the gilt-framed mirrors within mirrors that cast reflections of everything but the insult of my face. Meanwhile, costumed servants kept a close watch on the decorated porcelain eggs in a fragile glass case.

74 The Günzburgs were Russian-Jewish philanthropists

Time passed. The doors of the study remained shut. My temper began to rise. Not that, other than finding Pyavka, I had pressing business elsewhere. And I needed a pair of boots more than I needed my pride. But rather than sit there on display for the amusement of the domestic staff, I was ready to flee the hall of mirrors, shoes or no shoes, and let them see that even a degraded creature like me placed some value on his time. While entertaining those high-minded thoughts, I remained seated where I was.

At long last, an elderly servant approached bearing a dainty pair of patent-leather boots. He held them out to me with the air of someone cleaning up after a dog.

Overwhelmed by the mere feel of such delicate foot-gear, I forgot my manners, stripped off what was left of my boots, unwound my toe-rags and shoved my feet into the cool, painfully clean, new shoes. I could have saved myself the trouble, needing only one glance to tell me each of those excellent boots had room for barely three of my toes. But I was determined to believe that, with just a bit of breaking in, they would stretch enough to fit me.

The old servant watched in total absorption as I teetered with bird-flapping arms. Clearly, he was not prepared to shuttle back and forth to the stockroom until his customer was satisfied. There was nothing left to do but thank him, pick up the twin corpses of my old boots, and dance toward the exit.

At which moment I heard a cultivated voice call out from somewhere in the maze of sparkling glass, "Young man!"

I stopped. Afraid of toppling over if I shifted my feet, I merely twisted my head in the direction of the voice. Confronting me was an enchanting woman whose grace and bearing suggested that she actually lived in that wondrous palace. Even her frown of anger was exquisite, although I didn't know what, other than being in that room, I might have done to give offense.

She said, "Why didn't my husband offer you something to eat?"

I heard myself stuttering, "Thank you, dear lady, but I have dined already."

"Nonsense. You will sit down, at least, and take tea with me."

How could I say no? In Siberia the habit of hospitality is so ingrained that if you refused the offer of a drink in a *kretchma*, your host would fling it in your face, be it vodka or boiling tea. And while this angelic lady did not look like the type to fling hot tea at a beggar, my evening's schedule was not so crowded that I could not fit in one more engagement.

I nodded and mumbled something agreeable and, in my doll-sized footgear, tiptoed after her through a labyrinth of rooms large enough to stable a squadron of cavalry. Dementedly clutching my filthy boots, I strained not to crash into some priceless piece of furniture, while my hostess pretended not to notice the oafish way I deployed one foot in front of the other.

The house seemed to have a separate dining room for every meal. It even had a special area devoted solely to drinking tea. A samovar glowed and hissed on the sideboard, and a red-cheeked Russian maid brought me a steaming glass in a silver holder, along with the sort of sugary refreshments that required more tea to wash them down.

Madame Top Hat, if that was who she was, seemed not in the least bit offended by the speed with which I emptied the tray. Her bearing, in fact, put me so totally at ease that I began to behave like a real guest, rising to examine the paintings and photographs on the walls, and even leaning forward to study one of them more closely. It was a group photograph in front of a building, and it struck me as painfully familiar.

I finally recognized it as the Novocherkassky Barracks in Petersburg. As I looked more carefully at the large proportion of Jewish faces confronting the camera with mournful foreknowledge of their doom, I suddenly cried out, "Vasya!"

Turning to see my hostess' alarmed expression, I said, "Forgive me, dear lady, but this looks like a boy I knew in the army."

She followed my pointing finger with an indulgent smile. "That happens to be my brother-in-law," she said.

My heart raced. "Is his name 'Vassily Divanovsky?'"

"You know him?" Before I could stop my mouth, I blurted out that not only did I know him, but he still owed me 50 rubles. I burned with shame, but she only nodded.

"I believe he once mentioned something of the sort. What is your name?"

"Yakov Marateck."

"And you are sure he never paid you back?"

I was only able to nod as my throat was choked with foolish tears. How could I explain that, in my present circumstances, 50 rubles was a sum no more forgettable than $50 million would be to an American?

"I think I understand," she said in consolation. "He inquired through military channels, which advised him that his friend was dead."

"He could have written to my parents." In fact, upon my return to Vishogrod the previous year, I had sent a postcard to Vasya at his parents' address simply to let him know that I had survived. To this I got no response. Nor, some months later, to a printed card on which I wished him "to be Inscribed and Sealed for a Good Year." [75] And so I assumed that either the "inflammation of the heart" with which he had been generously diagnosed had been genuine, and killed him, or he had married and moved elsewhere.

Or, as rich men are apt to do, had forgotten both my name and the petty sum he owed one of his former comrades.

She looked at me closely. "Is it really possible that *you* were the one who saved him from the 'Convicts' Company' and loaned him the money to get home?" I felt like the frog that had turned into a prince.

But my hostess still couldn't grasp how a wealthy and educated boy like Vassily could have allowed himself to get into such a state of abject dependence on a ... whatever I was.

A frog, again. Telling her the full story would have taken all night, especially in my condition: lighthearted, leaden-eyed, and possibly a little feverish from the unaccustomed heat in the room.

But I could not leave her question totally unanswered, so I touched on some of the highlights: Our commanding officer, 'Haman,' who had, unaccountably, taken a particular dislike to Vasya. And that under his command, several men had been moved to take their own lives.

Having patiently heard me out, Madame Top Hat sighed, and rang for a maid to clear away the tea service. I assumed this meant that I was dismissed, but she waved me back into my chair.

"And now," she said, "I suppose you want to see your old friend and ask him to pay back what he owes you."

75 A traditional Jewish New Year's blessing

I confessed to her I would find it a great convenience to have 50 rubles in my pocket just then. I took the risk of further confessing that even a sum of that magnitude would only get my partner and me a fraction of the way back to Warsaw. Not to mention our dire need for passports and travel documents and other essential papers.

At this she shook her head. "I'm afraid you will not find it easy to get in to see him. Masses of people sit in his waiting room, day and night, in the hope of having just one word with him."

"You mean beggars like me?" I said bitterly.

"Businessmen," she corrected me. "Commercial travelers. Bankers. Exporters. From Moscow, Warsaw, even Shanghai. Will you believe me if I tell you he barely gets to see his own wife?"

I understood perfectly. Out of sheer kindness, she wanted to spare me of disappointment, perhaps even humiliation. Vassily Divanovsky had become hard and unapproachable, a slave to his own wealth.

"Don't misunderstand," she said. "Vassily is still, in many ways, the kindest, most generous of men. But the world changes and peoples' hearts change, as well. My brother-in-law is no longer the helpless innocent you had befriended back then. In fact, that is a period in his life of which he loathes to be reminded. You understand me?"

Flushed with anger, I wobbled to my feet and said, "I have no intention of imposing on Vas— Mr. Divanovsky. Other than the 50 rubles, he owes me nothing." And I turned my head into a kaleidoscope of mirrors, looking for the exit.

In the reflection of one, I saw her pained expression. "I would strongly advise you not to say a word about forged papers to Vassily. You see, to the local officials and bureaucrats it is intolerable that a Jew should be successful. One of the officials' favorite tricks is to send spies here, provocateurs who claim to be revolutionaries. The first time, Vassily fell for it. He was nearly sent to prison, and ended up having to pay a large bribe. Despite his wealth and prominence, a Jew here has no legal rights. The authorities can expel us at their whim. Ever since that incident, no beggar – forgive me, no one who appears to be in need – has been allowed near him. Surely you can't blame him."

"But he knows me! He can't fail to recognize my face. He can't believe that I'm a government spy."

"They will not let you get close enough for him to see your face."

"Madame," I said. "Do you believe my story?"

A blink of hesitation. But she nodded.

"Then could you not open a door for me?"

She evaded my eye. "I don't know if my husband would permit it. His own business depends greatly on Vassily's good will. And if I did anything to interfere ..."

I needed to hear no more. Balanced on my toes, I bowed to my hostess who, with a sad smile of apology, tugged a pink rope to ring for a servant.

As I left, she tried, with some awkwardness, to hand me two silver rubles. My impulse was to refuse, but I had the good sense not to be too proud.

Outside, the coach swayed in the wind. I climbed up the ladder. The driver set out to return me to the guest-house, but I felt a sudden surge of defiance. Had Vasya not assured me, repeatedly and with his whole heart, that he owed me his life? If I couldn't get in to see him, I didn't know what I'd do, but I felt capable of desperate actions.

I tapped the coachman on the shoulder and asked him to take me to the home of Mr. Divanovsky.

He looked at me curiously. Those were not his instructions. "What business do you have with him?"

I showed him a ruble. "Enough to make it worth your while."

"He'll likely still be in his office."

"Then take me there."

The ruble changed hands, and the wheels rolled in a different direction. Over his shoulder, the coachman said, "Brother, you're wasting your time. You could more easily get in to see the Czar."

I shrugged. Fortified with strong tea and sweet cakes, I was ready to risk everything, which admittedly wasn't much.

Still thinking about how I was going to get in to see Vasya, I didn't notice which way or how far the coach drove before two immense buildings appeared before me. One of them, surrounded by a wall, must have been a factory. The other was a department store. Although it must have been well past ten o'clock in the evening, both places buzzed with activity.

The coachman jolted us to a halt. "Good luck," he muttered into his beard.

Before I climbed down the ladder, I asked, "Will you wait for me?"

He gave me a pitying look. "I'll wait a minute or two. That's all it should take."

I knew he meant that was how long it would take until they threw me out. My audacity began to leak out like sawdust. What clerk or porter who valued his job would allow a soiled creature like me to set foot on his polished floors?

I thought about asking the coachman to take me back where I belonged, but he seemed to have fallen asleep. And if I gave up now, I'd be abandoning Pyavka every bit as cruelly as my former comrade seemed to have abandoned me.

My laughable new boots transported me headlong toward the entrance where I stopped. If I came doddering into that building like a second-rate clown, I would never get through the door. So I sat down on the wooden curb and put on my old boots in which, at least indoors, I could walk normally.

I had barely stepped over the threshold when a porter, sturdy as a tank, rose up to bar my way. Understandably, he was more interested in the state of my boots than my fanciful claim that I was there to see Mr. Divanovsky on an urgent personal matter.

He firmly shook his head even as he tried to keep from laughing in my face. And assured me that my request was quite out of the question. In fact, he started to help me leave rather more quickly than I had in mind.

Standing my ground, I threw off his hand, letting him feel enough of my arm to realize there was still some meat left under that threadbare sleeve. "Just tell him my name: Yakov Marateck. I'm an old friend."

The porter clearly had heard a hundred such preposterous tales. He tried, once again, to push me into the street. After scuffling for a while without progress in either direction, both of us were on the verge of violence when a tall, square-bearded man came down the stairs and demanded, "What is happening here? Who is this man?"

Before the porter could recover his breath, I said, "I've come to see Vassily Divanovsky. If you will kindly just tell him my name."

The tall man motioned to the porter to release my arm. "What business do you have with him?"

All at once, I felt tongue-tied and deathly weary. Had I forgotten that rich people had telephones, and if they called the police I was lost? Not meeting his eye, I mumbled, "It is a personal matter."

He noted my shredded footgear as well as the good shoes I was doltishly holding in my hand. Nevertheless, he answered civilly enough, "Mr. Divanovsky has a roomful of people waiting. If you wish, you can try again tomorrow."

I felt too defeated to argue. All I had strength enough to say was, "I can't wait until tomorrow. Please, just tell him that Yakov Marateck is asking to see him."

The name seemed to draw a flicker of recognition. Or so I imagined. Glancing past me to the splendid coach in which I had arrived, he motioned to me to follow him up the stairs.

As he ushered me into a high-ceilinged waiting room, I saw that the porter had not lied. I counted eleven people ahead of me. Some were cradling thick leather dispatch cases in their laps. My competitors for Vasya's attention refrained charitably from looking in my direction.

In the grip of such cheerless thoughts, I began to doze off. I was, in fact, about to topple off my chair when the inner door opened and the Director himself (could this truly be my pitiful old comrade?) stepped out, card in hand, to summon the next petitioner.

Before the other man could creak to his feet, I jumped up, threw my arms open and shouted, "Vasya!" I heard the others gasp at my impertinence.

For a brief but chilling moment, he stared at me from head to foot. Before the receptionist could intervene, I stepped forward and said more humbly, "Mr. Divanovsky, may I ask if you were once with the Novocherkassky Regiment in Petersburg?" Madame Top Hat had warned that he did not take kindly to being reminded of his painful past, but what choice did I have?

"And what is that to you?"

"In the 15th? The 'Convicts' Company'?"

My former comrade's glance down at my boots and then traveled back up to my face, but showed no sign of recognition. He nodded curtly. "Yes, and …?"

"Do you remember a soldier named Yakov Marateck?"

"I do, indeed. He died in one of the last battles of the war. His whole company was wiped out." He peered at me with a flicker of curiosity. "You knew him?"

"Vasya!" I shouted again. "Look at me!"

He took a step closer and stared shortsightedly into my eyes. Then, graceful as a falling tree, he toppled into my arms. Not to embrace me, but because he had fainted.

The waiting room was in an uproar. Clerks and executives poured out of every niche. One loosened Divanovsky's collar, one came running with a glass of water, another brought cognac, and yet another did his bit by giving me an accusing glare.

Finally, Vasya opened his eyes. "Yakov!" he shouted. "Yakov, my brother!"

I apologized for having upset him, for not having telephoned or written first. But …

"What need is there to apologize?" he shouted. "If only you knew how I suffered when I heard that you were dead!"

Before I could express how much the news had upset me, too, a doctor swept me aside. He took Vasya's pulse, unbuttoned his shirt, put some kind of horn to his chest, and went through all the flourishes by which doctors reminded you that your life was not in God's hands but in their own.

He assured Vasya that he was in exemplary health, but must avoid "unnecessary excitement." At this, his gaze condescended to take me in.

Vasya sat up, clapped for silence and announced, "The office is closed for the night. I am celebrating. My dearest friend has just returned from the dead." And he ordered a meal prepared for me at his home. To keep my appetite alive until then, his secretary plied me with brandy and cakes, which met little resistance from me.

After three or four drinks slurped down like water, the walls around me no longer stood still. In the midst of my struggle to stay upright, the door flew open. A majestic young woman swept into the room in a rustle of petticoats and silk. This could only be Madame Divanovsky. One look at her exquisite features and I felt the sharp tooth of the Commandment, "Thou shall not covet thy neighbor's wife."

With barely a glance in my direction, the lady demanded to know what had caused her husband to faint.

Vasya said, "It was nothing, my dearest." Then he decided, "No, it *is* something. A beloved old friend has returned from the dead. You've heard me speak of Yakov Marateck. I owe this man my life, not once, but a hundred times over. After the war, I had tried with all my heart to find him but was told he had fallen in battle. If not for him, you would not have me for a husband today."

At the sound of my name, Madame's smile turned toward me and she embraced me, rags and shaven head and all. "Is that your idea of a proper introduction?" she chided her husband.

Not for the first time since entering this building, I felt ashamed of my appearance.

With a dance-floor sweep of his arm, Vasya said, "Yakov Marateck, meet Zofia, my beloved wife."

She took my hand and held it. "So you are the man of whom Vasya never stopped talking." It was then he who looked embarrassed.

Reverting to protocol, Zofia raised her dainty hand for me to kiss. My nostrils filled with the odor of perfumed soap. I tried not to sneeze.

"After what I have heard about you from my husband, I consider you not only his dearest friend but mine, as well. No doubt you must feel some discomfort at the way you are dressed. But you are close to my husband's size, and until we can summon a tailor to take your measurements, you will share whatever is his."

The Divanovskys wanted to take me to their residence where dinner was waiting but, wretch that I was, it was not until that moment that I remembered Pyavka abandoned at the railroad station, tattered, lice-ridden, half-starved, and without papers or money. I feared I had become the kind of person who would allow his comrade to die of hunger rather than share his good fortune.

Which brought me a more troublesome thought. How could I bring a habitual thief into the unsuspecting home of these generous friends? Would I not be violating the biblical law of not making a "blind" man stumble by placing him in a position in which the impulse to steal would be beyond his powers to resist?

And yet, after all Pyavka and I had been through together, there was nothing else I could honorably do, regardless of consequences.

To give my new friends a chance to withdraw their offer, I said to Madame, "Shall I tell you how I came to be here?"

"People are in Siberia for many reasons. My own parents were sent here before I was born, and they were not criminals. We know the kind of man you are. And if you need documents or money to clear you in the eyes of the law, we can take care of that, too."

"I'm an escaped convict," I insisted. "A revolutionary. I escaped from a work camp together with a friend, a professional thief. A friend I cannot abandon now."

Madame's eyes widened with pity. "And where is this friend of yours?"

"At the railroad station. If he hasn't already been arrested."

"If he is your friend, he is our friend, too. Bring him here at once."

Madame sent someone to awaken the coachman, and have him harness the horses, apologizing in the same breath that their motorcar ran only in warm weather. I was prepared to go along, but my hosts wouldn't hear of it. "Until we can get you a passport, it is not safe for you to be near the depot."

I gave two of their clerks a detailed description of Pyavka, and asked for paper to write a note assuring him that it was safe to go with these men. It read, "A miracle has happened! We are saved!"

While waiting for Pyavka, I listened open-mouthed as Vasya and his wife discussed, with some heat, which of their twenty-odd guest-rooms was to be mine. Vasya tended to favor the large one at the rear overlooking the gardens, while Zofia demanded that I have a room closer to theirs. I tried to pay attention, all the while fighting the urge to fall onto the carpet and go to sleep.

But Vasya was not done with me yet. While Madame left to supervise my accommodations, my old friend unlocked a drafty passage to the adjoining building where he wastefully turned on the electric lights for all five floors. Our steps echoed across a vast, empty department store. "Are we allowed to be here?" I blurted out.

Vasya smiled and patted my arm. The manager came running. His nose couldn't help showing some reservations at the way I smelled. Especially when Vasya, without bothering to introduce me, instructed him to act as my personal fitter. My old friend and I strolled up and down the aisles, arms linked, followed by the flustered manager with a tape measure snaked over his shoulders.

At every other counter, Vasya stopped and ordered me to "buy" this or that item of clothing. I was too tired and too drunk to make choices. Impatient with my "indecisiveness," not to mention my provincial ignorance of the latest styles, Vasya unlocked a cash drawer and, to his manager's mute horror, snatched out a fistful of paper rubles that, uncounted, he stuffed into one of my ragged pockets.

I did my best to resist. For him to repay my loan there was plenty of time. Or so I hoped. And if I let him give me what may be far more than 50 rubles, would I not be guilty of accepting interest, which was against the *Talmud's* law pertaining to loaning money?

Before I could explain this to my generous but unlearned friend, he hauled me upstairs to a department that sold custom-fitted suits while his poor manager groped for some clue as to who I was or what sort of demonic power I held over his master. Made to kneel down and take my measurements, he started to fit me for a fine suit of heavy tweed woven in Łódź.

By now my head had turned to stone; I wanted only to put it down somewhere before it fell off. Next Vasya loaded my arms with silk shirts, a stack of warm underwear, a sable hat with earflaps, and an assortment of shoes ranging from heavy boots to delicate pumps, all without bothering to see if they fit. And since I could not go around in rags until my tailored suits were ready, he made me take one off the rack, which cost far less than the others and which, though I was too intimidated to admit it, I liked best of all.

In all this irresistible generosity, I saw one of Vasya's less attractive quali-
ties – the impatience of a rich boy accustomed to having his way. Which
might have been why some resentful clerk in the Army had shoved him
into the "Convicts' Company" in the first place.

A barber came to unearth my true face. When I saw myself, I was not
surprised to find that, over the past six months, I had grown to look less like
the son of Shloime Zalman Marateck and more like a common hooligan
or gangster. But at least now I looked like a respectable gangster. Once I
needed no longer to fear the police, maybe my face would lose its hunted
look and I would again resemble the ignorant boy who, once upon a time,
had set out for Warsaw to take on the world.

It was near two o'clock in the morning when lights began to be switched
off. While my limbs had turned to lead, my heart rattled with the fear that,
on account of my earlier laziness, Pyavka may have been arrested and sent
Heaven-only-knows where.

Just before three o'clock in the morning, a coach clattered over the
cobbled driveway under our window. I was about to run downstairs, but
Vasya held me back. "Wait … See if he will recognize you." It was not the
kindest thing one could do to a terrified friend at three in the morning, but
Vasya was giving the orders and, to be frank, I was also curious to see my
partner's reaction.

Moments later, Pyavka, flanked by the two servants, was marched into
the office. His face was ashen with terror. He clearly believed himself to
be in some sort of government building. After all, who else but the police
would be working this late at night?

Vasya came around the desk and offered his hand. Pyavka remained
frightened and mistrustful. He glanced for a moment in my direction but
didn't really see me. He finally blustered, "Where is the man who wrote
this note? What have you done to my friend?"

I felt touched and remorseful. Here he was in a state of mortal fear, and
yet his first thought was for me!

"Fool, don't you recognize me?" I said in Yiddish. At the sound of my
familiar voice, he lurched toward me, clutching my arm as though to make
sure I was real.

Still out of breath, the messengers told Vasya what a time they had had locating my friend. And even more, persuading him that my extravagant message was neither a police trap, nor something I had written in a fit of madness.

Drawing me aside, Pyavka nodded toward my old comrade and asked, "Who is this *Vanya?*"

Before I could explain, the '*Vanya*' tugged me in the opposite direction and wanted know to how I came to be friends with this peculiar creature. I suppose he had forgotten, or not taken seriously, my disclosure of my partner's criminal past. So, without lowering my voice, I told our host that Pyavka stemmed from a distinguished family, and that in certain quarters of Warsaw he was looked upon as a virtual "King." Until, owing to the malice of Czarist officialdom, he had ended up a prisoner like me. All this I said while looking sternly at my comrade in silent warning not to make me regret my words.

31

LINGERING IN THE LAP OF LUXURY

rom the awestruck manner in which Pyavka looked around Vasya's home, I saw that, for all his fancy airs, he, too, had never set foot in a place of such grandeur – except maybe in total darkness, when it was probably hard to appreciate the full splendor of his surroundings.

Madame Divanovsky made her entrance in what could have been a gown made for an empress. Majestic purple velvet draped her delicate body as if the fabric had been created for her, alone, with a neckline of lace that revealed the swell of her fair-skinned bosom, upon which rested a necklace with shiny stones that could only have been diamonds. Her waist was so narrow that it seemed to invite my hands to encircle it; I quickly clasped them behind my back. If Czarina Alexandra had walked in at that moment, wearing all of her jewels, I would not have noticed her.

Madame Divanovsky extended her fingertips to Pyavka, choosing to take no note of his disgraceful appearance or intolerable odor, to both of which I had suddenly become most sensitive.

She was the soul of grace. Which made me want to gag at the practiced ease with which my thievish comrade instantly turned on the full blaze of his charm. Especially when I noted the professional way he had already begun to appraise the rings on her feather-light, white fingers and the silver carelessly on display in cabinets a child could have motivated open.

After the meal, to which we did full justice, Madame escorted us to our room. Among the wonders it contained, she pointed with special pride to a white porcelain knob in the wall, as though no one living in Warsaw had ever seen such a miraculous thing as electricity. She also referred to a braided silk rope by which we may ring for a servant at any time of the day or night, although at that moment I could not see any circumstance under which I might dare to make use of such an insolent device.

A small quarrel broke out between Madame and Divanovsky, who had pushed in behind us. Our room, he reminded her, had only recently been furnished with electric power and some of the wiring may not yet be properly "shielded." In fact, he claimed to have heard of people who touched a naked wire and went up in smoke in an instant.

Madame scoffed at his backwardness. I could see that she was determined, after all the money it cost to install these devices, that their guests enjoy every modern convenience.

When they finally departed, Pyavka scouted the room, awestruck as a small boy in a candy store. I made a point of showing him how completely at home I felt under my old comrade's roof. Not only did I calmly turn off the electric light but, laughing at his plea to stop playing with fire, I switched it on and off again.

Then I emptied my bulging pockets. Pyavka gaped at the mass of rubles I scattered onto the dresser. "Where did you get all this money?" he whispered as one professional to another.

"Divanovsky," I said in my most casual tone.

Pyavka was both awed and fearful. "What if you'd been caught?"

"He gave it to me."

My partner complimented me with a grin of disbelief. "It seems I've been a better teacher than I realized."

"You think I stole it?"

"It's not for me to judge."

"He stuffed it into my pockets. To him, this is small change. Besides," I added with a nonchalant shrug, "he owed me some money."

"I'm not saying a word. But I warn you – I don't intend to go back to prison just because an amateur like you couldn't control himself."

This gave me the opportunity to remind him, again, not to dare abuse my friend's hospitality.

Pyavka sunk into his feather bed like an angel floating on cotton-wool clouds, and smiled at my stern warning. "After all we've been through," he said with a pained shake of his head, "how little you know me."

I chose, for the moment, to take this as reassurance. But then I caught a glimpse of his face and, even in the darkness, I could swear he was winking.

In the bright glare of morning, agitated hands interrupted my sleep. Pyavka's face hovered over me, white with indignation. "They've stolen our clothes!"

I sat up, startled, and looked around. There was no sign of them, nor of the rags that we had left on the floor.

Still rubbing my lids, I climbed out of bed. The giant wardrobe was locked. Before Pyavka could find a bent nail with which to exercise his skills, I spotted the key on the dresser.

Not only were all my new acquisitions neatly arranged on hangers and shelves, but the very shreds and tatters in which my partner and I had arrived had been lovingly washed and folded. Even my dismembered shoes had been shined to a military gloss.

Pyavka tugged at my arm. He was so agitated that the only words he could spit out were, "The money!"

I opened a drawer. As far as I could tell, everything was there.

A servant knocked, and entered with our breakfast tray, leaving Pyavka barely time enough to slam the drawer with our money and disguise the shocked look on his face.

About to butter a chunk of, bread, I noticed an envelope addressed to me wedged between two crystal jars of marmalade. In careless penmanship on crisp white paper, my old comrade apologized for not being present to greet us when we awoke, but he had had an urgent call from the office. Madame, also, would not be home before evening. Until then, his servants were at our disposal. But he ordered us not to leave the house for reasons he did not need to explain.

271

To my great shame, it was not until my third or fourth day of wallowing in the Divanovksys' hospitality that I thought to ask how to send a telegram to my parents to let them know I was alive.

Vasya's cheeks flushed dangerously. "That is quite impossible. And I warn you not to try it behind my back."

It took some minutes before my anger at being forbidden from doing something subsided, and I recognized that he was right. What better place than the telegraph office for the authorities to post a list of wanted men?

But the very next day, Vasya apologized for his outburst and assured me that my friend and I would shortly be furnished with forged documents. Then I would be allowed to send a cryptic wire to my married sister, Malkah, who was certain to recognize the childish nicknames I used for us both.

This brought up another matter weighing on Pyavka's mind: Divanovsky's "unaccountable" kindness and generosity. What normal human being, and a rich man in particular, behaved the way he did? Unless ..." His eyes narrowed with foreboding.

"Unless what?"

"There is something he wants."

I could barely keep from laughing in his face. "What could he possibly ask for that I wouldn't gladly give him a hundred times over?"

A gloomy expression overcame Pyavka's face, and he shook his large head. "I look at your trusting face, my friend, and I fear for you."

His earnestness was so preposterous that I could only shrug. Yet, when I next looked at my hosts, so open-handed and yet so self-important, I could not help wondering, for an unkind fraction of a second, what they could possibly want.

Other than making stealthy forays to the toilet, our only dealings with the servants was receiving, as humbly as prisoners, the crowded silver tray that carried our lunch. It held more food than either of us had eaten in four weeks, and Pyavka consumed his share with such speed that he was shortly writhing with cramps. Which did not stop him from examining the tray and pronouncing to be it pure silver.

More days passed in idleness like this before I got a moment alone with Vasya and had a chance to ask about our promised passports and travel permits.

His face puffed up with annoyance. "What is your hurry? Everything is being arranged. It's not as simple as you think." Then, looking offended, he demanded, "Don't you have everything here a man could possibly want?"

How could I explain to my old comrade that I simply didn't feel I belonged there, that living on his generosity made me feel like a parasite? But all I ended up saying was, "When I see your happiness with your wife, I feel the urge to start a family of my own."

Vasya burped his ironic, rich-man's laugh. "Is that all? I didn't want to excite you, but that, too, is being arranged."

"What? A wife?" He made it sound no more burdensome than finding a hat to match my overcoat.

"For the man to whom I owe my life, I want only the best. Just be patient a little longer."

I was not happy to have such matters arranged behind my back with no one troubling to ask about my likes or dislikes. This may be the Siberian style, but we were not talking about buying a horse or a goat. And yet the hot blood of youth made me eager to hear more. "Who is the girl? How old is she? Who are her parents?"

Vasya smiled, slapped me on the shoulder, and gestured that his lips were sealed. "Let it come as a pleasant surprise," he said, and held out his arms for his valet to insert him into his fur coat, which I took as my signal that the subject was closed.

At supper that evening, Madame was in a "mood," and barely responded to my attempts at conversation. I sensed something was going on. Though on the surface, Vasya was still as hearty as ever, even he acted too preoccupied for me to bring up the matter of our passports and travel permits, again.

Adding to my anxiety, Pyavka was also behaving oddly. Was it possible that, despite my fierce threats, he had resumed his old criminal practices? And that my hosts, too well mannered to bring the matter to my attention, were simply gritting their teeth till our departure? For whatever reason, we had overstayed our welcome.

I was tempted to walk out the door, leaving behind every ruble and every article of clothing my old comrade had lavished upon me. If nothing else, that would repair my pride. But the sad truth was that weeks of indolence and luxury had sapped my initiative and fattened my soul. Besides, where would I go? Back to the asylum for the homeless? Or, worse yet, to the railroad station, scratching and snarling among my fellow derelicts for every crust of bread, fearful day and night of being robbed, assaulted, or clapped in irons?

Rather than make a decisive move, I sat in our room day after day, playing listless games of cards with Pyavka, waiting for some unknown doom to descend upon me.

Finally one afternoon, I decided to take matters into my own hands. While my partner slept during the day, like a rich man, I told the servants that I was going for a walk around the garden. Which was what I did when I first set foot outside the house. After examining the leaves of various plants and bending over to smell the few flowers that still were in bloom, I was so thoroughly bored that I judged no servant assigned to observing me could have watched me any longer.

I was out on the street before I knew where I was going, but Vasya's reference to finding me a wife put me in mind of the last time I passed through this city. Last time it was as a soldier on his way home from the war. Not a war in which we had been victorious, but at least I was returning with my body intact. This time, I was an escaped convict, a revolutionary, a wanted man. Back then, I had been ready to offer my heart to the Siberian "Queen Esther." Now I would be ashamed to do so.

Although the city had felt unfamiliar when I debarked from the train, a few days of being treated like a human being made the landmarks recognizable, again. Even if I would no longer offer my heart to the Siberian Queen, I could, at least, visit her and let her know how much her generosity to Jewish soldiers had meant to us. And though I wouldn't make any decisions about it now, if I felt some familiar stirrings when I finally got to meet her …

It wasn't long before I found the Queen's mansion. It appeared more run-down than I had remembered it, but it was winter in Siberia, and I had previously only seen it at night. When I tapped against the door, the same 'general' answered. To my amazement, he claimed to remember me. But as I looked more closely, I was struck by the sag in his shoulders, the shriveled pallor of his face, and the barely-hidden shabbiness of his uniform.

With lurching heart, I stood there, like a fool, waiting for him to tell me what I already suspected: "Queen Esther" was dead. Death had, in fact, been slowly devouring her for years. Only the joy she derived from her deeds of hospitality had kept her alive. And when the war ended, and this solace was no longer available to her, she promptly resumed dying.

I was ashamed at not having considered a logical explanation for her mysterious absence. But I had been too weak, too hungry, and too in love with the picture of her that I had formed in my mind to wonder why neither I, nor the thousands of other Jewish soldiers whom she had fed throughout the years, had ever set eye on this modest and merciful creature.

32

AN ANGEL IN SIBERIA

A late-afternoon knock, too early for dinner, caused my pulse to leap with foreboding. The small silver tray in the servant's hand carried a message from Vasya. I was still so unaccustomed to the dizzying swing in our fortunes, and discomfited by Pyavka's interpretation of our situation, that I half expected my friend, having had his little joke, to give us five minutes to change back into our rags and clear out.

With trembling fingers, I clawed at the flap. In bewilderingly cordial tones, the letter begged my forgiveness if lately, under the pressure of business, he appeared to have been neglecting me. My heart quickened. What I had mistaken for coolness existed only in my overheated fantasy!

Without further explanation, he directed Pyavka and me to shave and dress at once, because a coach would arrive to fetch us in half an hour for a reception that evening at his in-laws, the Charlops, who were celebrating their 25th anniversary. In his casual scrawl, my friend had also added a post-script, more or less hinting that I might get to meet a certain "suitable" young woman who happened to be the Charlop's head bookkeeper.

Snob that I was, I confessed that the last part of his message left me with a thumping sense of letdown. Was this what Vasya meant when he vowed that, for me he would settle for "only the best?" Was a lowly head-book-keeper to be my consolation prize?

Shortly, a valet knocked discreetly and presented me and Pyavka with the kind of black suit you might see at a better-class gentile funeral, but worn by the corpse.

There were eighteen guests at the table, all of them, as Pyavka hand-somely acknowledged into my ear, of "a refined caliber." We were intro-duced as "old friends from Warsaw." But the guests' good-natured banter made clear they knew quite well what species of bird we were and under what circumstances we had landed there.

I had just settled into a delicate gilt chair when I felt a hush fall over the guests. All eyes were on the large double doors, which framed a most re-markable couple. The man was tall, arrow-straight, with a well-trimmed beard and the effortless assurance of a born nobleman. On his arm was a young woman whose very presence chilled my breath. And the bold, pene-trating manner in which her eyes swept the room made plain that, far from being anything as listless as a wife, she was triumphantly unattached. As to her other specifications, I will note only that the spun-sugar glow of her moonlit hair was the very shade I had, as a child, associated with angels.

My judgment addled by champagne, I told myself defiantly that, be she princess or head bookkeeper, I alone would determine my future. What was there to stop me from elbowing my way through that laughable siege of soft-handed rivals and carrying off my prize from under their pale noses? If this maiden's character was as pure and loveable as her face (and how could it not be?), I would, that very night, offer myself to her in marriage, as both husband and slave, content to live out my days in Irkutsk with or without Vasya's blessings.

But even with a torrent of sparkling wine foaming in my veins, all cour-age had departed me. While I might still have been able, in my condition, to charge a sputtering Japanese machine-gun, approaching this angelic creature was beyond my powers. I allowed my glass to be refilled until the overflow ran up my sleeve. By the time I reached the bottom of my glass, I felt like a different man, but one with an agreeable sense of having the ability to walk on walls.

Before the angel and I had time to undertake any kind of flirtation, Vasya clapped his hands for a Gypsy fiddler. Scarcely had I settled back to enjoy the performance when my host, in the manner of a man accustomed to obedience, invited me to perform the kind of *kazachok*[76] that had so often raised his spirits during his hellish months in Petersburg.

I was not overjoyed to be classed with the fiddler as a mere part of the evening's entertainment. But I also knew I had much to be grateful for. If a little dance would give pleasure to my old comrade and impress the heavenly creature who had just floated into the room, this seemed hardly the time for me to stand on my dignity.

Thus my flailing knees and elbows soon carved out a jagged space within which I circled on jackknifed legs that shot forth like Chinese firecrackers, executing acrobatic spins in joyous defiance of gravity. My feet touched the floor only long enough to propel me still higher and higher. While the band sweated to keep up with me, the guests clapped in tempo with the music, and my legs shot forth, weightless and inexhaustible.

Vasya watched me with such a glow of innocent pride that I thought this must have been his way of introducing me to Irkutsk society as an available bachelor who, even after months of squalor and hardship, was still bursting with masculine vigor.

The musicians ran out of breath not a moment too soon. I floated back to earth as a barrage of applause crashed over me, along with vain pleas for an encore. Men and women pressed up to me for the honor of shaking my hand. Among them, shyly waiting her turn, stood my blonde seraph.

"Never," she said in a voice I could liken only to a crystal bell, "have I seen such dancing." To which I instantly responded, "Never have I seen such beauty."

A maidenly blush illuminated her face. Moments later, with a benevolent nod from her father, I took her arm and drew her to the dance floor.

My partner's name was Slava, and she spoke a most educated Russian, along with a sprinkling of Yiddish idioms certain to charm my parents.

---

76 Also known as the Cossacks dance, it is a fast, Slavic dance with alternate squats, leg kicks and jumps

She also proved to be well informed about world events, that is, in Mother Russia, although it troubled her that certain "unruly" elements seem determined to overthrow our beloved Czar.

Even as she said this, her eyes twinkled, and I concluded that she was either joking or else disguising her honest, radical sentiments. I steered the conversation to safer ground: our families. That is, her family, mine being hardly the stuff of romantic anecdotes. Her father, she said, was a land surveyor who was obliged to travel a good deal. Ever since her mother died last year, she had kept house for him. And out of respect for her mother's memory, she lit two Sabbath candles every Friday night, a practice she had once confessed to her priest and had been told it was a superstitious custom.

An icicle pierced my heart. For the first time that evening, my tongue resisted my efforts to restrain it. "You go to church?" I stuttered.

"Only since my mother died." She tugged a gold chain out of her bodice. Suspended from it were a Shield of David and a cross. "That way," she said with a musical laugh, "When I go to Heaven, I will have two gates from which to choose."

A young man approached and bowed. Numbed, I allowed him to extract my partner from my unresisting grip. My head was spinning. I drifted to the sidelines where an unseen servant handed me another glass of something cold.

33
THE PRICE OF PAPER

On most evenings, the demands of his far-flung enterprises kept Divanovsky in his office until well into the night. On those occasions, I found myself called upon to be Madame's escort to cultural functions of which enjoyment she was determined not to be deprived.

To ease my discomfort in this role, Vasya assured me, repeatedly, that he could think of no one else to whom he would so readily entrust his "dearest treasure."

Still, for the sake of propriety, I asked Pyavka to accompany Madame and me. But he declined with a shameless wink, saying, "Good brother, in your game, you need no partners."

A *troika* deposited us at the Opera House where we learned that the train that was bringing the Harbin Opera Company to Irkutsk, had been stranded en route, not an uncommon occurrence, upsetting to no one except those at the station who were left without heat for long hours.

I consoled Madame by telling her that I had seen the Harbin Opera, and could get along nicely without it. But her heart was set on going out, and it became my task to escort her to a hastily substituted play by a resident amateur troupe. As it would not start for another hour, I asked if she would like to spend the time in the warmth of a nearby café. Instead, she wanted to tour the surrounding countryside.

Back in the coach, bundled up heavily in our furs and blankets, I tried to keep an arm's length distance between us. But the coachman made a sudden turn and Madame lurched against me. To keep her from being flung about, I put my arm around her waist while she, for added safety, clung to my neck.

Sweating guiltily, I asked, "Shall I tell him to slow down?"

"If you wish. But it might make us late getting back to the theatre."

"Then shall I tell him to go faster?"

"Whatever you think is best."

This left me puzzled. Madame was not normally in the habit of leaving such decisions to anyone else. "Won't you mind being late?"

She smiled at my earnestness. "It's an old play. I've seen it twice before."

"Then do you really want to see it again?"

"It doesn't matter."

Somewhat alarmed by her strangely docile manner, I ordered the coachman to head back toward the city. The *troika* flew and bounced over the uneven ground, and Madame and I struggled not to be pitched out of our seats. Now and then, our faces nearly collided, but she did not flinch. Her scent burned in my nostrils and I tried not to sneeze. Soon, I had nowhere left to retreat, although it was possible that I didn't try hard enough. I felt horridly disloyal to Vasya. But was it my fault that Madame and I were late for the theater?

Snowflakes pounded like fists against our windows, but not half as loud as my thundering heart. To distract myself from wrongful thoughts, I tried to focus on what Madame was saying. But while her lips moved, her words hung mutely in the frozen air, waiting for the fire in my ears to melt them. Not for the first time, I reminded myself that I was a guest in her home, dependent for my very life on both her and her husband's good will.

At the theater, the performance had long been under way. Refusing to check our expensive coats, we squeezed into our seats. I settled back and tried to make some sense of what was happening on stage. But there were so many characters coming in and out, each with his own terrible story, that I found the plot impossible to follow. I was also distracted by the scenery, which was not the normal country-squire's drawing room that I had previous seen in plays, but a more familiar-looking, ill-kept shelter for the homeless.

I whispered to Madame that, thanks to her husband's generosity, the shelter in Irkutsk was in far better condition than that depicted on stage. And in my opinion it attracted a somewhat classier clientele.

"Yes," she said with a strangely bitter smile. "My husband is a generous man."

Moments later, she determined that she had seen enough.

As the *troika* plowed homeward, Madame suddenly dug her nails into my wrist. Having thus attracted my attention, she declared that she did not love her husband.

Had my eyes been open, I suppose this revelation would not have come as a great shock. But my ignorance of married life was such that all I could think of was to suggest we had probably both had too much to drink at the theater. In fact, I guaranteed that, by morning, we would both have forgotten this whole conversation.

Her eyes blinked, and tears glistened down her marble cheeks. Bewildered, I asked if I had said something to give offense. She shook her head so vehemently that one of her tears splashed my nose.

That night, although my head lay on my pillow as heavily as a cannonball, I did not close an eye. The heat of Madame's breath near my cheek had singed my skin. Through sheer, unforgivable negligence, I had fallen in love with someone forbidden to me. From that moment on, every hour I spent in that unhappy house would be a torment, as much for her as for me.

A servant's knock summoned us to an early breakfast with our hosts. Numb with apprehension, I set my feet on the icy floor and struggled to pull on my trousers. Pyavka, following me down the stairs, humorously noted that I walked like a condemned man.

The Divanovskys had nearly finished their meal. Both were reading the newspaper. Vasya looked up and asked whether I had enjoyed the previous night's performance. One glance at Madame's face alerted me to be on my guard.

I told him truthfully that I was so charmed to have an escort like Madame that I hardly paid attention to the action on stage.

Later that morning, Madame and I had a moment alone. She told me how, as a girl, she had been wildly in love with a poor student. But her parents would not hear of the match, and the student had run off in despair to America. She never heard from him again, and could only assume that he was dead. Then, at a cousin's wedding in Kiev, not yet recovered from her broken heart, she met the dashing young Divanovsky, fresh out of the Army, and was swept off her feet. "But the moment I stood under the canopy, I knew I had made a bitter mistake." And, to this day, not a night had passed that she did not mourn the ghost of the boy she had loved.

When I first appeared in her husband's office, looking barely human, she had almost fainted because, for a flicker of a moment, she thought it was he, the ghost, the *dybbuk*, of her beloved returned to claim her.

I reminded her that I knew her husband long before she did and had always found him to be a kind and honorable man.

"Oh, yes, he is a kind man. Kind to all the beautiful women."

"Madame, there are none more beautiful than you."

"And what good is a silver cup if it is filled with tears? Or my beauty, my money, when it cannot give me a child? If I had that, at least, my life would have some purpose."

"You have only been married for three years. Surely it's too soon to give up hope."

She shook her head with finality. "We have both been to doctors, specialists as far away as Vienna. I am capable of having a child, but he is not."

I squirmed at being burdened with such intimate details, and felt relieved when she looked at the clock and said she had to go out.

Wonderful news! Our passports were finally ready. My new documents, cunningly aged and faded, were in the name of "Yakov Marmeladov." My only small objection was that the paper did not appear to be of sufficiently poor quality to pass as "authentic."

Pyavka, though, was greatly displeased with his new surname, Duda. When I heard what name had been chosen for him, I laughed uncontrollably. "It's a perfect name," I said.

Pyavka shook a finger at me. "You put him up to it." I had not. I didn't know how the passport forger had come up with either of our names, though one had to appreciate the irony that the new surname chosen for Pyavka meant "one who makes a lot of noise."

"Why didn't they have the courtesy to ask me what I wanted to be called?"

Out of patience with Pyavka's delicate feelings, I told him that he was welcome to order a new set of papers with a more attractive name, but that I was taking the first train back to Poland.

At dinner, Vasya announced that from that night until I left, he would stay home to make up for all the days he had shamefully neglected his old comrade. I felt relieved to know that he would be present as a chaperone, whether he knew it or not.

That night, he and I played cards, while Madame sat mutely in a corner, embroidering. I could tell that Vasya's mind was elsewhere. Near midnight, he threw down his hand and declared that he was going to bed.

Pyavka went to sleep early, again, complaining of various aches in his body, but refusing to let us call a doctor.

Left flagrantly alone with Madame, I struggled not to offend her by yawning. Long minutes passed, with neither of saying a word. At long last, she was ready to say good night. I waited until I heard the click of the key in her bedroom door, and then went up to my room. Pyavka was asleep, his face covered by a three-week-old newspaper from Warsaw. As I undressed, I realize I had left my gold watch, a farewell gift from Vasya, in the card room.

In my nightshirt, I raced down the stairs. A chill gripped my heart when I saw that the watch was gone.

I started to climb back up to my room to check my pockets once more. Halfway up the stairs, I encountered Madame. With a lit candle in her hand, and in a nightdress as filmy as a spider's web, she descended in ghost-like silence, stopping on the step above me.

We stared at each other in silence. Her eyes haggard with reproach, she handed me the watch while I stood motionless, shivering in my half-unbuttoned shirt.

Simply to break the endless silence between us, I was about to ask her what was wrong when Madame said, "Are you my friend?"

I found the question astonishing, and could only mutter, "Of course."

"There is a favor I want to ask you, but I fear you will say 'no.'"

"I promise you, I will not."

She looked suddenly aged and weary. "I want you to give me a child."

I felt myself being drawn into quicksand. It took me some moments to recover my balance. Then, in as neutral a tone as I could manage, I said, "Dearest Madame, do you know what would happen? I would fall hopelessly in love with you, and ..."

"Why 'hopelessly'?"

The words in my head tripped over each other before I was finally able to extract, "And as for your faithful and devoted husband, neither of us would be able to look him in the eye."

"Faithful?" she echoed with a bitter laugh. "Where do you think he stays until three o'clock in the morning? In his office, checking the books?"

"I don't know what your husband does at night, but I have known him long enough to be convinced that he is an honorable man. And, as much I feel drawn to you, I will not violate his trust."

Her face quivered. Anger, irony, self-pity? I was too confused to judge. "I have told you my husband is not capable of fathering a child. But the truth is more painful than that. He refuses to have relations with me. There is something about me that repels him." She wiped her cheek. "And now I have made a fool of myself with the only man I respect."

I tried to interrupt. "Dear lady, not at all."

"But rather than be doomed never to experience motherhood, I swear I will divorce my husband and marry someone else."

"I plead with you not to even think of doing that."

"Then the matter is in your hands."

"I don't understand."

She lowered herself until we were on the same step. "If you give me a child, I promise you, I will go on living with my husband. With love or without. For the sake of our child. You would be responsible for saving your friend's marriage. What greater act of friendship could there be than that?"

As she spoke, her perfume seemed to wrap its arms around me and draw me closer. I struggled to direct my eyes away from her translucent nightdress My resolution melted. I was ready to do whatever she asked.

Then a curious thing happened. The image of my father rushed through my brain. And something that I had not believed possible for a normal man happened. All desire suddenly drained out of me.

Madame's voice was dry as tinder as she asked, "Promise me you will at least think about it? Until tomorrow?"

I agreed, wordlessly, and with the most intense discomfort. Feeling as though I had already betrayed my friend, I went up to my room.

Pyavka was still awake. Being no fool, he saw at once that something had been going on. I suppose he expected me to gossip about it, as men are apt to do. But I shut off the light and told him to go to sleep.

In the middle of breakfast, while Pyavka slurped his sugared coffee and Madame and I strained to avoid each other's glance, Vasya was called to the telephone.

He came back looking distracted, if not evasive. I looked at him and realize that, should he ever have an inkling of what Madame and I had been discussing, or should she turn and lodge an accusation against me, my old comrade would, without a moment's pity or hesitation, sling me out into the street. And then, for all my popularity, every door in Irkutsk would be closed to me. Except one: the local prison.

Pyavka, aware that some strange game was being played, sat hunched in his chair, flicking his eye from one of us to the other, careful not to draw attention to himself.

Vasya drank his coffee standing up. He held the newspaper to his face in his other hand. (I had stopped reading the local gazette with its gleeful accounts of the latest pogroms. Nor was there much comfort to be found in the Yiddish papers from Warsaw, which conveyed either a sense of utter helplessness, or breathed defiance with the facetious humor of impotent old men.)

An ugly quarrel suddenly broke out between Divanovsky and Madame. She wanted him to drink sitting down, as good manners required. He, in turn, demanded that she quit "dictating" to him. The quarrel grew more bitter, more personal. I was desperate to escape from the room before some of their venom spilled over onto me.

As quickly as it started, the quarrel was over. Paying no further attention to his wife, Divanovsky motioned to me to step outside. There was something he must tell me privately. My heart thundered with guilt. He suspected! He *knew*! She had told him everything!

In his bookless "library," he shoved a cigar into my mouth, lit it for me and demonstrated how to inhale.

"All is in readiness," he said.

For a brief, terrible moment, I thought he was talking about Madame and me.

"Your train is due to leave at ten-thirty tomorrow morning."

Overwhelmed with relief, all I could think of saying was, "Nothing sooner?"

"You sound as though you can't wait to leave us."

Had I offended him, or was he toying with me?

"Surely you don't begrudge us one more day of your company." His smile left me feeling that he was holding something back. "You would not consider staying in Irkutsk a bit longer?"

"Why?"

"Why not? Has anyone done anything to make you feel unwelcome?"

"Heaven forbid! No one could have been better hosts than you and Madame. But my parents have not seen me in over six months, and who knows how much longer I will have them?"

"Is that your only reason?"

I felt like a prisoner given one last chance to make a full confession – a familiar sensation. "No. To be truthful, I don't feel I belong here, not in your house, nor among your friends. Whatever I had once done for you, you have already repaid a thousand times over."

For a long moment, his eyes reflected the glowering tip of his cigar. "What if I were to offer you a full partnership in my firm?"

"You're mad!"

"A millionaire's life doesn't tempt you?"

"Of course, it does. But …" My mind had gone blank. "I don't know what to say."

"Say 'yes'."

"Maybe one day, when I am no longer a fugitive, when I have a wife of my own …" My tongue stumbled.

His shrewd glance seemed, again, to signal that he knew all, that he was testing me. But then his former boyish smile returned, and he allowed me to help him into his overcoat.

For the rest of that day, whenever Vasya was out of the house, Madame and I took care not to be alone in the same room.

At dinner, no place was set for him, so Madame, Pyavka and I ate in silence, measuring each other's every breath. Feeling banished from our wordless conversation, Pyavka announced that he was ready to retire. I told him that I planned to retire early, too, but he was already on his way to the stairs. I noticed in passing that his face had taken on the color of moldy bread. But I was too preoccupied with my own situation to give it much thought.

My new belongings had been packed in leather trunks so fresh from the factory that they seem not yet to have lost the smell of the animal from which they had come.

Pyavka finally made peace with his new name and would be traveling with me.

We stood in the entry hall, hovering protectively over our trunks, waiting for Vasya. Both of us were so thickly bundled up, I didn't see how we and our belongings would all fit into the same coach.

Earlier that morning, Vasya told us that he had cancelled all other appointments so that he might escort us to the station. Following which, he promptly disappeared. Now and then, I heard him through closed doors, shouting into the telephone.

Thus far, I had dodged the awkwardness of saying goodbye to Madame. Now, flinching at the click of her descending footsteps, I knew I could not put it off any longer.

My mind groped for something agreeable yet impersonal to say in parting, but my tongue had turned to stone.

Her head motioned me to follow her into her husband's study. For a moment, I saw her once more as the grand and fearsome lady who had first confronted me in Divanovsky's office, and I braced myself for what she might have to say.

"I want you to swear to me you will forget what passed between us the other evening."

"There is nothing to tell."

"Words were spoken."

"They will go no further."

Her throat released a dry sob. "I will never forgive myself."

"For what?"

"Driving you away."

"Truly, Madame, it has nothing to do with you."

Her wounded eyes branded me a liar. I stood, encased in my bulky fur coat, and felt the sting of perspiration as it glided down my neck. Now even my bones were sweating.

I looked at my gold watch. We were late! The train must already be at the depot. But no one seemed to be in any hurry. Other than Pyavka and me.

At long last, Vasya made his ponderous way downstairs, even as Madame presented me with her pulsing, almost weightless hand. Vasya observed this without expression. He merely reminded me that although the train was scheduled to depart at ten-thirty that morning, one could never be certain whether this once, just for spite, it would hold to its pitiful schedule.

The coachman helped Pyavka and me into the carriage and piled our luggage in after us. The last item to be loaded was a farewell gift from Madame, an immense basket, whose warm, meaty aroma overpowered even the icy winds.

While we contorted ourselves to make room for Vasya, he suddenly commandeered a cab. It seemed he had forgotten to take care of a certain matter at the office. I wondered if this was his way of showing displeasure at the length of time I had held his wife's hand.

Late as we were, Pyavka and I climbed out again and trooped back into the house to await his return. Madame ordered the butler to bring us hot tea. I tried to avoid her look of desolation.

Pyavka whispered, "Why can't we go without him?"

I reminded him that our host had our tickets in his pocket. He paid for them, and that gave him the right to make us miss the train. At worst, there would be another one two days from now.

"In two days a lot can happen."

"Like what?"

He gave me the look of a man who knew more than he let on.

I sipped hot tea with jam, and wondered whether everyone in this house knew more than I did.

While Pyavka made use of the toilet for the second or third time that morning, Madame looked at me as though expecting some memorable pronouncement.

"At least neither of us has any cause to be ashamed."

She nodded, her eyes damp with resignation. "Go in peace. Rejoice in your parents, while you have them. They have mourned and suffered long enough. Only promise me you will be careful. Stay clear of your old comrades. Remember, to the police you are still a marked man. All it takes is for one person to recognize your face and denounce you."

Her words left me chilled. Had the luxury of the receding few weeks dulled the edge of the fear that had been my constant companion since escaping from Siberia? Perhaps I was acting too rashly. Much as I longed to see my parents, I was seized with a sudden dread of leaving the shelter of Divanovsky's home.

And this time, there would be no one to come to my aid. Once, an unknown girl at the train station in Warsaw had picked up my scrap of paper with its silent scream for help, and saved me. She was not likely to be there, again.

But being still young and reckless, I made light of Madame's fears in the next breath. "Dear Madame, being an outlaw is the only trade I know."

"Come back to us," she said with more emotion than I found comfortable. "You will be safe here. Cable my husband, and he will send you train fare. And his offer of a partnership remains open. I guarantee it."

"How did you know about that?"

"You thought he had acted behind my back? The wealth you have seen comes largely from my family. Oh, he too brought money into our marriage. But he destroyed himself with his evil lust for gambling." For a moment, the sadness bruising her features hardened to scorn. "Now he is nothing without me. I hold the whip. Come back and, much as it will torment me, I will help you find a bride. I need a friend with whom I can at least share what is in my heart. And you are the only true friend I have. I want your word. Will you come back?"

My face felt as though it had been thrust into boiling water. All I could say was, "If I am fated to return, I'll return."

"You will if you want to, if you are my true friend. I want your most solemn promise." While saying this, she tried to press a thick bundle of money into my hand. "Your return fare to Irkutsk. Now there will be nothing to hold you back."

I tried to refuse the gift. Or rather, the conditions attached to it. "Your husband has already given me more than I need. How can I accept this behind his back?"

"Take it," she commanded. "Take it, or you will leave me with no hope at all."

Before I could protest any further, Vasya returned. He and his wife exchanged a dark look whose meaning escaped me. As though to defy his wife, Vasya openly handed me, along with our train tickets and travel permits, another five hundred rubles.

Pyavka had been standing outside, stamping his feet to keep warm. I saw him, through the open door, waving his arms with impatience. By now it was well past ten-thirty. For all we knew, the train might have long since departed.

Pyavka and I climbed into the carriage once again and were joined by Vasya, leaving barely enough room for a deep breath. Our driver was about to start when Madame came fluttering toward us in a cloud of furs. She knocked on the carriage door and demanded that we make room for her, as well.

Poor Vasya. It occurred to me that this lady, for all her beauty and wealth, might not be an easy woman to have for a wife.

34
THE COST OF MONEY

The carriage flew at a fearful speed, churning up a spray of snow as high as our windows. I took a stealthy look at my watch. I was nearly eleven o'clock in morning. I shared Pyavka's annoyance with Vasya and Madame. Not only did they make us late, but I had hoped to have a quiet word with my friend in private to impress upon him that he had been shamefully cold toward his wife.

At the station, we skidded to a halt so sharply that the carriage nearly tipped over. The train was still there, but impatient puffs of steam were hissing out from under its belly.

Although I was strongly tempted to ignore convention, for people of our rank, arriving as we did by coach, it would have been unthinkable to leap out and run along the platform. So we sat back and waited, with varying levels of calmness, for the driver to dismount from his box. Then Pyavka and I were obliged to watch as he shuffled to open our door with all the grace of a snowman come to life, which exposed us to a blast of cold air. Next, he carefully removed and folded the valuable fur blankets covering our laps and legs, and placed them on his seat. Finally, we had to stand by and observe him unloading our immaculate new luggage, repelling with a dog-like snarl the helpful hands of half a dozen idle porters. At last, gasping like a bellows, he carried each trunk to the train, and from there to our first-class car at the far end of the platform.

By the grimy and indifferent station clock, all of this took another fifteen minutes. During this time, our train squatted on its trestles, excreted foul-smelling clouds, and waited for us to do it the kindness of boarding.

Protocol, at last, allowed us to head for our car, unhurried and unburdened with luggage, as befitted our first-class tickets.

Headed toward our car, I swallowed a sudden taste of fear. Three uniformed men were leading a string of chained prisoners down the platform. From the way the victims were dressed and tonsured, they might well have escaped from our camp. I averted my face and nudged Pyavka to do the same.

Sensing my discomfort, Madame laughed. She whispered that I needn't worry. For one thing, no one looking at Pyavka or me would find a speck of resemblance to the barely human specimens who had turned up in her husband's office weeks earlier. And if some uniformed thug on the train should dare to question our documents, "all you need to do is send a telegram and—"

"Madame," I said respectfully. "I've been arrested before, and in a civilized city like Warsaw. By the time I was able to bribe one of the guards to let me write a message, I was already on my way to the execution wall."

She frowned with annoyance. My quibble seemed not to fit the high opinion she had had of my resourcefulness. I could only hope that, when the Revolution washed over Irkutsk, her husband would have had the good sense to see it coming and take her far away.

I was just about to board when Vasya pulled me aside. He wanted to speak with me, alone. *Now*?

He said that he planned to lose himself in the crowd. And when the train left, he would be on it, too.

I gaped at him stupidly. "What about your wife?"

"She knows how to find her way home."

"But she won't know where you are. She'll be frantic."

"I doubt it very much. But if it will make you happy, I'll send her a message." I couldn't say that I much liked his casual compromise.

The conductor chanted his final warning of imminent departure. Vasya tipped him a ruble, handed him a slip of paper, and strolled along the platform.

Madame, caught in a rush of last-minute passengers, elbowed her way toward the train and peered through each window, her eyes roving for her husband. She saw me and waved. Her lips formed words I could not decipher. All I could do was curve my hand behind my ear, shrug and shake my head.

By the time Pyavka and I were entrenched amidst our barricade of heavy luggage, the wheels were already pounding under our feet. I had just begun to wonder whether Vasya had changed his mind when our door slid open.

My old comrade, his nose and mouth theatrically muffled, motioned me to follow him to the dining car.

Pyavka, with an accommodating smile, rose to join us. But Divanovsky's brusque gesture made clear the invitation was meant for me, alone.

We threaded our way down a succession of jolting corridors. While we waited to be seated in the dining car, I expressed my concern that Madame might still be searching for him at the station, not the safest place for a lady to be on her own.

Vasya looked at me with a bitterness I had not seen since his days under the fist of the arch-fiend, Lieutenant 'Haman.'

"She is not the dear, helpless creature you seem to think she is," he said.

My heart pumped a warning. Could one of the servants have been spying on Madame?

But he said nothing further until we were seated at the table and a bottle and two glasses before us. To set my mind to rest, he said that Madame would have already received his message informing her that he would return by train at two o'clock in the morning, and to have his carriage waiting. He said that he often went away on business without telling her in advance.

Then he filled my glass and cleared his throat. He had something serious to speak to me about, but didn't know how to begin.

I put a heavy hand on his elbow and said, "Good brother, let me begin for you. You have a wife who is one in a million. And yet you treat her as though she didn't exist. Before I say goodbye to you for good, I want to know why."

Trees scoured and stunted by the winds flashed past our window. Vasya ordered another bottle. We drank several glasses in sullen silence.

Fearful of meeting his eye, I picked up the new bottle, but his hand covered the rim of his glass.

"Our tragedy is common enough," he said. "She is desperate for a child. And why should she not be?"

"Then what the devil is stopping you? I remember, in Petersburg, the times you stayed out all night. And not merely drinking and gambling."

But this was not an aspect of his sad time of which he liked to be reminded, either. Especially by me, a witness to his degradation. "That is exactly my tragedy. One of those low women gave me a disease. And now I am so fearful of passing it on to my wife, I use every possible excuse to avoid being with her. Even if I were cruel enough not to care, the disease has advanced so far that it has left me incapable of fathering a child."

"You've been to doctors, of course."

"The best. Each had his own procedures, usually painful and humiliating. Nothing helped. All they did was make me lose whatever respect I had for doctors."

"Then why not tell her the truth? Admit you are avoiding her, not from aversion, but out of your love for her."

"You don't know her family. If they ever suspected what a libertine I had been, not only would she put an end to our marriage but her father would ruin me."

"You would prefer that Madame believe you hate her?"

His bones sagged. "At one point, we developed a plan: we would choose another man to father our child." I felt pinpricks of sweat bursting from every pore.

"You look shocked," he said. "But that was how much I loved her. The only problem was finding the right man."

"You do your wife an injustice," I tried to say without sputtering.

Vasya laughed at me outright. "She told me the whole story, herself, the very next morning. How you had fled from her as though she carried the plague." He chuckled as though, for once in his life, he had gotten the better of me. "I never doubted you were an honest man, Yakov, but you're a fool. Why do you suppose I made you wait so long for your passport? Why did I even offer you a partnership? She and I thought we had found the perfect candidate. What normal man would have passed up such an offer?"

I felt a shiver of disgust. "You sent her to me?"

He grinned. "I know, I know. 'A horse and a wife you don't lend.' But, oh, she was willing enough, more than willing. How I hated you for that! And yet, if anyone in this whole business behaved decently, it was you."

A chill ran down my back. I was glad, at least, that we hadn't had this conversation before I left Irkutsk. "And what will you do now?"

"Nothing. It's over."

"You can't mean that."

"Your sudden arrival was like a miracle. A last chance to revive our marriage. I could see she was drawn to you. Not that she ever, in so many words, said she loved you. But you were the only man of whom I ever heard her speak without contempt. I thought, finally, the two of you would give me a child. And now I have no hope left at all." Damp-eyed, he refilled his glass and drained it in one gulp. "When I get home tomorrow night, I'll tell my wife she can have her divorce. If she accepts, she would marry you in a second."

"How can you know that?"

"Because she told me so. The only question was your interest."

I didn't know whether to feel pity or rage, and had to force myself to keep from shouting, "Are you asking me to marry your wife?"

Vasya laughed. "You sound terrified. Not that I blame you. Thus far, you've seen only her gentler side. There are other times when the sting of her tongue would send the Angel of Death howling for mercy." Yet he said this with a peculiar kind of pride.

Needled by curiosity, I asked, "You wouldn't be jealous?"

"I would die of envy. But I swear to you, I would cherish your children like my own."

Moments later, he murmured drunkenly, "Will you at least consider it?"

I was inclined to fling the contents of my glass into his face. But my response was shamefully civil. In those unsettled times, who knew what I would find in Poland? Was it really unthinkable that I might, one day, be glad to escape back to Irkutsk?

After about three hours, the train stopped and Vasya got off. We embraced like brothers and promised faithfully to write to one another. But we both knew we were lying.

Pyavka sat sprawled in our compartment with his boots up, a snowy napkin tucked into his vest, his cheeks brazenly chewing on the contents of the basket Madame had packed for us both. Undaunted by my disapproving look, his only observation was, "You are still on the train?"

"Where else would I be?"

"I thought you and your old comrade were staging this whole masquerade to be rid of me."

"You don't think I want to see my family as much as you do?"

"It seemed to me you already had a 'family' in Irkutsk. A partnership in a great business, and another kind of 'partnership' with Madame."

My impulse was to put a fist through his face. Rather than wondering what he knew, I tried to understand whether what I felt was honest indignation or the sly sting of regret.

I tucked a napkin into the front of my vest and applied myself to the roast goose. A moment later, the first mouthful nearly stuck in my throat. At the bottom of the basket lay a letter in Madame's inflated handwriting. It was addressed to me.

I was seized by the temptation to tear it up, unread, and scatter the pieces out the window. Perhaps Vasya was correct about my being fool for passing up such an opportunity.

For a fraction of a moment, I longed for Madame so keenly that I wanted to leap from the speeding train.

Pyavka said, "What's wrong? Your face is turning green."

I pretended I had choked on a bone.

Later, while he dozed, I slipped the letter into my sleeve and stood outside the cabin to read the letter in privacy. My head whirled. What if she begged me to take the next train back? What if she offered me … I didn't know what? Would I have the resolve to continue on to Vishigrod?

Blindly tearing open the envelope, I held the letter close to my blurring eyes.

Her message was brief. "Hearty appetite!" Nothing more.

35
RETURN TO WARSAW

My heart leapt in anticipation as much as in fear. Until now, our forged papers, first-class tickets, stylish clothes and rich men's demeanor may have shielded us from being challenged. But here, in these tense and bloody times, the terminal was certain to be swarming with policemen who would be somewhat less impressed by English tailoring.

The moment we set foot on the platform, Pyavka's old regal demeanor put iron into his spine. This was truly his kingdom. But instead of surveying the environment opportunistically, he snapped his fingers and summoned a porter to help with our trunks. Barely troubling to glance back over our shoulders (as who would dare steal from the "King of Thieves?"), we crossed the waiting room unchallenged.

While Pyavka summoned a motor-taxi, I glanced behind me. Our porter, panting under the weight of our bags, had not yet caught up with us. But suddenly two unmistakable police types were walking alongside him, showing indecent interest in our expensive luggage.

The porter shrugged and looked about him, then he pointed in our direction.

I shoved Pyavka into the cab, piled in behind him and told the driver to whisk us to the Hotel Bristol, the first name that came to mind.

Looking back, I could see our bewildered porter scratching his head. Poor man, he had been cheated of his tip. But I daresay our luggage and its contents would more than make up for his loss.

Let off at the Bristol, we pushed our way through the crowded lobby and, having made sure no one followed us, left by another exit.

The second cab took us to Pyavka's home. There another surprise awaited me. The royal "mansion" I had expected to see was, in fact, no more than an unremarkable two-story brick house with a pair of haughty "Greek" columns flanking the entrance.

Pyavka begged me to come in with him long enough to at least meet his wife and children. But now that I was back in the normal world, I could not ignore the fact that this was Friday and, according to my new watch, the arrival of *Shabbos* was but minutes away. There was barely enough time to reach my brother's home before sunset.

But I promised Pyavka I would visit him on Sunday, and then told the driver to speed me to number 72 Pavia Street, Mordechai's last-known address.

My final glimpse of my partner was of him facing a pale, plain-looking woman in the open doorway who stood there only for a moment before collapsing at his feet.

By the time we reached 72 Pavia, the sky had already been punctured with stars. I climbed out of the cab, ashamed to be seen by Jews in their Sabbath clothes. Apprehensive, I mounted the four flights to Apartment 5, uncertain whether my brother still lived there. It was too dark to read the name-plate, but as I pressed my ear to the door I heard voices joined in a familiar Sabbath melody. The tune brought up a rush of tears.

I tried the handle. The door was not locked. I tiptoed through the unlit corridor and, through foggy eyes, as in a dream, observed the people at the table: My brother, Mordechai, and two married cousins. His wife, Dvorah, was about to serve the fish. The first to see me, she screamed and dropped the platter. Moments later, I was embraced from all sides. Forced into a seat at the table, I was served so many portions of the *Shabbos* dinner that I needed to eat with both hands just to keep up.

My eyes opened to the curiously soothing pop-pop-pop of small-arms fire. It was *Shabbos* afternoon, normally the most peaceful of times, even in Warsaw. I had been lying on my brother's bed, watching webs of dusty sunlight spill through the lace curtains. I tried to resist, but finally professional interest won out, and I stood by the window to observe the outside action.

Four stories below, lightly armed men in grimy street clothes were running, first in one direction, and then in the opposite, periodically remembering to take cover. Faint puffs of smoke issued from a variety of old rifles and pistols, as the combatants advanced and retreated with all the tactical discipline of schoolboys kicking a football. A dozen years ago, on any day other than *Shabbos*, this might have been me and my friends playing soldier, the only difference being that the firearms in the present picture issuing their noisy reports were real.

Suddenly, as if they'd all heard the same dinner bell, the combatants drifted off in various directions, and a horse-drawn ambulance ground over the cobblestones to collect the fallen.

From the doorway, my brother and his wife saw me at the window and decided that, in view of my persistent fascination with armed combat, something had be to be done quickly to keep me from sliding back into my old, lawless ways.

I tried, vainly, to convince them that, after what I'd lived through – good and bad – I had lost my appetite for disorderly conduct. Nevertheless, to help determine my future, first thing Sunday morning my parents arrived from Vishogrod along with my sister, Malkah.

All agreed it would not be wise just now for me to show my face in Vishogrod. Not that anyone would inform on me. But the Czar had just appointed a new *natchalnik* to rule over our city, a curious creature who was neither married nor a drunkard, and people had not yet determined whether he was corrupt (that is, greedy), or corruptible (meaning humane).

But if I stayed in Warsaw, what were my prospects for a career? The only professional skills I could claim were marksmanship and Cossack dancing. And where, in all of Warsaw, was I likely to find an employer who would not recoil at the mere sound of my name, remembering the baby-faced agitator, the organizer of riots and strikes, the 'terrorist' responsible for broken windows and black eyes?

In the end, we all agreed there was only one safe place for me – America, that fairytale continent of noble red men and cloud-scraping cities, with a statue in its harbor welcoming immigrants, including Jews.

Best of all, my brother Chayim, whom I had last seen presiding over his pitiful "department store" in Łódź, already lived in Shenandoah, Pennsylvania, where he had found steady employment as a haberdasher. While not as wealthy as most Americans, he already lived in a three-room house with electricity, and wooden floors in every room.

Not, as my mother reminded me, that all the things one heard about America were reassuring to a parent's heart. To shield me, in my innocence, from falling into the hands of a whiskey-guzzling, cigarette-smoking American woman of uncertain ethics, my parents insisted that I not set out for the New World until properly armed with a wife. My groans of protest were a mere formality.

Early Monday morning, in a sudden rush of guilt, I recalled my promise to visit Pyavka. Without telling my family, who might not care to see me maintain this link to my disreputable past, I took a cab to his house. Hearing the address on Nowy Swiat, the driver gave me a curious look. Or was it a wink of complicity, as from one crook to another?

To my surprise, Pyavka's front door was half open, as though the police had just been there and left nothing worth stealing.

With a sense of foreboding, I mounted the front steps and peered inside. Seated at one end of the parlor in formal attire were a number of unmistakable specimens of the criminal persuasion, some of whom crossed and uncrossed their legs, as though too delicate to get up and ask for the toilet.

I headed for a low chair in a spot where none could pick my pocket. Immediately, I felt a familiar sense of discord that I didn't allow myself to recognize. Only once I was seated at the dark end of the room did I notice the middle-aged woman who had collapsed upon Pyavka's arrival.

I didn't know what manner of wife I had expected him to have, but it was a shock to see her up close, an exhausted woman in stocking feet, eyes raw with grief, her leaden hair matted in disarray.

Stupidly, I asked her, "Forgive me, but are you Madame Pyavka?"

"And who would you be?" she said wearily. "Another of his 'colleagues'?"

Before I could respond, she looked at me more closely and her tone suddenly grew animated.

"No. I know who you are: Yakov Marateck. Even in his final hours, your name was on his lips, and how, without your friendship and your strength, he would have gone into the earth where none would ever know."

Pyavka – gone into the earth? I felt the breath squeezed out of my lungs, and trembled with remorse. So all the times he had complained of weakness or gone to sleep early, he had been bravely concealing the pains of a mortal illness, afraid to call a doctor or go to the hospital where the first organ they would likely have wanted to examine was his passport. All those times I had threatened him that, unless he followed me quickly, I would leave him to die where his family would never find his grave, he had been slowly dying, like the magical "Queen Esther." The only explanation for my blindness was that I had been too self-focused to recognize my friend's suffering.

"They called him a 'King'," his widow suddenly burst out. "The highest officials were proud to be invited to our home. But for his burial, I had to go begging to scrape up ten men. Even his son could not be found." And she wept anew.

Tears clogged my throat. This "King of Thieves" had been the instrument of my escape, a faithful partner in my adventures, and yet, having at last returned to his family, he lived only long enough to be lowered into a Jewish grave.

I needed to mourn for him privately to fix in my memory the times we enjoyed together when we weren't, at that moment, fearing for our lives. It would take recalling many such occasions to dislodge my recollection of how shamefully I had behaved toward the one man whose company had sustained, and alternately amused and infuriated, me since we met on the way to Siberia. What I hadn't recognized was that he was essential to my survival. Sometimes it was only my sense of responsibility for my partner, and maintaining his optimism, that allowed me to find more and more outrageous ways to keep us both alive.

I promised Pyavka's widow that I would return at some future time to relate some of the incidents he and I had shared, stories I was sure would make her proud. And I had fully intended to do so.

But by the time I remembered this promise, my life had already taken quite another turn.

36

THE REDHEAD

To my surprise, most of the matchmakers who scaled the narrow four flights to my brother's apartment didn't take long to decide that it was a waste of their time to try to meet my "outlandish" specifications, namely for a girl both beautiful and intelligent, pious and worldly, good-natured, yet able to assert herself.

Only Leibush, the tireless old-timer who had tracked me to Warsaw, had not given up on me. And since I really did want to get married, I applied my most respectful attention to each of the finger-marked photographs he slapped down on the table, like a gambler playing his ace, confronting me with a row of young women whose mournful smiles and moist black eyes seemed to plead for compassion from the photographer's indifferent lens.

Much as I struggled to concentrate on the prospective brides being set before me, my attention began to blur and I was forced to confess that none of those sad and trusting faces captured my heart. None even aroused a flicker of a sinful thought.

Leibush angrily scooped up his gallery of clients and made ready to leave, accusing me of having too high an opinion of myself. Which I couldn't dispute. My palate may well have been jaded from months of exposure to snowy-fingered beauties, like Slava, and the formidable Madame Divanovsky, both now forever beyond my horizon.

But in an effort to convince Leibush that I was not a hopeless bachelor, I agreed to meet a few of his clients for a coffee or a walk in the Botanical Garden. But even the briefest of conversations revealed their outlook to be so cruelly stunted by poverty, their modest demands on life so uncertain, their minds so ill-schooled in either sacred or secular writings, that I felt able to talk with them only in the most general and stilted terms.

In the end, I was left with but one possibility, a well-dowered redhead from Łódź. Although we had not yet met, her photograph intrigued me with the ironic curl of her lips and the twinkle of what could portend either a spirit of mischief or a temper as clipped as the fuse of a grenade.

Seeing me take a second look, and then a third, Leibush cautioned me shrewdly that this creature needed a "real man" to tame her.

Stung by his suggestion and the challenge, I demanded to meet her at once, but she had to come to Warsaw since, as I asked Leibush to explain, owing to a small misunderstanding with The Law, it was not altogether safe for me to travel.

But nothing would move The Redhead to meet me in Warsaw, a stand I found admirable, if inconvenient.

For several days, telegrams, phone calls and letters flew back and forth like mortar shells from opposing trenches. But the more eagerness I showed to meet this principled young woman, the more her father was convinced that I was not only a wanted criminal but a fortune-hunter holding out for a larger dowry.

Determined to prove him wrong, I impulsively took a train to Łódź and, unannounced, knocked on his door.

To my surprise, The Redhead's father seemed neither startled nor offended to find me on his doorstep. In fact, he'd been expecting me, thanks to a mysteriously prophetic telegram from Leibush.

The Redhead, on the other hand, needed some time to be persuaded that my blunt arrival did not indicate a "lack of respect."

For my part, while I found her somewhat bossy as well as a few years older than advertised, I considered her a definite possibility. In part, because Leibush had made me fear that I was holding out for an unattainable ideal, and this young woman with her pretty features and charmingly scolding voice, may have been the best I could hope to do.

Especially when, after a day or two of cautiously becoming acquainted, she confided in a whisper that she also found me not unacceptable.

My talks with The Redhead's father, under Leibush's prodding, soon turned to such practical details as the size and location of the grocery store that would be my means of supporting a family. Train schedules were consulted to arrange for my parents to come to Łódź and meet their future in-laws.

But one thing held me back. A totally crazy idea. Which was that I had never thanked the girl from the railroad station in Warsaw, the one who had picked up the piece of paper that I dropped on the way to my execution. The girl who had saved my life.

I tried to explain this to my almost-fiancée, but she lost patience with my "indecisiveness" and snapped, "Then why don't you go and marry *her*?" And shut the door in my face.

I returned to Warsaw with a delirious sense of freedom, and promptly asked my brother and his wife for the name and address of the girl who had delivered my note.

Silence.

In all the confusion, neither one of them had thought to ask the girl who she was or where she was from. I was incensed by their negligence.

I suddenly also had Leibush under foot, complaining that, after all his efforts, I had gone back on my word, and he was not at all certain that my reputation, at least within the borders of Russian Poland, could still be salvaged.

My brother, too, was annoyed. "Fine. I should have asked her name. But I thought it was more urgent to get you a good lawyer. Tell me I was wrong."

"Well, what did she look like?"

"You saw her, too. Didn't you notice?"

"I was on my way to get shot. I had other things on my mind."

"You can't just play with a young woman's feelings," Leibush insisted.

"What young woman?" Mordechai asked.

"The one from Łódź!" Leibush said.

"She threw me out," I added.

"Nonsense. Her father said if you went back and apologized, she might reconsider. Shall I send a telegram?"

"Yes. No. Wait; I'm not sure."

"You would rather go chase after some unknown female from the railroad station? You know what kind of women hang out at stations?"

"Novy Dvor," my brother's wife burst out. "That's where I think she said she was from."

"Novy Dvor," the matchmaker said mockingly. "Two hours by train. Ever been there? A nothing of a town. And when you get there, you'll do what – go from door to door and ask for a girl whose name you don't know? For a boy from a fine family like yours to go prowling after a female who picks up letters from criminals …"

"*I* was the 'criminal,'" I reminded him.

"So, who's blaming you?"

My brother, trying to calm me down, remembered that we had a great-aunt in Novy Dvor named Hana-Tova who, as it happened, had done rather well as a matchmaker in her younger years.

Leibush scoffed, "Hana-Tova! Who doesn't know Hana-Tova? Fifty, sixty years ago, sure, she would have matched you up in five minutes. But now? Listen, we all get old."

He finally left, vowing, unasked, to bring me a favorable answer from the girl in Łódź. "I will remind her father what the Almighty said to Eve when he presented her to Adam. You remember the verse? 'And he shall rule over you.'"

Since I could well imagine how The Redhead would respond, I raised no objection.

To fill the profound silence left by Leibush's abrupt departure, my brother shyly opened his billfold and showed me a muddy scrap of paper.

"What's this?"

"You don't recognize it?"

It was the very piece of paper on which I had blindly written my desperate appeal. He carried it with him as a reminder of the brother he had never expected to see again.

I squinted at it in the afternoon light, and could barely make out the scrawl. It could have been written by a cripple or a blind man. I didn't even recognize the handwriting. The text, however, had a familiar ring: *"Jews, have mercy and run quickly to 72 Pavia, Apartment 5. I am on my way to execution get me a lawyer whatever it costs tomorrow will be too late."* To which I had courteously added, "thank you," but forgotten to sign my name.

I was astonished at the letter's length, scribbled in Egyptian darkness.[77] Only, what had made me address the letter to Jews, alone? Had I not considered that gentiles also had compassion? But I suppose, in my despair, I could not picture anyone but a Jew bending down to pluck a scrap of paper out of the mud.

At once, I was filled with determination to find this remarkable girl, regardless of the obstacles.

Evening. Friends and cousins, intrigued by my romantic quest, gathered in Mordechai's apartment. Each knew exactly what I should do when, and if, I located this mysterious creature.

A neighbor said it would be a nice gesture to present her with a pair of silver candlesticks.

Dvora objected that such a gift might be taken as a marriage proposal. "And what if she says 'yes?'"

A cousin said the most respectable thing would be to bring her flowers, and maybe a postal order for 50 rubles. Someone else wondered why twenty rubles wasn't enough. This started a dispute between those who thought 50 was too extravagant and those who considered it too little.

Another relative pointed out that giving someone a material reward for a *mitzvah* diminished his or her reward in the World to Come.

I broke in to remind them I still didn't have a clue as to who she was or where she lived.

Dvora said, "Why not ask her cousin?"

I exploded out of my chair. "What cousin?"

"She mentioned that she had come to Warsaw to visit a cousin named Golde, a wig-maker, who lived on Smocza, corner Gesia."

"Why didn't you say so before?"

Turning away, she said, "So who listens to a woman?"

77 A reference to one of the Ten Plagues, which was Darkness

Mordechai claimed not to have heard the girl say any such thing. But the rest of us, smelling a challenge, jumped up and clattered down the stairs, headed for Smocza.

Like any intersection, this one had a building on each corner, five stories each, two apartments per story, a total of forty apartments, not counting attics and cellars.

Smocza being that kind of a neighborhood, some of the people who answered my knock either mistook my intentions and closed the door in my face, or offered me a ready substitute – a hairdresser, a manicurist, even a dress-maker, although none were named Golde.

At the third house, a severe young housewife said, "I am a wig-maker, but my name is Guta, not Golde. Also I don't touch men's hair."

Before she could shut the door on me, I hastily asked, "Do you have a cousin in Novy Dvor?"

"What has that to do with you?"

"Last year she did me a great kindness, and I want to thank her."

"It took you a whole year to remember?"

"I was away. In Siberia."

"For what?"

"For nothing. I was innocent. It's not your business, anyway."

She suddenly widened her eyes and leaned forward to stare at me in a better light. "Are you the young man in chains who was on his way to being shot?"

"That's me!" I said, perhaps too proudly. "What is her name?"

Guta wrinkled her nose. "You couldn't find a clean piece of paper to write on?"

"I was in jail."

"She showed it to me, for my opinion. Did I think it was a joke? I told her it's either a joke or written by a lunatic."

"I am the lunatic! Now can you please tell me her name and where I can find her?"

"It would do you no good."

"Why?" I had a sudden sense of fear I would learn, as I had twice in the recent past, that I was too late.

"Her father doesn't let her meet just anyone."

"All I want is to look at her face and say, 'thank you'."

"It starts with an innocent 'thank you', and who knows where it ends up?"

"And what if it does?"

"Take my word for it; you're not the type he's looking for."

Before I could knock my head against the doorpost, Dvora smoothly intervened, "You are quite right. My brother will write her a nice letter. If you will kindly give us her name and address."

With a suspicious glance in my direction, Guta said, "Her name is Bryna Migdal. I don't know her address because I don't need to; I recognize the house."

I raced blindly down the unlit stairs, five at a time. Out in the street, I tried to hail a cab to the station. While I frantically waved my arms, as if that would make a cab suddenly appear, Dvora took my arm and dragged me back to her apartment so I could polish my boots and put on a clean shirt.

Somehow, Leibush already knew I was going to Novy Dvor, and before I reached Mordechai's door, he was waiting there wearing a benign smile to let me know he was traveling with me, at his own expense.

"What for?"

"To handle the negotiations."

"What negotiations?"

"Don't be a child. You're single, she's single. Who knows what can happen? A look leads to a word. A word leads to another. If you don't have someone to stand up for your interests, you'll end up with nothing."

"How do you know she's single?"

"If not, I have two other girls for you in Novy Dvor. Twins. I already spoke to the father ..."

Even as my brother politely escorted him out, Leibush assured me that, when I came back, he would surely have at least a "hopeful" decision for me from The Redhead in Łódź.

The train was marked Express, but its speed could not keep up with my racing heart.

Resting on my lap was a gift, heavily wrapped. I won't tell you what it was or how much it cost, but it was not a pair of silver candlesticks.

To contain my impatience, I strode up and down the rattling corridors. This got me to my destination no more quickly, but got me there with tired feet.

I didn't have my great-aunt, Hana-Tova's, address, but my driver not only knew where she lived, but confided that she had the largest Jewish-owned store in Novy Dvor, employing as many as two shop-assistants at the same time.

Although I had not seen Hana-Tova since childhood, she remembered me at once. That is, she had heard that one of her nephews named Yakov had been, for some whimsical Czarist reason, sent to Siberia. And she was not only pleased to see me back, but also touched that I had traveled all this way to let her know.

Her next question was, "Are you married yet?"

"No."

"Why not?"

"I haven't had time."

She did not consider this a serious answer. She was all the more intrigued when I explained that I had come to Novy Dvor to meet a particular girl.

"Who?"

"Bryna Migdal. Maybe you know her?"

She looked me up and down with what I took to be sympathy, if not pity. "How did you hear of her?"

"She saved me from being shot."

My great-aunt nodded shrewdly, as if that were the most natural thing in the world for this particular girl to have done.

Elya, her husband, strolled in from the storeroom as our voices had awakened him. Hana-Tova introduced me as "Shloime-Zalman's son, just back from Siberia."

He shook my hand. "And what are you doing in Novy Dvor?"

"He wants to meet Bryna Migdal."

My great-uncle sighed and patted my arm.

I asked, "What's wrong?"

"Nothing. What should be wrong?"

At dinner, I told them how this total stranger had, no doubt at some inconvenience, saved me from the firing squad. And that, indicating the parcel on their sideboard, I had come to express my thanks.

"Fine. I'll have it sent over," said Hana-Tova.

"Why can't I give it to her myself?"

Uncle Elya sighed once more. "Don't take this as anything personal, but her father, like any good *Hasid*, holds to certain standards for the sort of young man he will allow his daughter to meet."

I kindly challenged my uncle to point out in what respects I fell short.

Both he and Hana-Tova assured me, with all possible delicacy, that it was not simply a matter of my fine English suit being of a color other than black, nor that the brief train ride from Warsaw had allowed me insufficient time to grow a beard. It was just that, through no fault of my own, I had spent some years in a world of lawless, violent men, shedders of blood, and probably was forced to do this-and-that and who-knows-what-else to stay alive. And while Elya could see that none of this had left its shadow on my soul, a man of such penetrating insight as Rabbi Migdal might, at the very least, regard me as a man who, begging my pardon, had seen something of life.

"And why should that be held against me?"

"No one is holding anything against you. It is just that Jews in Novy Dvor are serious people, and a young man cannot simply walk in off the street and hope to be introduced to a treasure like Bryna."

Having nothing left to lose, I shifted to the offensive. "Then why is she not married, yet? Could it be there is something wrong with her?"

"Heaven forbid," Hana-Tova said. But I didn't fail to spot her anxious eye consulting with her husband. She finally confessed, "Since we know what kind of a family you come from, and I can see your interest is not frivolous, it would be only fair to mention one small blemish, at least in some peoples' eyes, especially since she, herself, makes no secret of it."

"Ah," I said, but my heart quaked with apprehension.

"This girl, you understand, has been offered some of the finest matches in the country, brilliant scholars, eldest sons of Hasidic dynasties. Only ..." She looked to her husband for permission to continue. Elya shrugged, resigned to having it come out. "The fact is, she has one indulgence. She reads secular books. Not only in Yiddish, but in Polish and Russian and

I think even in German. What is more, she has let it be known that the man she marries can not dictate to her what she may or may not read." Hana-Tova sadly shook her head. "Already any number of fine young men, hearing such a condition, have declined to meet her. But she will settle for nothing less."

Throughout the meal, I brooded and schemed for some way to meet this elusive young lady. About the only thing that came to mind was to ask Hana-Tova to send one of her girls with a message to Bryna Migdal that she had just received a bolt of cloth that would go perfectly with her complexion. "And when she comes into the store, simply introduce me as a relative from Warsaw, and I will casually ask her advice on something to buy for my mother, which will indicate I am a serious person, and if the conversation goes well, then I might ask if I can buy her a coffee, and ..."

Hana-Tova silenced me with an uneasy, "Yes, but what if she actually wants to buy the cloth?"

"What's wrong with that?"

"I will have sold it to her on false pretense."

I was ready to tear out my hair. But Uncle Elya was on my side. He reminded his wife that making matches is regarded as so urgent a Commandment that it is permitted even on *Shabbos*. She can also sell her the material at cost or give the profit to charity.

So Hana-Tova relented and sent off one of her shop-assistants while I, already burning with impatience, stood at the window and watched a rusty sun drown behind a horizon of chimneys and tiled roofs, in dread that night would fall too quickly and the girl whose presence I craved would choose to come tomorrow, a lifetime from now.

What seemed like hours later, the little bell on the door to my aunt's store pealed and my aunt's messenger sidled into the store, alone. My teeth cut into my lip with disappointment. She said nothing, so I blurted out, "What did she say?"

Ignoring my rude question, the salesgirl reported to Hana-Tova. Miss Migdal will come over, but not now. Then when? Later. How much later? When she has finished giving her father his dinner. I tried to master my impatience. A good daughter, after all, was apt to make a good wife.

Another half an hour crawled by. But suddenly time stopped. A graceful shadow was headed this way. Her face, as yet, was only a tantalizing blur. But the manner, demure but decisive, in which she placed one foot in front of the other was enough to stop my heart. In all my life, I remembered only one person I'd seen walk in this manner, and that had been outside the railroad station in Warsaw.

The blue flame of a streetlight stroked her cheek and I glimpsed, or maybe even recognized, a crown of rich dark hair, a perfect nose, and eyes dancing with zest.

I wanted to fling open the door and shout, "Please, walk a little faster."

Only when she was about to enter the shop did I become aware of my oafish posture at the counter and forced myself to turn aside and look natural, even bored, like someone waiting for his order to be wrapped.

The little bell deafened my ears. My chest rumbled with apprehension. I was shocked to hear Hana-Tova greet this girl as casually as if she were some ordinary child from the street.

Smiling in anticipation, Bryna said, "What is this surprise you have for me?" Her velvety voice sent the blood thumping in my ears. Thankfully, up to this moment, she had taken no notice of my insolent stare.

"Oh, and my nephew just arrived from Warsaw. He brings regards from your cousin Guta."

"Oh?"

I had to pretend that my shoulders were made of stone, which was how my head felt, in order to keep from turning toward her too quickly. But now that I faced her, what could I possibly say to this girl that would hold her attention for more than a second?

Just then, a customer lumbered in and demanded that my aunt wait on her in person.

It was up to me, alone. As King Solomon wrote, 'Life and death lie in the power of the tongue.' My future, and the future of my children and children's children, hung in the balance. But not a word escaped my lips.

Seeing Hana-Tova occupied, the girl dismissed me with a nod and said, "Tell her I'll stop in again tomorrow."

I heard myself cry out, "Don't go!"

This rated me only a look of mild curiosity.

"Do you remember, last year, in Warsaw, by the railroad station, a column of prisoners in chains? One of them dropped a letter, and you picked it up and delivered it to my brother ..." All of which tumbled out of my mouth in less than one breath.

She nodded, frowning. Had I made her angry?

"I was that prisoner! I wrote that letter! I am the one whose life you saved!" I shouted, alarming the other customer. "I would have thanked you sooner, but I got back only this week."

Unthinkingly, I tried to seize her hand. She drew firmly out of my reach. And, as though to spare me further embarrassment, she nodded and exited, leaving me to berate myself as the prince of fools.

The gift in my hand turned to lead. Why could I not, like any normal bachelor, have brought flowers or a box of chocolates? And what evil demon had prompted me to identify myself, at once, as the convict in chains?

Despairing, I was ready to take the next train back to Warsaw, but Hana-Tova persuaded me to stay at least until Sunday. I accepted. But, to avoid the torment of false hopes, I went to the station and bought my return ticket to Warsaw for Sunday morning.

Upon the conclusion of *Shabbos*, my married cousin Zena, considered the most "worldly" of Hana-Tova's children because she covered only part of her hair, left on an errand while Laizer, her husband, shyly asked me to walk with him in the park because he was curious to learn how it was possible to survive for even a day in a place like Siberia, that is, in a place without Jews.

But, even as I tried to describe how the Almighty had arranged our dispersion so that one may stumble upon Jews in the most unlikely places, I recalled the chill of impermanence I had felt in Irkutsk, the sense that, while we lived in Exile at the sufferance of men in high boots, no matter how much blood, money and sweat we poured into alien soil, neither the dead nor the living could ever rest easily.

From out of a labyrinth of leafy darkness, we came suddenly face-to-face with Zena, out for a stroll with another young lady, whose name you will already have guessed.

Once again, my voice betrayed me, while Laizer and Zena suddenly remembered that they had small children at home, leaving me no choice but to offer myself as an escort to the girl who already owned my heart.

37

A REFORMED REVOLUTIONARY

What more is there to tell? In the course of what became an almost night-long conversation, I felt able, for the first time, to bare every corner of my heart. I also assured her that, despite the burden of chains in which she had seen me being marched through Warsaw, I was not a hoodlum, nor a terrorist or a thrower of bombs, although in my younger years, perhaps foolishly, perhaps not, I had been prepared to give my life to help bring about the birth of a more just society.

Then I asked what prompted her to pick up a note dropped by a filthy convict.

Crimson-cheeked, she said that, to this day, she herself couldn't understand what made her do it; it was as though some Higher Power had guided her steps.

I claim this proved we were truly a *zivug*, a pairing of souls whom Heaven had pre-ordained for one another before we were born, and that it was surely to fulfill this destiny that my life had been spared.

Overwhelmed by a rush of emotions I could not control, I kissed her cheek. I saw at once that it was the first kiss any man had ever come close enough to attempt, and she drew back as though from a blazing furnace – abruptly, yet without anger.

But the punishment for my rashness was immediate. A frail spell of magical harmony had arisen between us, and I, in my crude haste, had shattered it.

Too ashamed to apologize, all I could say was, "If you don't want my kiss, then please be good enough to give it back."

She laughed. Her face was radiant, again. I was forgiven.

That is not to say we had forgotten her parents. What, after all, is a love story without some towering obstacle to test the young couple's dedication – be it jealousy, a misunderstanding, or the collision of heedless youth and immoveable old age – those essential staples of Yiddish melodrama?

As I should have known, my beloved's father and stepmother were neither tyrants nor fools. From the instant they saw our glowing faces, having been daringly awakened by my future bride, they understood it was not for them to fly in the face of Prophecy, and that the Almighty had wrought one of those feats more miraculous than cleaving the Red Sea, namely matching their cherished daughter to the very lunatic with whom she had been fated to dwell all her days in loving friendship.

THE END

EPILOGUE

When my father returned from Siberia, he met and married the girl who became my mother. And although he had been urged to abandon Poland for his own safety, he found it difficult to leave the family that he loved.

But it soon became clear that there was no future for Jews in Poland (especially for those individuals with a record of revolutionary activities). And at risk of being conscripted again, my father left for America to join two of his brothers who had preceded him to Columbus' country: Berel, an older brother who had a haberdashery store in Shenandoah, Pennsylvania, and his younger brother, Avrohom. As was typical in those days, my parents decided that my father would go on ahead and get established, and then send for my mother and their two young children.

In the "goldeneh medina" (the country where 'the streets were paved with gold'), my father started out as a peddler, going door-to-door with what he hoped was useful merchandise. Just off the boat and not yet familiar with his new language, he was advised that, if asked a question, he should reply with the only English sentence he knew: "Look in the basket." Resourceful and optimistic, it would not take very long before he could send for his wife and children.

Once he had saved enough money, he sent steamship tickets, which my mother never received. It turned out that someone in the post office had stolen them. Undeterred, my father worked even harder to earn the money for replacements. Before the tickets arrived, the Great War had suddenly broken out, and my mother and the children were trapped in Poland until it ended. They suffered great deprivation during those years. My oldest sister, Edith, remembered not being able to play in the snow with her friends one winter because she had outgrown her shoes, and my mother's health was greatly damaged.

Somehow, they survived, but then a terrible blow struck. My brother, Chaim Mordechai, became ill. As there was no doctor in Vishogrod, my mother took the children to the train station to travel to a town that she knew had one. Despite her pleas, the railway guards refused to let them board. One of them said, in a phrase that was too prophetic, "We will get rid of all of you Jews. And if we don't finish the job, our sons and grandsons will."

Eventually, probably as a result of scraping together enough money for bribes, they were finally permitted to travel to the next town, but it was too late. My brother died of tuberculosis. He was four-and-a-half years old.

It took some time before my mother and sister, the surviving child, were finally able to travel to America. By the time they arrived at Ellis Island, my sister no longer recognized the man she was told was her father, and initially would have nothing to do with him. And my mother, who had been robust and healthy, had developed a serious heart condition. And every Friday before sundown, when she lit the Shabbos candles, she cried for the little son she had lost, the brother I never knew.

My sister, Rose, was seven, and I was two years old when my family moved to New York. There was a high rate of intermarriage in Shenandoah, and, as my sister Edith was a teenager, they were concerned about her opportunity to meet young Jewish men. Also, the mines in the Shenandoah Valley had failed, and my parents' general store lost many of its paying customers, although they gave people credit for as long as they could. Many years later, during World War II, there was a knock on our apartment door. A young soldier who had somehow tracked us down thanked my parents for keeping his family from starvation in Shenandoah as they had done for many other families, too.

In spite of being unable to keep his store in Shenandoah, my father's cheerful personality never wavered. He made the best of his circumstances, whatever they were. Arriving in New York just in time for the Depression, he got a temporary job with the Work Progress Administration (WPA) shoveling snow. It was hard work, yet when the men took a break, Poppa would dance the *kazachok* to entertain them, as he had once done for the Czar. The men stomped their feet, and clapped their hands to keep warm. When we attended weddings, the highlight was always my father's incredible dancing. People would get off the dance floor to watch him.

The Depression also gave my father time to finish writing about his activities during the war, and life as a Jew in Russian-occupied Poland. Ultimately, he filled 28 handwritten, marbleized, black-and-white composition notebooks with the adventures he had begun recording in 1904, and retold during all the years since then. On Sunday mornings, he used to read us what he had written during the week, including such tales as how the conscripts needed to pretend fierce loyalty to the Czar, even kiss the portrait of Czarina Alexandra that hung in the barracks. Hearing these stories remains one of my fondest memories of childhood.

One evening in 1950, my father asked me if I would help him translate his diaries from Yiddish into English. I was delighted; we were to begin the next evening. But at one o'clock in the morning, he woke me and said, "Don't wake Momma. I don't want to upset her, but there's pressure in my chest." He was more concerned about her heart condition that about what might be happening to his own.

As there was no 911 to call at the time, I phoned the hospital and begged them to send an ambulance. It took many repeated calls until one was dispatched. When my mother heard us and ran into my room, he said to her: "Calm yourself." Those were his last words, because by the time the ambulance showed up, my father had already passed away.

I suppose we all forgot about the diaries until 1953 when I brought my then-future husband, Shimon Wincelberg, to meet my mother towards the end of her life. Knowing that he was a writer (he was the first Orthodox writer in Hollywood), she whispered to me, "Show him Poppa's diaries."

The diaries had been handwritten in Yiddish, but as a labor of love, the late Rebbetzin Faigy Wasserman typed the manuscript. My sister, Edith, of blessed memory, translated a rough, first draft, and then Shimon and I translated them in greater detail. Then we divided up the sections of the first twelve notebooks, compared what we had written and then chose the best. Each of us took special care to preserve my father's unique voice and reflect his humorous outlook on even the most horrendous circumstances. It was my father's sense of humor and unique perspective that helped him survive, and what make his stories so compelling.

We set to work organizing my father's accounts of his experiences, and in 1976, the Jewish Publication Society published stories from the first twelve of the 28 notebooks as <u>The Samurai of Vishogrod</u>. Between jobs writing for television and the stage, Shimon continued working on the remaining sixteen diaries, intending to publish them too, but he passed away before he could complete the job. Before his death, I promised him that the diaries would be published.

How appropriate it was that, when I worried that I might not be able to fulfill my father's, my mother's, and my husband's dreams, that the job was taken on by my daughter, Bryna, who was named after the young girl who had saved my father's life so many years ago.

AUTHOR'S NOTE

A s the third and final author of this book, I approached the task differently than my parents had when they produced The Samurai of Vishigrod, based upon the first twelve of my grandfather, Jacob Marateck's, 28 diaries. While they had been faithful to the translation of the diaries, I didn't have access to the original translation but rather to what my father had done with it, so I began with that and directed the narrative to follow a storyline of which the multiple death sentences formed the spine. The objective was to create an entertaining and enlightening narrative without changing the story.

Creating a cohesive story line occasionally necessitated combining incidents that made the same point. I also eliminated redundancies and corrected discrepancies, and excised chapters or scenes that did not fit with the storyline and were distractions. Sometimes, it was necessary to develop additional material based upon what I knew or could surmise from the text in order to fill in gaps. I also tightened the narrative, while expanding on the dialogue and description in areas where I felt it was lacking. On occasion it was also necessary to relocate certain scenes to better emphasize the point they made. What I hope is not obvious from reading this book is where my grandfather's or father's words end and where mine begin.

For contextual understanding, and often to satisfy my own curiosity, I tried to identify some of the historical individuals referenced in the book.

(To my great disappointment, I was unable to locate or identify Captain Mikhailoff, my grandfather's rescuer on one occasion, or "Left-handed Stepan." I am also aware that some of the names had been changed, but other than Pyavka's, I don't know which ones.) Later, by following clues in the text, I tried to figure out the location of the transit camp from which my grandfather had escaped, merely for the purpose of showing, on the map, his journey home from Siberia. Yet none of these changes affected the essence of my grandfather's stories.

As my mother recognized, it was important to include some background information about my grandfather so that the reader would understand who Jacob Marateck was and how he ended up in the positions in which he found himself. To provide this context, I reused and rewrote some material that had previously been published in The Samurai of Vishigrod.

While my grandfather didn't live long enough to produce more than a first draft, it is his unguarded, unedited personal thoughts and feelings that give his story its unique intimacy. Although the original purpose of keeping a diary had been to leave something behind for his parents in the event that he didn't survive the war, what he left, instead, is something that brings each of us closer to his heart.

Bryna Kranzler

GLOSSARY

Banzai – (Japanese) A war cry

Chanukah – (Hebrew) Holiday commemorating the rededication of the Old Temple in Jerusalem following the Maccabean victory (165 B.C.E.). The eight-day holiday, which begins every year on the same date on the Jewish (lunar) calendar, falls on a different date on the secular calendar each year, either in late November, or December

Drozhky – (Russian) An open carriage

Dybbuk – (Hebrew) In Jewish folklore, a malicious spirit of a deceased person that attaches itself to a living one

Eydem oyf kest – (Yiddish) Supported or 'kept' son-in-law

Faworki – (Polish) Ribbon-shaped pastries (often known as "Angel Wings") that are fried and then coated with confectioners sugar

Gemara – (Aramaic) Rabbinical commentaries on the Talmud

Golem – (Hebrew and Yiddish) In Jewish Folklore, the golem was created from mud, and became animated when the name of God, written out, was placed in its mouth

Gubernya – (Russian) Province

Hasidic – (Hebrew) Pertaining to a Hasid, a member of a strict sect of Orthodox Jews

Izvoshchik – (Russian) Taxi driver

Kaddish – (Aramaic) Prayer said by relatives of the deceased so that the deceased benefits from the merit earned by its recitation

Katzap – (Russian-Yiddish) Nationalistic term for a Russian person; someone who is wholly Russian, not a hybrid with another nationality

Kazachok - (Russian) "Cossacks Dance." (also known as 'Kazatzka'). It is a fast, Slavic dance with alternate squats, leg kicks and jumps

Kol Nidre – (Aramaic) Prayer said on the eve of Yom Kipper, before beginning the Service, pertaining to vows made during the previous year

Kretchma – (Yiddish) Tavern or bar

Macher – (Yiddish and German) A person of influence; a big shot

Marranos – (roots in Spanish, Portuguese, Aramaic-Hebrew) "Secret Jews" who had been forced to convert to Christianity but still practiced Judaism privately

Musaf – (Hebrew) Additional prayer said on Sabbath and holidays

Misheberach – (Hebrew) A prayer said for someone who was ill.

Mitzvah – (Hebrew) A good deed

Natchalniks – (Russian) Authority or official

Natchalstva – (Russian) Officialdom

Okhranka – (Russian) The Russian secret police

Polkovnik – (Russian) Colonel

Purim – (Hebrew) The holiday celebrates the Jews' reprieve from Haman's plan to annihilate the Jewish people of Shushan, which was in western Iran

Rosh Hashanah – (Hebrew) The Jewish New Year (Literally, the "Head of the year")

Schnorrer – (Yiddish) Beggar (implies 'professional' beggar)

Shabbos – (Yiddish) The Sabbath

Shaliach tzibur – (Hebrew) Intermediary of the Congregation

Shema – (Hebrew) Short for Shema Yisroel, a central Jewish prayer: "Hear O Israel, the Lord is our God; the Lord is One" (Literally, "Hear, Israel")

Shiva – (Hebrew) Seven-day mourning period for the dead (from the Hebrew word "sheva," meaning seven)

Sholom aleichem – (Hebrew) A Yiddish greeting

Shul – (Yiddish) Synagogue

Tallis – (Yiddish) Prayer shawl

Talmud – (Hebrew) Composed of Jewish law and commentary of the great rabbis from centuries past

Tehillim – (Hebrew) Psalms. Also, The Book of Psalms

Tefillin – (Hebrew) Phylacteries. They consist of leather straps, and two square leather boxes containing four sections of the Torah written on parchment

"Thirty Six" – (Hebrew) According to the rabbinical commentaries in the *Talmud*, in every generation there are 36 individuals who greet the Divine's presence daily. Later literature suggests that they sustain the world. (They are also known as the "Lamed Vavniks," from the Hebrew letters "lamed" and "vav," which are assigned the numerical values of "thirty" and "six")

Troika – (Russian) Carriage or sled drawn by three horses

Vanya – (Russian) A nickname for 'Ivan;' used as a general term referring to all Russians

Yankel – (Yiddish) Nickname for Jacob or Yakov

Yetzer hara – (Hebrew) Inclination to sin

Yeshiva – (Hebrew) Jewish educational institution at elementary or high school level, or beyond

Yom Kippur – (Hebrew) The Day of Atonement

Yom Tov – (Hebrew) Refers to any Jewish holiday (Literally, a "Good Day")

Zhydovska morda – (Russian) JewFace, or more precisely: JewSnout

INDEX

H

I

K

L

M

N

O

P

Q

R

S